THE PRODUCTS OF BINNS ROAD

A general survey

Peter Randall

FRANK HORNBY
1863–1936

New Cavendish Books

LONDON

*This edition is dedicated to all those who worked
at Meccano's Binns Road factory in Liverpool.*

**First edition published in Great Britain
by New Cavendish Books – 1977.**

**Revised and reprinted – 1981
Second reprint – 1991.**

Specification: 224 pages, 170 b/w illustrations
and 102 pages in full colour.

The Publishers express their thanks to Meccano Limited and particularly,
to J. D. McHard and W. B. Warncken.
The names *Meccano* and *Dinky Toys* have been used by courtesy of *Meccano Limited*.
The name *Hornby* has been used by courtesy of *Rovex Limited*.

All archival material by courtesy of M. W. Models, Henley-on-Thames.

The Publishers express their thanks to:
W. E. Finlason, Keith Waldron, and Roy Hallsworth for their loan of original colour
catalogue material and to David Nathan for his extensive enquiries in tracing a copy
of The *Book of Hornby Trains and Meccano Products*.

The Hornby Companion Series

Design – John B. Cooper
Text production and supervision – Narisa Chakra
Edited by Allen Levy

Copyright – © – New Cavendish Books & PBA Enterprises 1977
All rights reserved, this book, or parts thereof, may not be reproduced in any form
without permission in writing from the publisher.

Filmset by Filmtype Services Limited, Scarborough
Colour Separation by Spectraplan Limited, London
Printed and bound in Thailand by Amarin Printing Group.

New Cavendish Books, 3 Denbigh Road, London W11 2SJ.

ISBN 0 904568 06 7

Contents

Preface

IT IS A LATE SUMMER EVENING in the year 1931. A nine-year-old boy has been playing trains on the front lawn, but now the green engine and its coaches *Marjorie* and *Aurelia* stand deserted, as the boy looks anxiously down the road. Suddenly a bigger boy appears on a bicycle and hands an evening paper to the younger lad. He knows immediately, from the weight, that his precious *Meccano Magazine* is folded inside.

Newspaper tossed aside, the boy sits on the grass engrossed in his favourite periodical. On the coloured cover is a picture of an African elephant, but two inside pages grip his attention. One gives news of a completely new range of Hornby Trains which will be available in the autumn, while the other tells of additions to the Meccano system. By now the light is fading, but the boy reads on, oblivious to the gathering dew.

Forty-four years on, and now more portly, he stretches himself after an hour's weeding, sinks gratefully into a deck chair and picks up the Meccano Magazine Quarterly which arrived that morning. With a pleasure undiminished by the passing years, he reads about a super Meccano model locomotive, built by an enthusiast in Argentina.

That boy was, of course, the author, and if I can impart to my readers a small fraction of the pleasure 'Meccano Products' have given me over almost half a century, then this task will have been more than worthwhile.

Peter Randall
Bedford

An early box top which expresses
'The Spirit of Meccano'

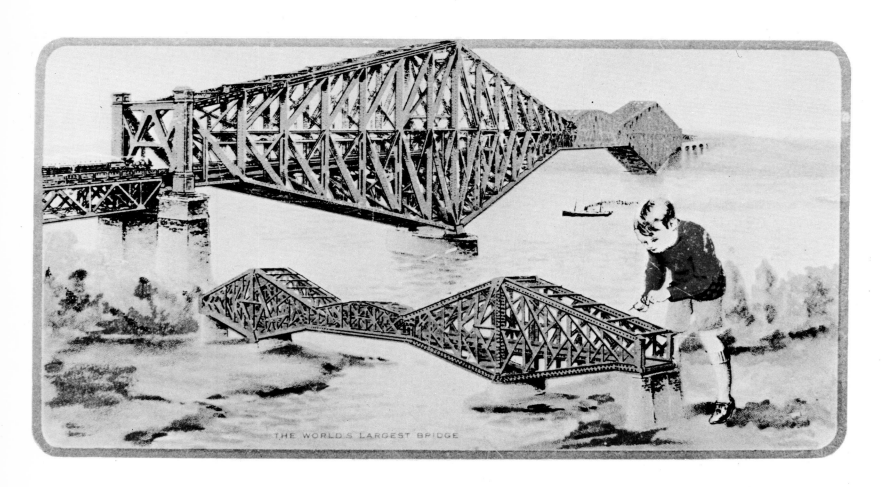

THE WORLD'S LARGEST BRIDGE

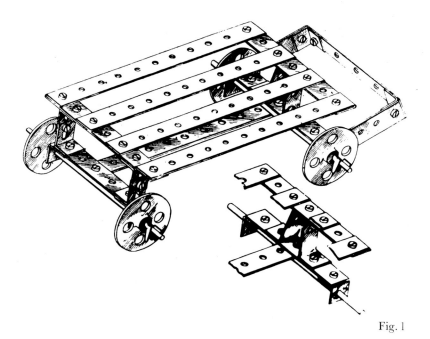

Fig. 1

Frank Hornby worked in a shipping office in Victorian Liverpool, but his overriding interest was his workshop. As a young man he had patented many ideas. Fired with enthusiasm after reading of other inventors' struggles, he even tried to devise a machine to solve the problem of perpetual motion!

After he was married with boys of his own, Frank Hornby turned his attention to making mechanical toys for them. When a model crane presented special difficulties, he considered what a waste of labour it was to make special parts which only served one purpose. So the idea of perforated metal parts gradually formed in his mind. These parts could be bolted together to make a model (Fig. 1) and later dismantled and reassembled as a different structure. By hand he laboriously cut out and perforated strips of copper in various lengths. The original dimensions he used, the size of the holes and the distance between them have not changed to this day.

On the 9th January 1901, a patent was granted for the invention, to which Frank Hornby gave the name *Mechanics Made Easy*. Local dealers, at first with some doubts, agreed to sell the tin box containing an assortment of strips, rods, wheels, nuts and bolts. In September 1907, the name was changed to *Meccano*, (although the precise derivation and circumstances surrounding the 'invention' of this name remain unrecorded, heresay evidence suggests that George Jones was the originator) and by 1910 it was available in a series of seven outfits ranging in price from 3/6d to 126/-. Sets now contained Angle Girders as well as Strips, and these parts were nickel-plated, while the wheels were of polished brass. The next few years saw the introduction of many new important parts.

The *Meccano Magazine*, was first published in September 1916. Its stated aim was 'to help Meccano Boys to have more fun than other boys', and Frank Hornby twice published the Company's history in its columns once in 1917 and again in 1932. In spite of the War, the system had been considerably

THE PRODUCTS of the famous firm of Meccano Ltd, Binns Road, Liverpool, represented far more than hobbies to boys of the 1930s; they were a way of life. Boys who grew up in the inter-war years had never known a world without Meccano or Hornby Trains, and to find such a world without either, one would need to return to the year 1900.

Youngsters and adults are now as keen as ever on Meccano, and this is reflected in the considerable expansion of the system over the years. It seems that Meccano is all set to see the turn of the twentieth century, thereby out-living several generations of its adherents.

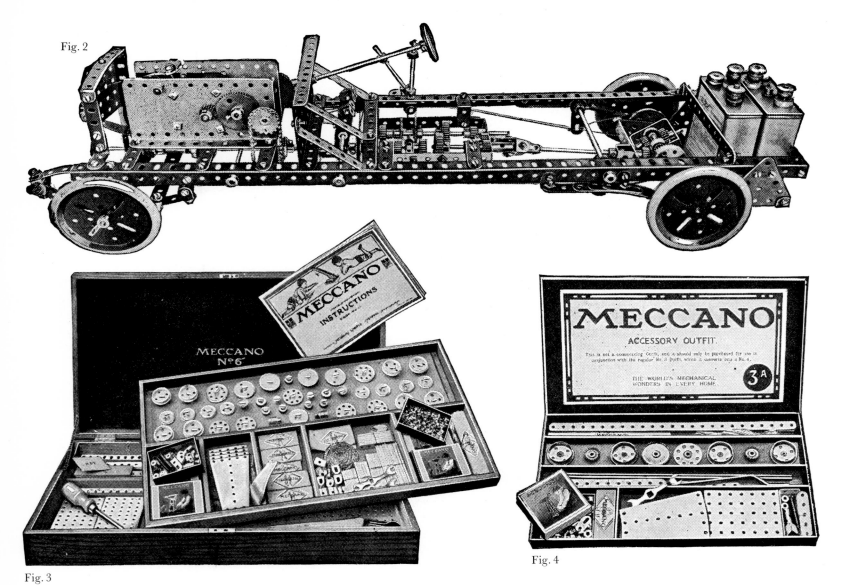

Fig. 2

Fig. 3

Fig. 4

6

extended. The magazine showed new parts including Braced Girders, Spoked Wheels, Sprocket Chain and Sprocket Wheels. An Electric Motor was described, to be used for driving models as an alternative to the Clockwork Motor already included in the system. One interesting model pictured (Fig. 7) and described, was a loom which could actually weave cloth. There was also a machine called a *Meccanograph* which produced intricate designs on paper, and was the forerunner of many similar models.

After Mechanics Made Easy, Meccano can be divided conveniently into historical periods, and the first of these – up to 1926 – is usually known as the 'nickel period', the parts receiving a nickel plate finish during that time (Fig. 2).

Meccano has always been sold as a series of outfits with the idea of progressing from one to the next by the addition of an Accessory outfit. Thus, a boy could begin with a small outfit such as a No. 3, and the later purchase of a 3A outfit (Fig. 4) converted his set into a No. 4. This progressive system has remained substantially the same throughout Meccano's history and was always emphasised in the Company's advertising material. The latter included, in addition to catalogues and the *Meccano Magazine*, special booklets which were published from time to time. Such a publication is *'The Story of Meccano by the Meccano Boy'* dating from 1912. Although it contained pictures and phrases which now seem dated to the present day reader, the remarkable thing about the book is how much of it is true of *contemporary* Meccano. Of course, Frank Hornby was anxious to sell his product, but he also sincerely believed that it had a place in the development of a boy's mind and skills, especially a boy with an aptitude for mechanics. Meccano was claimed to be 'Real Engineering in Miniature', and the serious aspects of it were always stressed in Meccano literature.

The 1925 catalogue reveals that there were now nine main outfits in the series, numbered from one to seven plus two smaller sets numbers 00 and 0. These smaller sets were intended for younger boys, and enabled simple models to be built. With a No. 4 Outfit, more advanced models were possible, and Outfits 5 and 6 were optionally available in oak cabinets instead of cardboard boxes. Set No. 7, established towards the end of the nickel era, remained the largest in the series for many years. Priced at 370/- in 1925, it was beyond the reach of all but a few fortunate boys.

Fig. 5

Fig. 6

Fig. 7

A WEAVING
LOOM

Fig. 9

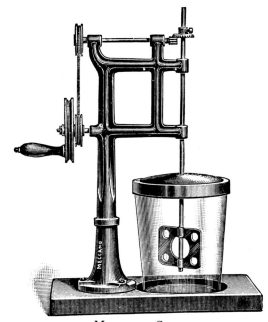

MECCANO CHURN   Fig. 10

MECCANO STEAM ENGINE

Fig. 11

Fig. 8   *The Paris Eiffel Tower.*

MECCANO SAW BENCH

A browse through the instruction manuals of the nickel period illustrates models which mirrored those times, while others, with little change, still appear in the manuals of the 1970s.

Until the introduction of Flat Plates, nickel Meccano models presented a skeletal appearance, and cardboard was sometimes used as platework. The accent was always on working models, of which cranes were the most popular. Naturally, with the larger sets more advanced models could be built. The No. 7 Manual illustrated a Motor Car Chassis complete with gearbox, clutch, differential and rear-wheel brakes. Another complicated and spectacular model was the High-Speed Ship Coaler. Although illustrated in the manual, fully detailed instructions were only available separately for building these two large models.

A special series of parts, introduced into the Meccano system in the early days, was known as the *Hornby System of Mechanical Demonstration*. Hooks, Weights and spring balances used with standard parts, enabled experiments in mechanics to be undertaken. Intended primarily for use in schools, these special parts were included for a time in the Meccano system.

Although instructions for making a whole range of models were always included in Meccano Outfits, the primary intention was for boys to create their own inventions. From earliest times, Meccano Ltd held competitions, which were divided into grades, so that young boys with small outfits could compete with a fairer chance of winning. Prize-winning models frequently became official models in new editions of the manuals.

In order to provide power various Meccano Motors were available. The earliest – spring-powered – was made in Germany by Märklin et Cie for Meccano Ltd, and introduced into the system in 1912.

The following year a high-voltage Electric Motor was introduced which could be plugged into the house mains. In spite of the obvious dangers to children, HV motors with exposed working parts were included in the system until the late 1920s, though, 4-volt Motors (Fig. 6) for use with accumulators were also available from 1916. Small, stationary steam engines, used for driving models were popular in the early years of the century, and one with the archetype vertical boiler (Fig. 9) was added to the Meccano system in 1914. In the same year a more unusual motor, powered by water pressure from the domestic tap, was also introduced. It cannot have been very popular, as it was withdrawn three years later.

Special-purpose accessories have always been included in the Meccano system. In the early 1920s, two Electrical Outfits were available (Fig. 5) containing Bobbins and wire for making coils; Terminal Nuts, Lamps, and the like.

Meccano also marketed a range of non-constructional models amongst which were the Butter Churn (Fig. 10) and Circular-Saw Bench (Fig. 11) which actually made butter and cut wood.

Fig. 12

A CERTAIN AMOUNT OF CONTROVERSY surrounds the dating of the principal changes in the Meccano system. Obviously when a company ceases production of an item on a given day, both their own and their dealers' stocks are not exhausted overnight; there being a transitional period, with no precise date for the withdrawal of any given item.

In the latter half of 1926, certain Meccano parts were sprayed in light red or green instead of being nickel plated. This fact was mentioned in Meccano advertisements, and a special full-colour leaflet entitled 'The New Meccano' was issued (Fig. 12). As late as July 1927, a *Meccano Magazine* page about accessory parts said 'Steel Meccano parts are now brightly coloured in red and green . . . if nickelled parts are preferred however, they may be obtained from your dealer at the same price as the coloured parts'. For the previous six months, sets contained a mixture of nickel and coloured parts, but by the end of 1927 all coloured Meccano had arrived in darker shades of red and green. A whole-page advertisement on the inside cover of the November 1927 *Meccano Magazine* referred to it as 'the New Meccano – all coloured!' A free book, in colour, was also mentioned, to introduce boys to red and green Meccano for the Christmas season of 1927.

Strictly speaking of course, it was not really 'new' Meccano, and several times in later years, usually just before Christmas, Meccano Ltd changed the colour, introduced a few new parts, modified the contents of some sets and announced 'the New Meccano'. Whilst sales undoubtedly improved, some Meccano enthusiasts were against these colour changes as they were unable to buy parts to match their existing outfits.

Colour changes apart, there were many landmarks in the world of Meccano during the latter years of the 1920s. Some of these were the result of new introductions, but others evolved as a result of the Company and model builders discovering new ways of using Meccano parts. This process is continuous, in fact the limit of Meccano's potential will never be reached. It is

Run your Models with the Meccano Steam Engine

Height 7 ins.
Length 7 ins.
Width $4\frac{1}{4}$ ins.

This Powerful Engine is specially designed to build into Meccano Models

You have already experienced the thrill of building real engineering models with Meccano . . . imagine the crowning joy of operating your models with the Meccano Steam Engine, in exactly the same way as their " big brothers " are worked in real life !

The powerful Meccano Steam Engine, which is fitted with reversing gear, is the latest Meccano achievement. The base and side plates are pierced with the standard Meccano equidistant holes, thus enabling it to be built into any Meccano model in the exact position required.

Steam is admitted to a single cylinder of the oscillating type through a special reversing block. Operation of the reversing lever enables the crankshaft to run in either direction.

The boiler is of heavy gauge brass and is fitted with an efficient safety valve. The cylinder, reversing block, crank disc, and pin, are machined from solid brass and steel. The base, side plates, and spirit container are enamelled in colour and the boiler casing is of oxidised brass finish. *Price 21/-*

Fig. 13

12

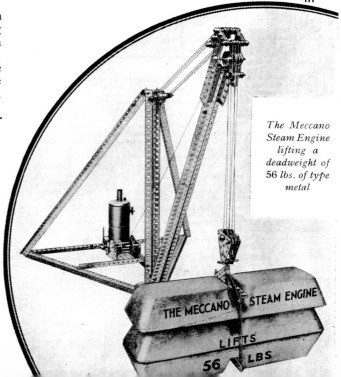

The Meccano Steam Engine lifting a deadweight of 56 lbs. of type metal

certainly true however, that this period was the one in which Meccano, as a medium for building a series of toys, expanded to Meccano as a means for constructing large-scale reproductions of the wonders of real engineering.

During 1926 and 1927 there was a long series of articles in the *Meccano Magazine*, entitled *Meccano Standard Mechanisms*. This was later reprinted in book form and revised from time to time to incorporate new ideas, or uses for new parts. The intention was to show boys how a particular mechanism could be incorporated in a model of their own design. Some of these examples, such as the 'simple hand brake' and the 'worm and chain steering gear' will be familiar to all old Meccano 'boys'; others, like the 'four speed and reverse planetary gear box', were decidedly aimed at the embryo engineer.

Another *Meccano Magazine* feature which ran from early times was the 'Suggestions Section' edited by 'Spanner' – a pseudonym for a succession of staff writers. The suggestions were ideas – mainly for mechanisms – built in Meccano and submitted by readers. Prizes were awarded for ideas which were published, and some readers' suggestions were included in the later editions of *Meccano Standard Mechanisms*.

Meccano Magazine readers were also encouraged to suggest new parts which the company might include in the system. It is interesting to read these pages in the old magazines to see which suggestions were eventually adopted. For example, flexible metal plates, a feature of present-day Meccano, were suggested as long ago as April 1928, while in September of that year a suggestion for blue and yellow Meccano, the colours of the 1970s, was turned down by Meccano Ltd.

Between 1927 and 1936, Meccano Ltd issued a series of *'Super Model'* Leaflets. In each of these were instructions for building one model, which in many cases, had previously been included in the *Meccano Magazine*. Pride of place among these must surely go to the famous Block-Setting Crane, a very large and complex model calling for considerable skill in its construction. Completion of this Model required more parts than were included in the largest set in the series, the No. 7. By contrast, some of the 'Super Models', like the Hydraulic Crane, were small and simple, although incorporating ingenious mechanisms.

Many of these models called for new parts to be introduced into the system, and some of these were larger, and less abstract, than the existing standard parts. In August 1928, the

Geared Roller Bearing, (Fig. 14) the largest and most complex Meccano part, made its appearance in the system. It consisted of a pair of twelve-inch diameter races between which was placed a Ring Frame fitted with sixteen Flanged Wheels. This bearing was used in the construction of the Block-Setting Crane and for similar very large rotating models. A much smaller but very useful ball bearing unit (Fig. 17) was also introduced in the same month.

During this period, other special parts were introduced including realistic rubber Tyres for model vehicles, a Boiler, an increased range of Gears and a Digger Bucket (Figs. 15 & 16) for model excavators. This last item was a part with a limited use, one of many which the Company added to the system in the late 1920s. Contrary to their stated policy that Meccano parts should have several applications, Meccano Ltd were now bringing in parts with very little apparent use *at all*. If one wished to make a loom, then Shuttles, Reed Hooks and Healds were of course necessary, but at the same time there was a series of twenty-six Ships' Funnels, each identical except that it was finished in the colours of a different shipping line!

By 1932, the range of sets had been increased at the bottom end to include No. 000. Outfit No. 7 was now priced at 450/-, the sets having been modified to include new parts, and a more attractive presentation. Instruction manuals supplied with the sets had been brought up to date, and included many models representing contemporary cars, lorries, cranes, etc, although, as previously mentioned some models had been retained from the pre-1914 manuals.

Motors for driving the models had also been improved. Towards the end of the red-green era, 20-volt and 6-volt motors were available, which were driven from the same transformers as supplied with Hornby Train Sets. In 1928, a superior Steam Engine appeared and was extensively advertised (Fig. 13). Unlike the 1914 model, this one had a great advantage: it was possible to build it into Meccano Models. Its vertical boiler had an outer jacket, the engine boasted a reversing lever, and steam was realistically puffed out the chimney. The 1928 Steam Engine was probably the most exquisite item ever to emerge from Binns Road, but for all that, it could not have been as popular as the Clockwork or Electric Motors, as it was withdrawn in 1935, to the everlasting regret (or delight!) of present-day collectors.

No. 167, Geared Roller Bearing

PART No. 167 comprises the following units: two Roller Races, each 12″ diam. and dished to form a rim near their peripheries; one Ring Frame, 10″ diam.; one special Pinion, 16 teeth; sixteen ¾″ Flanged Wheels; sixteen Pivot Bolts and Nuts; two Bush Wheels; one 9½″ Strip; one 1½″ Rod; ten nuts and bolts. When assembled these parts form a complete Roller Bearing.

The Meccano Roller Bearing is designed to facilitate the building of large models of swivelling structures, such as giant Hammerhead Cranes, Rolling Bridges, etc. The Roller Races are provided with teeth around their peripheries, so that they may be engaged by the special Pinion. In this way a realistic and efficient means of rotating the superstructure is provided.

Above: The complete Roller Bearing unit, with box. On Right: A Meccano giant Block - setting Crane, showing the Roller Bearing Unit used as a swivelling base for the boom.

Fig. 14

The Roller Races are enamelled grey, except the toothed edges, which are given a nickelled finish. The Ring Frame is enamelled grey throughout.

Price of Geared Roller Bearing complete, as detailed above, packed in carton; 20/-

No. 169, Digger Bucket

This is a very useful and realistic accessory. It is designed principally, of course, for use in Meccano steam shovels, or mechanical navvies, etc. The mouth of the Bucket measures about $1\frac{7}{8}''$ by $2\frac{1}{4}''$, while the depth (over cutting teeth) is $2\frac{1}{2}''$. The bottom of the Bucket is mounted on hinged levers and normally is held in place by a sliding lever, the end of which may just be seen in the illustration, that engages with a slot in the front of the Bucket. A cord may be attached to the lever and on pulling this the floor falls open and so discharges the contents of the Bucket.

The Digger Bucket is of very sturdy construction, the principal parts being secured together by nuts and bolts. It is beautifully enamelled in steel blue, except for the sliding lever, which is nickel-plated. Price 2/–.

Fig. 15

Fig. 16

No. 168, Ball Bearing

Part No. 168 comprises the following units : one Ball Race Flanged, one Ball Race Geared, and one Ball Casing, complete with Balls. The over-all diameter of the part is $4''$. It is designed for use in models of swivelling structures where the Roller Bearing (part No. 167) would be too large. Its use reduces friction to a minimum and enables the moving part to be turned easily and smoothly about its pivot. The Flanged and Geared Ball Races are enamelled green, and the Ball Casing is nickel-plated throughout. Price, complete, 3/–.

Fig. 17

The components of the Ball Bearing will be listed separately, as follows :—

No. 168a, Ball Race, Flanged, price 6d.
No. 168b, Ball Race, Geared, price 9d.
No. 168c, Ball Casing, complete with Balls, price 1/9.

In 1932, Meccano Ltd introduced the 'X' Series Outfits (Fig. 18) to compete with the Trix constructional sets then being sold by Woolworths. Both systems were based on a ¾-inch-wide strip with rows of three perforated holes across it. The pattern of holes was different in the two systems, but the chief difference was in finish, the Trix parts being unpainted. Two Meccano 'X' sets were available, X1 and X2 costing respectively 1/3d and 2/-. The *Meccano Magazine* of the period ran several articles on 'X' parts and showed how large models could be built by combining 'X' and standard parts. An 'X' clockwork motor was produced which survives to this day, in slightly modified form, as the 'Magic' Motor. 'X' series parts and sets became obsolete in 1936, but two parts, a ¾ inch and a 1¼ inch disc were retained in the standard system, the former surviving to this day.

Two monthly features in the *Meccano Magazine* during the 1930s were 'New Meccano Models' and 'Model Building Contests'. The former showed instructions for building several models each month, or occasionally one large one. Frank Hornby himself commented on the contests, which featured the work of boys and adults and was usually divided into grades. As time went by, some magnificent models were entered, needing very large collections of parts to build them. By the middle 1930s the first prize in major contests had risen to five guineas (£5.25), a sizeable sum for a boy to win in those days. Many prize-winning entries were included in the yearly *Meccano Book of New Models*, to be re-built all over the world. As the *Meccano Magazine* said, this in itself was sufficient reward to the original designers.

As the first red-green era came to an end, models were more complicated and performed most of the mechanical movements seen in real life. Yet many could not have been described as realistic. With the exception of cranes – for which Meccano has always been an ideal medium – road vehicles, locomotives and ships built with Plates, Strips and Girders still presented a very 'perforated' appearance, but already someone at Binns Road was working on this problem.

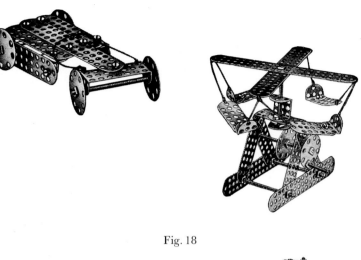

Fig. 18

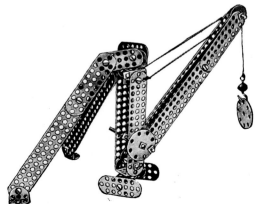

THE *Meccano Magazine* FOR NOVEMBER 1934 CARRIED a further advertisement announcing 'The New Meccano'. This time however, a major change was to occur – the introduction of metal and fibre Plates perforated around the edges only. This enabled models to be made which looked more solid than before. Moreover, the fibre plates could be bent into curves and other shapes, enabling structures such as aeroplane and ship bodies to be modelled. The colour of the Strips was changed to gold and that chosen for the plates was blue, the latter having

one plain side and a pattern of gold cross lines on the other. Although not the finish of real ships or locomotives, models built with Meccano in these colours certainly presented a very attractive appearance.

To begin with, the contents of the sets – now in sequence A to L instead of 00 to 7 – were based upon the old sets, but included an appropriate supply of the new parts. Thus, most 'Super Models' which could be built with the old No. 7 set could still be built with the blue/gold 'L' set. However, in the Autumn of

Fig. 19

Fig. 20

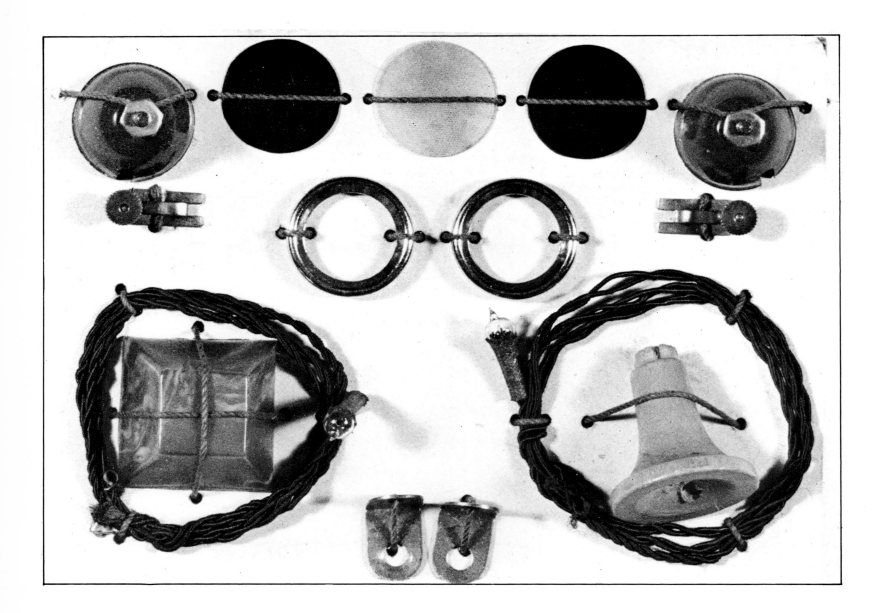

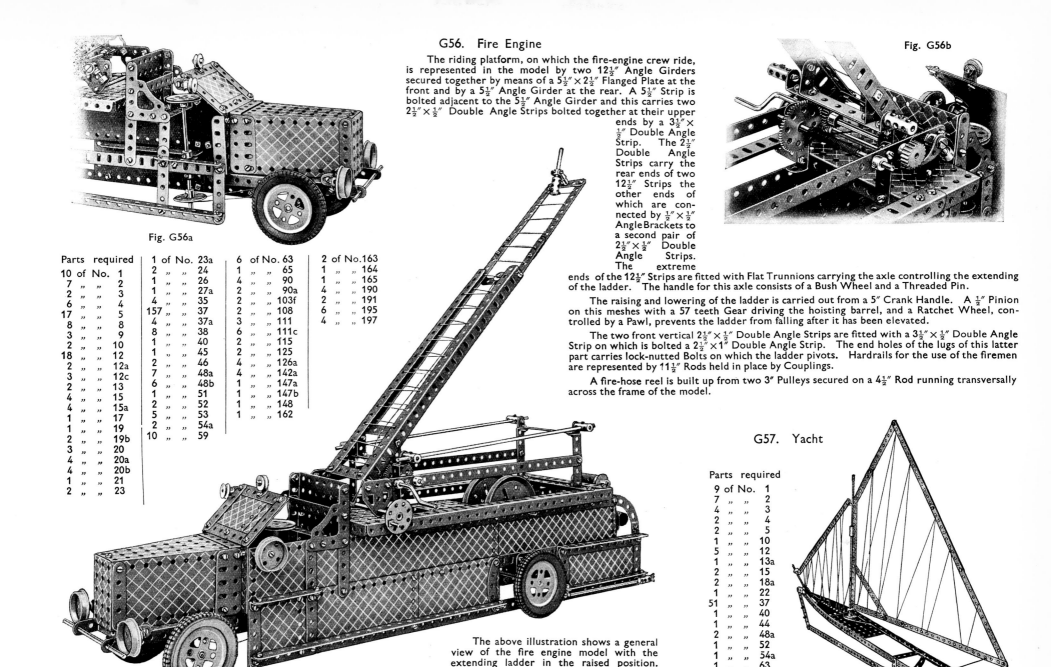

G56. Fire Engine

The riding platform, on which the fire-engine crew ride, is represented in the model by two 12½″ Angle Girders secured together by means of a 5½″ × 2½″ Flanged Plate at the front and by a 5½″ Angle Girder at the rear. A 5½″ Strip is bolted adjacent to the 5½″ Angle Girder and this carries two 2½″ × ½″ Double Angle Strips bolted together at their upper ends by a 3½″ × ½″ Double Angle Strip. The 2½″ Double Angle Strips carry the rear ends of two 12½″ Strips the other ends of which are connected by ½″ × ½″ Angle Brackets to a second pair of 2½″ × ½″ Double Angle Strips. The extreme ends of the 12½″ Strips are fitted with Flat Trunnions carrying the axle controlling the extending of the ladder. The handle for this axle consists of a Bush Wheel and a Threaded Pin.

The raising and lowering of the ladder is carried out from a 5″ Crank Handle. A ½″ Pinion on this meshes with a 57 teeth Gear driving the hoisting barrel, and a Ratchet Wheel, controlled by a Pawl, prevents the ladder from falling after it has been elevated.

The two front vertical 2½″ × ½″ Double Angle Strips are fitted with a 3½″ × ½″ Double Angle Strip on which is bolted a 2½″ × 1″ Double Angle Strip. The end holes of the lugs of this latter part carries lock-nutted Bolts on which the ladder pivots. Hardrails for the use of the firemen are represented by 11½″ Rods held in place by Couplings.

A fire-hose reel is built up from two 3″ Pulleys secured on a 4½″ Rod running transversally across the frame of the model.

Fig. G56a

Fig. G56b

The above illustration shows a general view of the fire engine model with the extending ladder in the raised position. Note the hose nozzle at the top of the ladder for directing "water" on to upper stories.

Fig. 21

Parts required

10 of No. 1	1 of No. 23a	6 of No. 63	2 of No. 163
7 ,, ,, 2	2 ,, ,, 24	1 ,, ,, 65	1 ,, ,, 164
2 ,, ,, 3	1 ,, ,, 26	4 ,, ,, 90	1 ,, ,, 165
6 ,, ,, 4	1 ,, ,, 27a	2 ,, ,, 90a	4 ,, ,, 190
17 ,, ,, 5	4 ,, ,, 35	2 ,, ,, 103f	2 ,, ,, 191
8 ,, ,, 8	157 ,, ,, 37	2 ,, ,, 108	6 ,, ,, 195
3 ,, ,, 9	4 ,, ,, 37a	3 ,, ,, 111	4 ,, ,, 197
2 ,, ,, 10	8 ,, ,, 38	6 ,, ,, 111c	
18 ,, ,, 12	1 ,, ,, 40	2 ,, ,, 115	
2 ,, ,, 12a	1 ,, ,, 45	2 ,, ,, 125	
3 ,, ,, 12c	2 ,, ,, 46	4 ,, ,, 126a	
2 ,, ,, 13	7 ,, ,, 48a	4 ,, ,, 142a	
4 ,, ,, 15	6 ,, ,, 48b	1 ,, ,, 147a	
4 ,, ,, 15a	1 ,, ,, 51	1 ,, ,, 147b	
1 ,, ,, 17	2 ,, ,, 52	1 ,, ,, 148	
1 ,, ,, 19	5 ,, ,, 53	1 ,, ,, 162	
2 ,, ,, 19b	2 ,, ,, 54a		
3 ,, ,, 20	10 ,, ,, 59		
4 ,, ,, 20a			
4 ,, ,, 20b			
1 ,, ,, 21			
2 ,, ,, 23			

G57. Yacht

Parts required

9 of No. 1
7 ,, ,, 2
4 ,, ,, 3
2 ,, ,, 4
2 ,, ,, 5
1 ,, ,, 10
5 ,, ,, 12
1 ,, ,, 13a
2 ,, ,, 15
2 ,, ,, 18a
1 ,, ,, 22
51 ,, ,, 37
1 ,, ,, 40
1 ,, ,, 44
2 ,, ,, 48a
1 ,, ,, 52
1 ,, ,, 54a
1 ,, ,, 63

A Message to all Readers

The news of the death of my father, Frank Hornby, has been received in all quarters, and especially in that great and wonderful country called Meccanoland, with the deepest regret, and I wish to thank very sincerely all those who have written to express their sympathy.

As the inventor of Meccano, and the head of the Meccano Guild and the Hornby Railway Company, the great organisations founded by him, he came into close and affectionate contact with the youth of the whole civilised world. The responsibility of maintaining this contact falls upon me as his elder son and the first Meccano boy, and I accept this responsibility as a great and sacred trust. I look back to the days when my father first began to see dimly the outlines of his great invention; and I recall vividly the wonderful evening when I helped him to cut out from a sheet of copper the very first Meccano parts.

I send my cordial wishes to readers of the "Meccano Magazine," to members of the Meccano Guild and of the Hornby Railway Company, to all Meccano boys, and to all to whom my father's invention and its developments have brought pleasure. I assure them that I shall do my utmost to further their interests and to carry on the high traditions associated with the name of Frank Hornby.

Yours very sincerely,

Roland G. Hornby.

Fig. 22

Fig. 23

Frank Hornby explaining the manufacture of Meccano Parts to the Duke of York, on the occasion of His Royal Highness' visit to the Meccano Factory in 1930.

1937, further change took place: the outfits in the series A to L were replaced with a new numbered series, the largest set of which was the No. 10. The new No. 10 was somewhat smaller than the 'L' set but, of course, a keen model builder was not restricted to any particular set, and spare parts were readily available to enable any model, past or present to be constructed.

However, to return to 1934, the December *Meccano Magazine* described 'the New Meccano' in detail, and the fairly simple models illustrated showed the considerable advance the Company had brought about. In the same issue a new accessory set for lighting models (Fig. 20) was also described. This remained in the system until the war, and consisted of two Head Lamps which could be mounted in various positions (Fig. 19), two pea bulbs with flex and Terminals and, somewhat surprisingly a table lamp of the doll's house variety.

On Monday, 21st of September 1936, following an operation at the David Lewis Northern Hospital in Liverpool, Frank Hornby died. It was too late to include an obituary in the next *Meccano Magazine*, but the November editorial was devoted to this. A message from Roland Hornby, (Fig. 22) who succeeded his father, told of letters of sympathy from boys all over the world. It is amazing how the invention of one man had affected the lives of so many, and in spite of being an active Member of Parliament he was fully involved in company policy right up to the time of his death.

During 1938, the *Meccano Magazine* ran a regular series called 'In search of new models'. Each article had a theme – road vehicles, aeroplanes, etc – and although several models were illustrated, instructions for their construction were not given. This may have been to encourage boys to invent their own models, rather than to have them depicted in detail, as had previously been the practice.

Meccano has always had a serious application in such fields as experimental engineering and scientific laboratory work, and a very unusual 'model' of this kind was described in the Magazine for June 1938. Invented and built by Dr Axel Saugman, it was an Arc Lamp (Fig. 24) used with considerable success in the treatment of skin tuberculosis.

Meccano Model-Building Contests, on which Frank Hornby had been so keen, were continued, and during the late 1930s some quite spectacular prize-winning models appeared, as builders of giant models took full advantage of the new parts to

Fig. 24

A powerful arc lamp constructed mainly from Meccano parts. It was designed and built by Dr. Axel Saugman, Odense, Denmark, and has been used with great success in the treatment of skin tuberculosis.

achieve remarkable realism. To the fortunate few with vast quantities of Meccano – to say nothing of the necessary time and skill – the new parts had opened up interesting possibilities of building realistic large-scale models of actual locomotives, ships and other engineering wonders of the period.

During the summer of 1939, the 'new models' section of the Magazine was devoted, appropriately enough, to ships, aeroplanes and tanks of the fighting services, and in August, a Special Meccano Army set was introduced, to which I shall refer again later.

Like most other firms, Meccano Ltd now turned their attention increasingly to Government work. In the October 1939 issue of the *Meccano Magazine*, the Editor expressed the hope that the magazine would continue and, although a smaller format was adopted, publication of the Magazine continued, uninterrupted, throughout the war. On another page of that same issue, a notice warned of possible increases in prices but not of shortages! The war was to bring about tremendous changes in Meccano products, as in so many other things.

The beginnings of serious Meccano shortages however came in December 1940 with an announcement that 'certain Meccano parts are no longer available owing to wartime conditions'. The manufacture of Meccano was gradually phased-out at Binns Road as the war progressed but, stocks still existed both there and in the shops. On 30th September 1943 however, a Government Order prohibited the sale of any new or secondhand models and toys made from metal. From that date the Meccano advertisements in the Magazine and elsewhere stated that although Meccano could not be supplied, it would be available again after the war (Fig. 25).

So the blue/gold era was a relatively short one, which came to an end through circumstances outside the Company's control. However, the blue/gold finish continued to be marketed by Meccano (France) SA until recent times. It was to be more than three years before Meccano was seen again in British shops, at which time it reverted to red and green.

Fig. 25

MECCANO

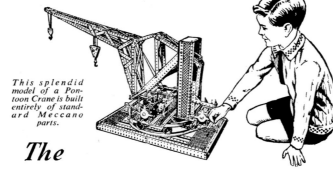

This splendid model of a Pontoon Crane is built entirely of standard Meccano parts.

The World's Greatest Toys

We regret that we cannot supply these famous toys to-day, but they will be ready for you again after the war. Look out for the good times coming.

HORNBY TRAINS

A Hornby Passenger Set passing under a Gantry Signal.

MECCANO
DINKY TOYS
HORNBY TRAINS
DUBLO TRAINS

Here is what you are looking for—
THE FIRST GOOD NEWS.

A limited supply of the smaller Meccano Outfits
and a first instalment of Dinky Toys will be
ready during December.

Obtainable ONLY from Meccano dealers.

MECCANO LIMITED - BINNS ROAD - LIVERPOOL 13

A NOTICE ON THE BACK OF the December 1945 issue of *Meccano Magazine* headed 'The First Good News' (Fig. 26) announced that a supply of smaller Meccano outfits would be in the shops that month. Some of these might have been 'unfrozen' war-time stocks and therefore in blue and gold.

The first illustration of a post-war Meccano Set appeared on the back of the November 1946 issue, where a red and green No. 4 Set was illustrated, although with the contents arranged differently from the pre-war version.

As well as the smaller sets, supplies of separate Meccano parts gradually became available during 1948. Some parts, such as the Geared Roller Bearing and Digger Bucket were not re-introduced, but the majority of the three-hundred-odd parts in the Meccano system did return.

Throughout 1948 and 1949 no new Meccano items were introduced, and the Company was hard-pressed to keep up the supplies of sets and spares. By January 1950, the No. 10 Set was still shown in the list as 'available later', but the No. 9 Set had returned. Contents in the post-war No. 9 Set were similar to the pre-war equivalent, except that the set did not now include a Clockwork Motor. In January 1950, a new Gears Outfit (Fig. 31) was added to the system which enabled owners of smaller sets to drive their models through Gears or Sprockets and Chain.

For giving models motive power, two Clockwork and two Electric Motors were made available, one of which – the No. 1 Clockwork Motor – was completely re-designed. The Electric Motors and transformers were now made only in 20 volt versions.

During the early 1950s, prices began to escalate setting an irreversible trend, and worse still, national shortages of steel and brass caused further difficulties. However, the 1952 catalogue showed the complete range of sets once more, with the price of the No. 10 now triple its pre-war listing. This

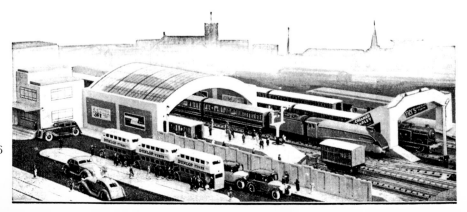

Fig. 26

MECCANO

This splendid model of a Traction Engine is built entirely of standard Meccano parts.

Fig. 28

Here are two pictures to remind you of the happy days you used to have before the war. It will not be long now before the good times are here again.

The small supplies our dealers will have during December are only a beginning.

HORNBY TRAINS

Here is the famous Hornby S.R. Locomotive "Eton" hauling an express passenger train.

MECCANO LIMITED
BINNS ROAD, LIVERPOOL 13

Fig. 27

Fig. 29

Fig. 30

Fascinating...NEW... Meccano Special Models

We have recently published twelve Special Leaflets—part of a series of twenty—each containing clear illustrations and detailed building-instructions for a new and attractive model that can be built with Meccano Outfit No. 10. The present range is listed below; other leaflets are in preparation and will be available soon.

Leaflet No.								Price
Leaflet No.	1	(6-pages)	Railway Service Crane	..	..	..	..	1/3
,,	2	(6-pages)	Sports Motor Car	..	..	..	..	1/3
,,	3	(4-pages)	Coal Tippler..	..	..	..	..	1/-
,,	4	(6-pages)	Cargo Ship	..	..	..	..	1/3
,,	5	(6-pages)	Double Deck Bus	..	..	..	..	1/3
,,	6	(6-pages)	Lifting Shovel	..	..	..	..	1/3
,,	7	(5-pages)	Block-setting Crane	..	..	..	..	1/3
,,	8	(6-pages)	Beam Bridge..	..	..	..	..	1/3
,,	9	(4-pages)	Dumper Truck	..	..	..	..	1/-
,,	10	(6-pages)	Automatic Gantry Crane	..	..	..	1/3
,,	11	(3-pages)	Automatic Snow Loader	..	..	..	1/6
,,	12	(8-pages)	4 4 0 Passenger Locomotive and Tender	..	..	1/6

Obtainable from Meccano dealers, or direct from Meccano Limited, Binns Road, Liverpool 13 (postage 1½d. extra).

MECCANO 4-4-0 Passenger Locomotive and Tender

MECCANO Automatic Snow Loader

MECCANO Automatic Gantry Crane

MECCANO Lifting Shovel

The above set of 12 Leaflets in an imitation book cloth wallet costs 15/- (plus 1/1d. post if ordered direct).

NOTE
The postage rates indicated apply only in the United Kingdom.

economic trend was also apparent in Model Building Contests; for example, the competition announced in December 1952 offered £50 as the first prize. Of the models entered several set a new standard in Meccano construction and included a Juke Box (Fig. 28) and a Duplicating Machine, (Fig. 29) both of which functioned like their prototypes.

Early in 1955, a series of twelve special leaflets (Fig. 30) showing new models for the No. 10 Outfit was produced. Later, the series was extended to 20, and replaced the No. 10 Manual which was still being included in the Outfit up to 1955.

At the end of 1959, the Mechanisms Outfit appeared (Fig. 32). Whilst being complete in itself, this new set could also be used in conjunction with a standard set.

The 1962 up-dating of Meccano did not this time come just before Christmas, but instead in March. The main new parts added on this occasion were a series of red and transparent plates in flexible plastic. Plastic Plates spring back to their original shape when unbolted, and the transparent variety were, of course, used to represent windows and glass panels. In the re-styled outfits – which included these new parts – new manuals were issued which showed models in an 'exploded' form without any instructions. The big advantage of this was that translations were no longer necessary, however some people found the new-style diagrams harder to follow than previous fully annotated instructions.

The smaller of Meccano's two Electric Motors now became obsolete, and its place was taken by the 'Emebo', a tiny motor of considerable power, capable of being driven from a dry battery.

In May 1963, the Elektrikit developed by Meccano (France) SA the previous year, was introduced to Meccano enthusiasts in Britain. This set contained electrical, lighting, insulating and magnetic components of an entirely new design for use with the standard Meccano parts.

The second red-and-green period ended in the summer of 1964 when the 'new look' Meccano was announced. Strips and Girders were now finished in silver instead of green, Flat Plates became yellow, and Flanged Plates – with certain other parts – were sprayed black. Meccano Ltd claimed that the new colours made Meccano models look more like the real thing, and certainly, yellow and silver were colours frequently seen on building sites and road construction projects throughout the country.

25

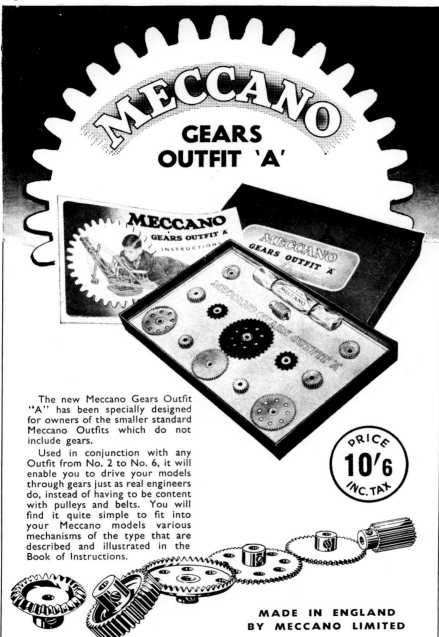
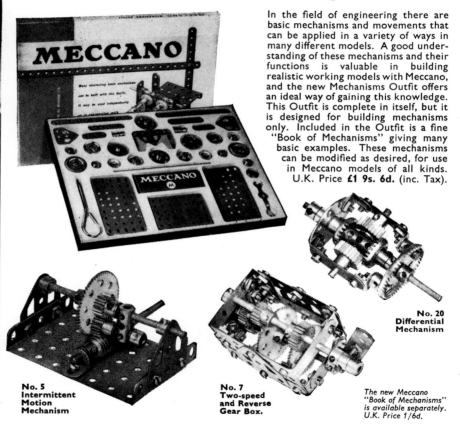
26

Fig. 33

Fig. 34

Fig. 35

Fig. 36

Sets 1 to 9 were now given thematic titles; for example, No.6 became 'Ocean Terminal Set'. As far as separate spare parts were concerned, the colour changes were gradual, and depended on the speed with which dealers' stocks were replenished. In fact, some red-and-green Meccano could still be found in shops well into the 1970s.

During 1965, new power units were added to the Meccano Range under the general name of 'Power Drive': these included two Electric Motors, the larger having a six-ratio gearbox with nylon gears selected by a knob which could be locked in position. These new motors both had plastic bodies.

The other item in the family was a Steam Engine, made for Meccano Ltd by Malins (Engineers) Ltd, manufacturers of the well-known 'Mamod' range. It resembled the 1928 Meccano Steam Engine except for its horizontal rather than vertical boiler.

A noticeable trend during the late 1960s was the return of a general interest in complex Meccano models, and this was reflected in contemporary *Meccano Magazine* articles. Included were such models as a Binary Counting Machine, a Remote-Controlled Tank, and several working models of machinery which catered for advanced model-builders with a large supply of Meccano parts at their disposal.

In March 1970, Meccano adopted the slogan 'Meccano for the Space Age' and the Company revised the sets once more, dropping the thematic titles and the No. 9 Set, renumbering sets 0–8 as 1–9, and packaging these renumbered sets in eye-catching dark blue cartons with silver lettering. New coloured manuals were also produced, using the same 'exploded' form. Several new parts were introduced, including an ingenious plastic Multi Purpose Gear Wheel. Colour changes this time were not so drastic; in the main black parts became blue, while yellow and silver parts remained unaltered.

By this time however the silver paint was replaced by bright zinc-plating, and this finish was also used for all parts previously nickel-plated and a few that had previously been coloured. Another addition to the system was the Electronic Control Set, containing a Photocell and a Relay, by means of which even those with no knowledge of electronics could control their models by light beams. The next interesting addition to the system was the Pocket Meccano Set of 1971 (Figs. 33–36). Containing only eighteen standard parts, (exclusive of Nuts and Bolts) it put inventive youngsters (and some adults!) to work, discovering the ingenious models that could be made within the tight limits of the Set.

The Meccano story is brought up to date with the price of the No. 10 Set currently standing at around £200. What appears to be a history of constant change was in fact a long history of very minor changes, and it could be said that Meccano has, in a sense, never changed. Undoubtedly Frank Hornby would instantly recognise his product in the seventies, as most of the original parts are still in the system, unchanged, except for their colours.

Recently, Meccano Ltd celebrated their 75th anniversary, and it is interesting to reflect how Frank Hornby's original concept has withstood the test of time.

The Meccano Crystal Radio Receiving Set.

Fig. 37

Fig. 38

MECCANO
AEROPLANE
CONSTRUCTOR
OUTFITS

Every boy should know how aeroplanes are designed and constructed, and should be able to recognise the different types of machines at a glance. These fine Constructor Outfits contain a range of aeroplane parts by means of which boys are able to design and build their own Aeroplanes quite easily.

Price List of Aeroplane Outfits

Standard Series

No. OO Outfit	...	...	3/3	No. 1 Outfit	7/6
No. O Outfit	...	...	4/6	No. 2 Outfit	12/6

Special Series

No. 1 Special Outfit	... 12/6	No. 2 Special Outfit ...	21/-

Note. The parts in the No. OO and No. O Outfits are not intended for use with the larger Outfits.

AT VARIOUS TIMES DURING the history of Meccano, special sets have been produced with the limited purpose of constructing models of one type only. These have often consisted of standard parts, sometimes in non-standard colours, plus some special parts; certain sets were however made up entirely of special parts. A brief chronological review of these special sets will reveal that they span the years from the early 1920s to the present day.

Radio Sets

In 1922, Meccano Ltd produced their first two radio sets (Fig. 37) which were obtainable either as finished receivers or a kit of parts. Separate spares were, of course, available. The radios were 'crystal sets' typical of the period, and some standard Meccano parts were used in their construction. Single headphones were supplied at first, but pairs appeared later when an aerial outfit (minus pole!) was produced.

Following technical objections by the Postmaster General, Meccano Ltd revised these sets, and from 1923 the No. 1 Set was sold complete, and the No. 2 Set as a kit of parts for experimental purposes, for which an experimental licence was needed. By 1930, advances in radio made the Sets obsolete, and

the Company sold off remaining stocks at reduced prices during that year.

Aeroplane Constructor Outfits

In October 1931, Meccano Ltd announced the new Aeroplane Constructor Outfits (Fig. 38). There were two sets, No. 1 and No. 2, with a No. 1A to convert the smaller to the larger. With the exception of a few standard Meccano parts, aeroplane parts were entirely new, and sprayed an aluminium colour. The price initially was 9/- for No. 1 Outfit and 16/6d for No. 2. Both contained body and wing sections, but the latter had additional parts such as die-cast engines, and seaplane floats. Six models – three monoplanes and three biplanes – were shown in the No. 1 Outfit Manual while an additional sixteen models of a more advanced type could be made with the larger set. In their advertising, Meccano Ltd stressed that by buying an Aeroplane Constructor Outfit, a boy could understand how real planes were made and recognise the different types. In addition, boys were able to build models of their own design, as spare parts could be purchased separately.

Soon after the introduction of the aeroplane outfits, two

MOTOR CAR CONSTRUCTOR OUTFITS

Now is the time to get a Meccano Motor Car Outfit. You will never grow tired of building and running the superb models that you will be able to build. Your days will be full of fun and thrills!

Perfect miniature reproductions of many different types of car can be built with these splendid Outfits, and a powerful clockwork motor, that gives the models a long run on one winding, is included in each Outfit.

Fig. 39

Prices of Motor Car Outfits

No. 1 Outfit ... ... 8′6	No. 2 Outfit ... ... 17′6

clockwork motors were made available for building into the models. The simpler of the two merely spun the propeller, while the larger motor also turned the landing wheels thus enabling the model to taxi along the ground.

Improvements to Meccano aeroplane parts were announced in December 1932. Formed edges were provided on the wings and tailplanes, giving them a more solid and realistic appearance. Fuselage sections and wing tips were enamelled red, and new-style wheels with spats were substituted for the original red Pulleys. These detail improvements gave the models a more lifelike appearance.

At about the same time, the Nos 00 and 0 Aeroplane Outfits were introduced to meet the demand for cheaper and simpler sets. There were fewer parts in these; for example the fuselage was in one piece, and as 6BA Nuts and Bolts were used, No. 00/0 Outfit parts were not interchangeable with those in sets 1 and 2.

During 1933, the No. 1 Special and No. 2 Special Outfits joined the series. They were launched in the October *Meccano Magazine* for that year by an advertisement headed 'Meccano

never stands still'. In addition to containing parts from the existing No. 1 and 2 Outfits, special parts included fuselage sides with passenger windows, pilots' cabins, wings with moving ailerons, and rudders with moving fins. The special Outfits were obtainable in either red and cream, blue and white or green and ivory colour schemes which also eventually replaced the aluminium colour of the standard sets. Twenty different models were illustrated in the No. 1 Special Manual and forty-four were shown for the larger set. At the same time, a model pilot was introduced for fitting into the open-cockpit models.

The No. 00/0, Standard, and Special series sets were all available up to the early part of the war. Later sets had civilian as well as military markings, and the No. 00/0 Series was, for a time, available also in military finishes. By 1941 all aeroplane sets were withdrawn and they were not to reappear.

Motor Car Constructor Outfits
The first Motor Car Outfit was put on the British market in September 1932 and was a superb production. Unlike any other special-purpose Meccano set before or since, no empty

holes showed on the completed model, and special flat 6BA Bolts were used. Models built from the set therefore resembled the non-constructional models in almost every respect. (Fig. 39).

Cars made with the first outfit were sports- or sports/racing-types, and their style could be varied, as alternative types of radiators, mudguards and body-tail sections were supplied with the outfit. Special features were correct Ackermann steering and an internal expanding rear brake with characteristic outside lever. A powerful clockwork motor was fitted, for which a run of 150 feet was claimed. The original set could be obtained with a red, blue or green body; the quality of paintwork was to the finest Binns Road standard. At 25/- the set was not cheap, and in the economic conditions of 1932, sales must have been limited.

In May 1933, a smaller Motor Car Constructor Outfit was introduced at 14/6d which was designated No. 1 while the original set became No. 2. The new set was to a smaller scale, had fewer parts and lacked some of the special features. However, saloon as well as open cars could be built from it, and the same rich enamelled finish was applied.

A few months later, improvements were made to the No. 2 Set. A driver, complete with helmet, was produced for fixing into the seat, the brake lever was fitted with a grip handle, and a metal spare-wheel cover replaced the earlier fifth wheel. A lighting set for fitting electric bulbs into the head-lamps was also made available as an extra item.

Motor Car Constructor Outfits did not appear to be very popular. In 1933, the back page and centre pages of several *Meccano Magazines* were devoted to advertisements for them. In 1935, the prices were reduced to 10/- and 20/- respectively for the two outfits. Various reasons for the relatively poor sales of this range include the comparative rarity of real cars in the 1930s and the fact that No. 1 and No. 2 Motor Car sets were not interchangeable with each other or with standard Meccano. The great rarity of surviving Motor Car Sets, compared with other old Meccano products, seems to indicate that only a small quantity were produced. The No. 1 Set was withdrawn in 1940 and the No. 2 Set in 1941. Like the Aeroplane Sets, they never re-appeared but entered the world of Meccano historians and collectors.

The Mechanised Army Outfit of 1939

In August 1939, appropriately enough, the Meccano 'Mechanised Army Outfit' was introduced. It consisted for the most part of standard Meccano items, finished in army green, with fewer holes. Special parts included a series of three Gun Barrels made of wood.

Multikit Sets

The story is brought up to date with the advent of the Multikit Sets in 1973. By this time, Meccano had established itself amongst the post-war generation while also attracting many older Meccano enthusiasts back to the hobby. The philosophy behind the introduction of the Multikit idea was explained by the Company in the April 1973 edition of *Meccano Magazine*.

The Multikit idea produced models which had an instant visual appeal whilst retaining all the advantages of Meccano. Initially there were two Multikit Sets, one in olive green for making army models, and one in yellow for modelling civilian road vehicles. New parts to be included in both sets (known as 'Army' and 'Highway' respectively) were a realistic Cab, wide Road Wheels and self-adhesive Stickers. These new parts, combined with a good selection of standard parts, and the one-colour effect, produced models which – whilst being instantly recognizable as Meccano – also had the appearance of ready-made steel toys. The new Multikit parts were of course interchangeable with standard Meccano. It was the Company's hope that a child first attracted to a Multikit would progress later to the Meccano standard sets. The full-colour manuals included with the sets gave step-by-step instructions in a series of pictures.

The sets have sold well, and additions to the range have recently been made. The first of these, the Super Highway Kit, is a development of the original and is slanted at road-construction models.

The next development, the Combat Multikit, was introduced as a result of the overwhelming success of the Army Multikit. It is also for making military models, albeit to a smaller scale, although it can be combined with the existing Army Set for building larger models.

In the year of Meccano's 75th Anniversary, yet one more Multikit was introduced – The Crane-Building Set – whilst being a subject new to the Multikit range, it has fittingly returned to the very first Meccano theme. With parts finished overall in yellow, and the introduction of a new Electric Motor, this anniversary outfit took the Multikit concept one stage further.

The Book of HORNBY TRAINS *and* MECCANO PRODUCTS

PRICE 9D

MECCANO LTD
BINNS ROAD
LIVERPOOL, 13.

MECCANO
PRODUCTS

Our 1935 Catalogue

This new Meccano Catalogue de Luxe contains full particulars of all the articles manufactured by Meccano Limited, and the majority of them are illustrated in actual colours. They have been arranged in such a manner that easy reference to any particular article can be made.

Under each Hornby Train Set illustration is stated the price of the complete Set with a Clockwork Locomotive and (where it is supplied) of the same set with an Electric Locomotive. The price of every unit of Rolling Stock, together with all information connected with each Set, is also given. In order to distinguish the Clockwork Train descriptive matter from the Electric, the former is printed in black and the latter in red.

This magnificent Catalogue is well worth keeping. Take it with you when you visit your dealer.

HORNBY ELECTRIC AND CLOCKWORK TRAINS

The Completeness of the Hornby Railway System

From the day of their introduction Hornby Trains have always represented the latest model railway practice. Designs are continually being improved and new items added so that the system is complete in practically every detail. There are Locomotives for all duties, driven by electric motors or by clockwork. There is Rolling Stock of all kinds, including Pullman Cars, ordinary Coaches and Guard's Vans for passenger services; and there are numerous and varied Wagons and Vans for freight working.

The Accessories are now better than ever before. Stations, Signals and Signal Cabins, Engine Sheds, Level Crossings and other items can be obtained wired for electric lighting. Miniature Trees and Hedging provide a splendid scenic setting for any layout; Cuttings and Tunnels add realism to the track; miniature Railway Staff and Passengers give "life" to station platforms; and there are Animals for lineside fields. There is practically no limit to the number of rail formations that can be built with Hornby Rails, Points and Crossings. A large variety is illustrated and described in the booklet "Hornby Layouts—One Hundred Suggestions," which is obtainable from your dealer, price 3d., or direct from Meccano Limited, Binns Road, Liverpool 13, price 4d., post free.

Perfect Miniature Railways

The splendid fun of running a Hornby Railway is real and lasting, because of the exceptional strength and reliability of Hornby Locomotives, the realistic appearance and easy running of the Rolling Stock, and the wide range of effective Accessories—all designed and built in proportion and all splendidly finished.

Hornby Electric Locomotives, of which there is a wide selection, are fitted with powerful and efficient motors capable of hauling heavy loads at high speeds, but always under perfect control. All Hornby Electric Locomotives can be controlled for speed, and for starting and stopping, from the lineside. The most complete control is afforded with the 20-volt locomotives with automatic reversing mechanism. This enables a train to be started and stopped, controlled for speed, and reversed from the lineside, without touching the locomotive at all.

Hornby Clockwork Locomotives are the longest-running spring-driven locomotives of their respective types in the world. The motors fitted are of the highest possible quality, being perfect mechanisms with accurately cut gears that ensure smooth and steady running.

In the following pages the components of the Hornby Series—Locomotives, Rolling Stock and Accessories, are fully described. Under each Hornby Train Set illustration is stated the price of the complete Set with a Clockwork Locomotive and (where it is supplied) of the same set with an Electric Locomotive. In order to distinguish the Clockwork Train descriptive matter from the Electric, the former is printed in black and the latter in red.

The Finish of Hornby Locomotives

Hornby Locomotives, with certain exceptions, are available finished in the passenger or the goods traffic colours of the four British railway groups. The passenger traffic colours are red for L.M.S.R., light green for L.N.E.R., and dark green for G.W.R. and S.R. The goods traffic colours are black for L.M.S.R., L.N.E.R. and S.R., and dark green for G.W.R.

Guarantee Every Hornby Locomotive is thoroughly tested and is guaranteed to be in good running order when it leaves our factory. Hornby Trains are manufactured by Meccano Limited, Liverpool, and are constructed throughout by expert craftsmen from the finest materials obtainable.

Run your own Railway! The Hornby System includes everything that is necessary to equip a complete miniature railway, either electric or clockwork, to be operated in exactly the same way as a real railway system.

Gauge 0, 1¼ in.

The MO Sets are made for clockwork railways only. The components are strongly built and well finished, and the Locomotives are fitted with a very efficient clockwork mechanism that gives a long run. The Sets can be obtained with the Locomotive and Tender coloured in either red or green.

MO CLOCKWORK GOODS TRAIN SET consists of a Locomotive and Tender (available in either red or green), two MO Wagons, and a set of Rails requiring a space measuring 2 ft. square. One rail is an MB9 Curved Brake Rail, by means of which the Train can be braked from the track. Non-reversible ... ... **Price 4/11**

MO CLOCKWORK PASSENGER TRAIN SET consists of a Locomotive and Tender (available in red or green), two MO Pullman Coaches, and a set of Rails requiring a space measuring 2 ft. square. One rail is an MB9 Curved Brake Rail, by means of which the Train can be braked from the track. Non-reversible ... ... **Price 5/6**

The components of the MO Train Sets are obtainable separately at the following prices:—

MO Locomotive (Non-reversing) ... Price 2/9	**MO Tender** ... Price 6d.	**MO Wagon** ... Price 6d.	**MO Pullman Coach** ... Price 9d.

RAILS FOR MO TRAIN SETS

BM Straight Rails ... ... Price per doz. 2/6	**M9 Curved Rails** (9 in. radius) ... ... Price per doz. 2/6
MR9 or ML9 Points, right-hand or left-hand ... Price per pair 3/–	**MB9 Curved Brake Rails**, 9 in. ... ... Price each 3d.

HORNBY ELECTRIC AND CLOCKWORK TRAINS

**Gauge 0,
1¼ in.**

*This is Hornby
EM16 Electric
Goods Train
Set (6-volt).*

EM120 ELECTRIC GOODS TRAIN SET (20-volt). This Train consists of EM120 Locomotive (non-reversing), M1/2 Tender, two M1 Goods Wagons (lettered L.M.S., N.E., G.W., or S.R.), and set of Electric Rails requiring a space measuring 3 ft. 3 in. by 2 ft. 6 in. One of the rails is the EMC20 Combined Switch Rail, incorporating a switch by means of which the train can be started or stopped. This rail provides also for the connection of the power supply (20-volt Transformer) to the track. The Locomotive and Tender are available in red (with wagons lettered L.M.S.), and green (with wagons lettered N.E., G.W. or S.R.). ... **Price 15/-**

EM16 ELECTRIC GOODS TRAIN SET (6-volt). This Set is similar to the EM120 Goods Train Set, except that the Locomotive is fitted with a 6-volt motor. An EMC5 Combined Switch Rail provides for the connection of the power supply (6-volt Transformer or accumulator) to the track ... **Price 15/-**

M1 CLOCKWORK GOODS TRAIN SET. The contents of this Set are as those of the EM120 and EM16 Electric Goods Train Sets, described above, except that the Locomotive is fitted with a reversing clockwork mechanism. The Electric Rails and Fittings are replaced by a set of Clockwork Rails, including a BB1 Straight Brake Rail, by means of which the Train can be braked from the track ... ... **Price 8/11**

The Locomotives and other Components of the above Train Sets can be purchased separately at the prices indicated at the foot of this page.

*This is Hornby
EM120 Electric
Passenger Train
Set (20-volt).*

EM120 ELECTRIC PASSENGER TRAIN SET (20-volt) consists of an EM120 Electric Locomotive (non-reversing), M1/2 Tender, two M1 Pullman Coaches and a set of Electric Rails requiring a space measuring 3 ft. 3 in. by 2 ft. 6 in. One of the rails is the EMC20 Switch Rail, incorporating a switch by means of which a train can be started or stopped. This rail provides also for the connection of the power supply (20-volt Transformer) to the track. The Locomotive and Tender are available in red or green ... **Price 15/-**

M1 CLOCKWORK PASSENGER TRAIN SET. The contents of this Set are as those of the EM120 Electric Train Set, except that the Locomotive is fitted with a reversing clockwork mechanism instead of an electric motor. The Electric Rails and fittings are replaced by a set of Clockwork Rails including a BB1 Straight Brake Rail, by means of which the Train can be braked from the track ... ... **Price 8/11**

M2 CLOCKWORK PASSENGER TRAIN SET. This Set is similar to the M1 Clockwork Passenger Train Set, but it has three Pullman Coaches instead of two, and the set of Rails requires a space measuring 4 ft. 3 in. by 2 ft. 6 in. ... ... **Price 10/6**

The components of all the above Train Sets are obtainable separately at the following prices:—

EM120 or EM16 Electric Locomotive, non-reversing (without Tender) ... ... **Price 8/6**		
M1/2 Clockwork Locomotive, reversing (without Tender) ... **Price 4/6**	M1/2 Tender ... ... **Price 9d.**	
M1 Wagon ... ... **Price 1/-**	M1 Pullman Coach ... ... **Price 1/-**	

For Electric and Clockwork Rails, Points and Crossings, see pages 30 and 31. Details of Transformers are given on page 42.

HORNBY ELECTRIC AND CLOCKWORK TRAINS

Gauge 0, 1¼ in.

M3 CLOCKWORK TANK PASSENGER TRAIN SET. This new Train Set consists of M3 Tank Locomotive (reversing) fitted with a long-running clockwork mechanism, three No. O Pullman Coaches and a set of rails requiring a space measuring 4 ft. 3 in. by 2 ft. 6 in. One of the rails is a BB1 Straight Brake Rail, by means of which the Train can be braked from the track. The Locomotive is available in the passenger traffic colours of the four British railway groups ... ... **Price 13/9**

The Locomotive and Pullman Coaches of the above Train Set can be purchased separately at the prices given at the foot of this page.

THE FINISH OF HORNBY LOCOMOTIVES

With certain exceptions, Hornby Locomotives are available finished in the goods or passenger traffic colours of the four British railway groups. The goods traffic colours are black for L.M.S.R., L.N.E.R., and S.R., and dark green for G.W.R. The passenger traffic colours are red for L.M.S.R., light green for L.N.E.R., and dark green for G.W.R. and S.R.

This is Hornby EM36 Electric Tank Goods Train Set (6-volt).

EM320 ELECTRIC TANK GOODS TRAIN SET (20-volt). This Train Set is composed of EM320 Tank Locomotive (reversible from the cab) fitted with a powerful electric Motor, Goods Wagon, Timber Wagon, Petrol Tank Wagon and a set of Electric Rails requiring a space measuring 3 ft. 3 in. by 2 ft. 6 in. A Terminal Connecting Plate with plug fittings is included for the connection of the power supply (20-volt Transformer) to the track. The Locomotive, which is fitted with an electric headlamp, is available in the passenger traffic colours of all four British railway groups ... ... **Price 24/-**

EM36 ELECTRIC TANK GOODS TRAIN SET (6-volt). The contents of this Set are similar to those of the EM320 Electric Tank Goods Train Set, except that the Locomotive is fitted with a 6-volt motor. A Terminal Connecting Plate with screw fittings is provided to connect the power supply (6-volt Transformer or accumulator) to the track ... **Price 24/-**

M3 CLOCKWORK TANK GOODS TRAIN SET. The components of this Set are as those of the EM320 and EM36 Sets, except that the Locomotive has a reversing clockwork mechanism, instead of an electric motor, and has no headlamp. The Electric Rails and fittings are replaced by a set of Clockwork Rails including a BB1 Brake Rail, by means of which the Train can be braked from the track ... ... **Price 15/-**

The Locomotives in the above Train Sets, and also the No. O Pullman Coaches of the M3 Clockwork Tank Passenger Train Set, are obtainable separately.

EM320 or EM36 Electric Tank Locomotive (reversible from cab) ... ... **Price 16/6**

M3 Clockwork Tank Locomotive (reversing) ... ... **Price 7/6**   **No. O Pullman Coach** ... ... **Price 1/3**

For Electric and Clockwork Rails, Points and Crossings, see pages 30 and 31. Details of Transformers are given on page 42.

HORNBY ELECTRIC AND CLOCKWORK TRAINS

Hornby No. EO20 Electric Passenger Train Set (20-volt).

HORNBY EO20 ELECTRIC PASSENGER TRAIN SET (20-volt). This handsome Train Set contains EO20 Locomotive (reversible from the cab) with an electric headlamp, No. O/1 Tender, two No. O Pullman Coaches, and a set of Electric Rails requiring a space measuring 3 ft. 3 in. by 2 ft. 6 in. A Terminal Connecting Plate with plug fittings is included for the connection of the power supply (20-volt Transformer) to the track. The Set is available with Locomotive and Tender in the passenger traffic colours of the four British Railway groups—L.M.S.R., L.N.E.R., G.W.R., and S.R. ... ... **Price 30/-**

HORNBY No. O CLOCKWORK PASSENGER TRAIN SET. The components of this Set are as those of the EO20 Electric Set, except that the Locomotive is fitted with a reversing clockwork mechanism instead of an electric motor, and has no headlamp. The Electric Rails and fittings are replaced by a set of Clockwork Rails, including a BB1 Straight Brake Rail, by means of which the Train can be braked from the track ... ... **Price 16/11**

The components of the above Train Sets can be obtained separately. For prices, see foot of this page.

Hornby No. O Clockwork Goods Train Set.

HORNBY No. O CLOCKWORK GOODS TRAIN SET. This realistic Train Set is composed of No. O Locomotive (reversing), No. O/1 Tender, No. O Wagon, No. 1 Timber Wagon, and a set of Rails requiring a space measuring 3 ft. 3 in. by 2 ft. 6 in. One of the rails is a BB1 Straight Brake Rail, by means of which the Train can be braked from the track. The Set is supplied with Locomotive and Tender in either the goods traffic colours or the passenger traffic colours of the four British railway groups ... ... **Price 17/6**

The components of the Train Sets on this page are obtainable separately at the following prices:—

Hornby EO20 Electric Locomotive, reversible from the cab (without Tender)		**Price 22/-**
Hornby No. O Clockwork Locomotive, reversing, (without Tender)		**Price 10/6**
Hornby No. O/1 Tender ... ... **Price 2/-**	**Hornby No. O Wagon**	**Price 1/6**
Hornby No. O Pullman Coach ... ... **Price 1/3**	**Hornby No. 1 Timber Wagon**	**Price 1/6**

For prices of Rails, Points and Crossings, see pages 30 and 31. Details and prices of Transformers are given on page 42.

HORNBY ELECTRIC AND CLOCKWORK TRAINS

Hornby No. E120 Electric Goods Train Set (20-volt).

HORNBY E120 ELECTRIC GOODS TRAIN SET (20-volt). This splendid Train Set contains a powerful E120 Locomotive (reversible from the cab) with electric headlamp, No. O/1 Tender, No. 1 Wagon, Brake Van and a set of Electric Rails requiring a space measuring 4 ft. 6 in. square. A Terminal Connecting Plate with plug fittings is included for the connection of the power supply (20-volt Transformer) to the track. Locomotive and Tender are supplied in either the goods traffic colours or the passenger traffic colours of the four British Railway. groups—L.M.S.R., L.N.E.R., G.W.R., and S.R. ... ... **Price 36/-**

Hornby No. 1 CLOCKWORK GOODS TRAIN SET. The components of this Set are as those of the E120 Electric Set, except that the Locomotive is fitted with a reversing clockwork mechanism instead of an electric motor, and has no headlamp. The Electric Rails and fittings are replaced by a set of Clockwork Rails, including an AB2 Curved Brake Rail, by means of which the Train can be either braked or reversed from the track ... ... **Price 22/6**

The components of the above Train Sets are obtainable separately. For prices, see foot of this page.

Hornby No. 1 Clockwork Passenger Train Set.

HORNBY No. 1 CLOCKWORK PASSENGER TRAIN SET. This very attractive Train Set consists of No. 1 Locomotive (reversing), No. O/1 Tender, two No. 1 Passenger Coaches, Guard's Van and a set of Rails requiring a space measuring 4 ft. 6 in. square. An AB2 Curved Brake Rail is included, by means of which the Train can be either braked or reversed from the track. The set is supplied in the passenger traffic colours of the four British railway groups. The Coaches and Guard's Van are of the latest improved design, and are fitted with lamp brackets and tail lamps ... ... **Price 25/-**

The components of the above Train Sets are obtainable separately at the following prices:—

Hornby No. E120 Electric Locomotive, reversible from the cab (without Tender) ... ... **Price 24/-**

Hornby No. 1 Clockwork Locomotive, reversing (without Tender)	**Price 12/6**	Hornby Guard's Van	**Price 2/6**
Hornby No. O/1 Tender	**Price 2/-**	Hornby No. 1 Wagon	**Price 1/9**
Hornby No. 1 Passenger Coach	**Price 2/6**	Hornby Brake Van	**Price 2/11**

THE FINISH OF HORNBY LOCOMOTIVES.

Hornby Locomotives, with certain exceptions, are available finished in the passenger or the goods traffic colours of the four groups. The passenger traffic colours are red for L.M.S.R., light green for L.N.E.R., and dark green for G.W.R. and S.R. The goods traffic colours are black for L.M.S.R., L.N.E.R. and S.R., and dark green for G.W.R.

For prices of Rails, Points and Crossings, see pages 30 and 31. Details and prices of Transformers are given on page 42.

Hornby E16 Electric Tank Goods Train Set (6-volt).

HORNBY E120 ELECTRIC TANK GOODS TRAIN SET (20-volt). This Set consists of E120 Tank Locomotive (reversible from the cab) with electric headlamp, No. 1 Wagon, No. 1 Petrol Tank Wagon, and a set of Electric Rails requiring a space measuring 4 ft. 6 in. square. A Terminal Connecting Plate with plug fittings is included for the connection of the power supply (20-volt Transformer) to the track. The Locomotive can be obtained in either the goods or passenger traffic colours of the four groups. **Price 36/-**

HORNBY E16 ELECTRIC TANK GOODS TRAIN SET (6-volt). The contents of this Set are similar to those of the E120 Electric Tank Goods Train Set, except that the Locomotive is fitted with a 6-volt motor. A Terminal Connecting Plate with screw fittings is included for the connection of the power supply (6-volt Transformer or accumulator) to the track ... ... **Price 36/-**

HORNBY No. 1 CLOCKWORK TANK GOODS TRAIN SET. The contents of this Train Set are as those of the E120 and E16 Electric Tank Sets, except that the Locomotive is fitted with a reversing clockwork mechanism instead of an electric motor, and has no headlamp. The set of Clockwork Rails includes an AB2 Curved Brake Rail, by means of which the Train can be braked or reversed from the track ... ... **Price 22/6**

The components of the above Train Sets can be purchased separately. For prices, see foot of this page.

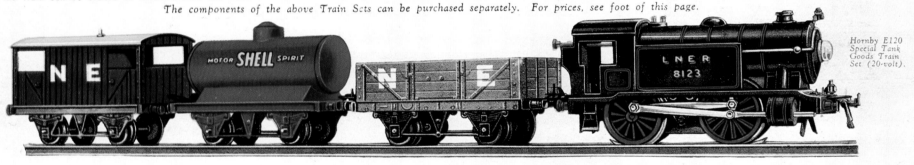

Hornby E120 Special Tank Goods Train Set (20-volt).

HORNBY E120 SPECIAL ELECTRIC TANK GOODS TRAIN SET (20-volt). AUTOMATIC REVERSING. This Train Set is composed of E120 Special Tank Locomotive (automatic reversing) with electric headlamp, No. 1 Wagon, No. 1 Petrol Tank Wagon, Brake Van, and a set of Electric Rails requiring a space 5 ft. 4 in. by 4-ft. 6 in. A Terminal Connecting Plate with plug fittings is included for the connection of the power supply (20-volt Transformer) to the track. The Locomotive is supplied in the goods or passenger traffic colours of the four British Railway groups—L.M.S.R., L.N.E.R., G.W.R. and S.R. **Price 42/-**

HORNBY No. 1 SPECIAL CLOCKWORK TANK GOODS TRAIN SET. This Set is identical with the E120 Electric Goods Train Set, except that the Locomotive is fitted with a reversing clockwork mechanism instead of an electric motor, and has no headlamp. The set of Clockwork Rails includes a BBR1 Brake and Reverse Rail, by means of which the Train can be braked or reversed from the track ... ... **Price 27/6**

The components of the Train Sets on this page are obtainable separately at the following prices:—

Hornby E120 or E16 Electric Tank Locomotive (reversible from the cab)		**Price 24/-**
Hornby E120 Special Electric Tank Locomotive (automatic reversing)		**Price 30/-**
Hornby No. 1 Clockwork Tank Locomotive (reversing)		**Price 12/6**
Hornby No. 1 Special Clockwork Tank Locomotive (reversing) Price 17/6	**Hornby No. 1 Petrol Tank Wagon**	**Price 2/-**
Hornby No. 1 Wagon ... ... Price 1/9	**Hornby Brake Van**	**Price 2/11**

For prices of Hornby Rails, Points and Crossings, see pages 30 and 31. Details and prices of Transformers are given on page 42.

Hornby No. E120 Special Electric Passenger Train Set (20-volt).

HORNBY E120 SPECIAL ELECTRIC PASSENGER TRAIN SET (20-volt). AUTOMATIC REVERSING. This excellent Train Set consists of E120 Special Electric Locomotive (automatic reversing) with electric headlamp, No 1 Special Tender, two No. 1 Pullman Coaches, No. 1 Pullman Coach Composite and a set of Electric Rails requiring a space measuring 5 ft. 4 in. by 4 ft. 6 in. A Terminal Connecting Plate with plug fittings is included for the connection of the power supply (20-volt Transformer) to the track. Locomotive and Tender are supplied in the correct passenger traffic colours of the four British railway groups—L.M.S.R., L.N.E.R., G.W.R., and S.R. ... ... **Price 47/6**

HORNBY No. 1 SPECIAL CLOCKWORK PASSENGER TRAIN SET. The contents of this Set are as those of the E120 Special Electric Passenger Train Set, except that the Locomotive is fitted with a reversing clockwork mechanism instead of an electric motor, and has no headlamp. The Clockwork Rails in the Set include a BBR1 Brake and Reverse Rail, by means of which the Train can be either braked or reversed from the track ... ... **Price 33/-**

The components of the above Train Sets may be obtained separately. For prices, see foot of this page.

Hornby No. E220 Electric Mixed Goods Train Set (20-volt).

HORNBY E220 ELECTRIC MIXED GOODS TRAIN SET (20-volt). AUTOMATIC REVERSING. This realistic Goods Train Set consists of E220 Special Electric Tank Locomotive (automatic reversing), with electric headlamp, No. 1 Wagon, No. 1 Cattle Truck, No. 1 Petrol Tank Wagon, Brake Van, and a set of Electric Rails requiring a space measuring 5 ft. 4 in. by 4 ft. 6 in. A Terminal Connecting Plate with plug fittings is included for the connection of the power supply (20-volt Transformer) to the track. The Set is supplied in the goods traffic colours of the four groups—L.M.S.R., L.N.E.R., G.W.R., and S.R. ... ... **Price 47/6**

HORNBY No. 2 CLOCKWORK MIXED GOODS TRAIN SET. The contents of this Set are as those of the E220 Electric Mixed Goods Set, except that the Locomotive is fitted with a reversing clockwork mechanism, instead of an electric motor, and has no headlamp. The Clockwork Rails in the Set include a BBR1 Brake and Reverse Rail, by means of which the Train can be either braked or reversed from the track ... ... **Price 35/-**

The components of the above Train Sets are obtainable separately at the following prices:—

Hornby No. E120 Special Electric Locomotive, automatic reversing (without Tender)				Price 30/-
Hornby No. E220 Special Electric Tank Locomotive (automatic reversing)				Price 32/6
Hornby No. 1 Special Clockwork Locomotive, reversing (without Tender) ...				Price 17/6
Hornby No. 2 Special Clockwork Tank Locomotive (reversing) Price 21/-	Hornby Brake Van ...			Price 2/11
Hornby No. 1 Special Tender ... ... Price 3/3	Hornby No. 1 Wagon			Price 1/9
Hornby No. 1 Pullman Coach Composite ... ... Price 2/9	Hornby No. 1 Petrol Tank Wagon			Price 2/-
Hornby No. 1 Pullman Coach ... ... Price 2/9	Hornby No. 1 Cattle Truck			Price 2/9

For prices of Rails, Points and Crossings, see pages 30 and 31. Details and prices of Transformers are given on page 42.

HORNBY ELECTRIC AND CLOCKWORK TRAINS

HORNBY E36 ELECTRIC METROPOLITAN TRAIN SET (6-volt). The contents of this Train Set are a Metropolitan Locomotive (reversible by hand) with electric headlamps, Metropolitan 1st class compartment Coach, Metropolitan brake-third Coach fitted for electric lighting, and a set of Electric Rails requiring a space 4 ft. 6 in. square. A Terminal Connecting Plate, with screw fittings, is included for the connection of the power supply (6-volt Transformer or accumulator) to the track ... ... **Price 57/6**

HORNBY No. 3C CLOCKWORK METROPOLITAN TRAIN SET. The contents of this Set are as those of the E36 Metropolitan Electric Set, except that the Locomotive is fitted with reversing clockwork mechanism, and has no headlamps. The Coaches are not fitted for electric lighting. The Clockwork Rails in the Set require a space measuring 6 ft. 3 in. by 4 ft. 6 in. A BBR1 Brake and Reverse Rail is included, by means of which the Train can be either braked or reversed from the track ... ... **Price 40/-**

The components of the above Train Sets may be obtained separately. The prices are given at the foot of this page.

HORNBY E320 ELECTRIC RIVIERA "BLUE" PASSENGER TRAIN SET (20-volt). AUTOMATIC REVERSING. This Set contains E320 Riviera "Blue" Locomotive (automatic reversing) with electric headlamp, No. 3 Riviera "Blue" Tender, Riviera "Blue" Dining Car and Sleeping Car, and a set of Electric Rails requiring a space 6 ft. 3 in. by 4 ft. 6 in. A Terminal Connecting Plate with plug fittings is included for the connection of the power supply (20-volt Transformer) to the track ... ... **Price 67/6**

HORNBY E36 ELECTRIC RIVIERA "BLUE" PASSENGER TRAIN SET (6-volt). The contents of this Set are as those of the E320 Electric Riviera "Blue" Train Set, except that the Locomotive is fitted with a 6-volt motor that is reversible only by hand from the cab. A Terminal Connecting Plate with screw fittings is provided for the connection of the power supply (6-volt Transformer or accumulator) to the track ... ... **Price 65/-**

HORNBY No. 3 CLOCKWORK RIVIERA "BLUE" PASSENGER TRAIN SET. The contents of this Set are as those of the E320 and E36 Electric Riviera "Blue" Sets, except that the Locomotive is fitted with a reversing clockwork mechanism, and has no headlamp. The Clockwork Rails include a BBR1 Brake and Reverse Rail, by means of which the Train can be either braked or reversed from the track ... ... **Price 57/6**

The components of the above Train Sets are obtainable separately at the following prices:—

Hornby E36 Metropolitan Electric Locomotive (reversible by hand) ...	**Price 30/-**
Hornby E320 Electric Riviera "Blue" Locomotive (automatic reversing) ...	**Price 35/-**
Hornby E36 Electric Riviera "Blue" Locomotive (reversible only from the cab)...	**Price 32/6**

Hornby No. 3C Clockwork Riviera "Blue" Locomotive (reversing) **Price 24/-**	Hornby Riviera "Blue" Tender ...	...	**Price 4/6**
Hornby Riviera "Blue" Sleeping Car ... ... **Price 12/6**	Hornby Riviera "Blue" Dining Car ...	...	**Price 11/6**
Hornby Metropolitan Coach E fitted for electric lighting (1st class or brake-third)	Hornby Metropolitan Coach C (1st class or brake-third)	...	**Price 7/6**
Hornby Metropolitan Clockwork Locomotive C (reversing) ... **Price 21/-**			

For prices of Rails, Points and Crossings, see pages 30 and 31. Details and prices of Transformers are given on page 42.

HORNBY ELECTRIC AND CLOCKWORK TRAINS

Hornby E220 Electric Special Pullman Train Set.

HORNBY E220 ELECTRIC SPECIAL PULLMAN SETS (20-volt). AUTOMATIC REVERSING. The Locomotives and Tenders in these Train Sets respectively represent the L.N.E.R. "Hunt" class, the L.M.S.R. "Standard Compound" class, the G.W.R. "County" class and the S.R. "L1" class. Each Set contains E220 Special Locomotive (automatic reversing) with electric headlamp, No. 2 Special Tender, No. 2 Special Pullman Coach, No. 2 Special Pullman Coach Composite, and Electric Rails requiring a space measuring 5 ft. 4 in. by 4 ft. 6 in. A Terminal Connecting Plate with plug fittings is included for connecting the power supply (20-volt Transformer) to the track.
No. E220 Electric Special Pullman Set, L.N.E.R., L.M.S.R., G.W.R., or S.R. ... ... **Price 75/–**

HORNBY No. 2 SPECIAL CLOCKWORK PULLMAN SETS. These Sets are similar to the Electric Sets above, but the locomotives have no headlamp and are fitted with a powerful reversing clockwork mechanism giving great length of run. The Set of Clockwork Rails includes a BBR1 Brake and Reverse Rail, enabling the Train to be either braked or reversed from the track.
No. 2 Special Clockwork Pullman Set, L.N.E.R., L.M.S.R., G.W.R., or S.R. ... ... **Price 65/–**

The components of the above Train Sets can be obtained separately. The prices are given at the foot of this page.

Hornby E220 Electric Passenger Train Set.

HORNBY E220 ELECTRIC TANK PASSENGER TRAIN SET. AUTOMATIC REVERSING. This new and realistic Train Set consists of E220 Special Tank Locomotive (automatic reversing) with electric headlamp, one first-third No. 2 Coach, one brake-third No. 2 Coach, and set of Electric Rails requiring a space 5 ft. 4 in. by 4 ft. 6 in. A Terminal Connecting Plate with plug fittings is included for the connection of the power supply (20-volt Transformer) to the track. Locomotive and Coaches are obtainable in the passenger traffic colours of the four British railway groups—L.M.S.R., L.N.E.R., G.W.R. and S.R. ... ... **Price 52/6**

HORNBY No. 2 CLOCKWORK TANK PASSENGER TRAIN SET. The contents of this Set are as those of the E220 Tank Passenger Electric Set, except that the Locomotive has a reversing clockwork mechanism, and no headlamp. The Rails include a BBR1 Brake and Reverse Rail, by which the Train can be either braked or reversed from the track. **Price 40/–**

The components of the above Train Sets are obtainable separately at the following prices:—

Hornby E220 Special Electric Locomotive, automatic reversing (without Tender), L.N.E.R. "The Bramham Moor", L.M.S.R. "No. 1185", G.W.R. "County of Bedford", or S.R. "No. A759" ... ... **Price 37/6**
Hornby E220 Special Electric Tank Locomotive (automatic reversing) ... ... **Price 32/6**
Hornby No. 2 Special Clockwork Locomotive (reversing), L.N.E.R., L.M.S.R., G.W.R., or S.R., as above ... ... **Price 27/6**
Hornby No. 2 Special Tender (L.N.E.R., L.M.S.R., G.W.R., or S.R. "No. A759") ... ... **Price 6/–**
Hornby No. 2 Special Clockwork Tank Locomotive (reversing) ... ... **Price 21/–**
Hornby No. 2 Special Pullman Coach "Loraine" ... ... **Price 13/–**   Hornby No. 2 Coach, first-third ... ... **Price 7/6**
Hornby No. 2 Special Pullman Composite Coach, "Verona" ... **Price 14/–**   Hornby No. 2 Coach, brake-third ... ... **Price 7/6**

For prices of Hornby Rails, Points and Crossings, see pages 30 and 31. Details and prices of Transformers are given on page 42.

Hornby No. E36 Electric Pullman Train Set.

HORNBY E320 ELECTRIC PULLMAN TRAIN SETS (20-volt) AUTOMATIC REVERSING. These Sets carry the names of famous British Expresses. Each Set consists of an E320 Locomotive (automatic reversing) with electric headlamp, No. 2 Special Tender, No. 2 Special Pullman Coach, No. 2 Special Pullman Coach Composite, and a set of Electric Rails requiring a space measuring 6 ft. 3 in. by 4 ft. 6 in. A Terminal Connecting Plate with plug fittings is included for the connection of the power supply (20-volt Transformer) to the track. Hornby E320 Train Set "Royal Scot" (L.M.S.R.), "The Flying Scotsman" (L.N.E.R.), "Cornish Riviera Express" (G.W.R.), or "The Golden Arrow" (S.R.) ... **Price 72/6**

HORNBY E36 ELECTRIC PULLMAN TRAIN SETS (6-volt). The contents of these Sets are as those of the E320 Electric Pullman Train Sets, except that the Locomotives are fitted with a 6-volt motor and are reversible only by hand. A Terminal Connecting Plate with screw fittings is provided for the connection of the power supply (6-volt Transformer or accumulator) to the track ... **Price 70/-**

HORNBY No. 3C CLOCKWORK PULLMAN TRAIN SETS. The contents of these Sets are as those of the E320 and E36 Electric Pullman Sets, except that the Locomotives are fitted with reversing clockwork mechanism instead of an electric motor, and have no electric headlamp. The set of Clockwork Rails includes a BBR1 Brake and Reverse Rail, by means of which the Train can be either braked or reversed from the track. **Price 62/6**

The components of the above Train Sets can be purchased separately at the following prices:—

Hornby E320 Electric Locomotive (automatic reversing), "Royal Scot" (L.M.S.R.), "Flying Scotsman" (L.N.E.R.), "Caerphilly Castle" (G.W.R.), "Lord Nelson" (S.R.) ... **Price 35/-**

Hornby E36 Electric Locomotive (reversible from the cab), "Royal Scot" (L.M.S.R.), "Flying Scotsman" (L.N.E.R.), "Caerphilly Castle" (G.W.R.), "Lord Nelson" (S.R.) ... **Price 32/6**

Hornby No. 3C Clockwork Locomotive, "Royal Scot" (L.M.S.R.), "Flying Scotsman" (L.N.E.R.), "Caerphilly Castle" (G.W.R.), "Lord Nelson" (S.R.) reversing (without Tender) ... **Price 24/-**

Hornby No. 2 Special Tender, L.M.S.R., L.N.E.R., G.W.R., or S.R. (S.R. numbered 850) ... **Price 6/-**

Hornby No. 2 Special Pullman Coach ... **Price 13/-** Hornby No. 2 Special Pullman Coach Composite ... **Price 14/-**

For prices of Hornby Rails, Points and Crossings, see pages 30 and 31. Details and prices of Transformers are given on page 42.

HORNBY EPM16 SPECIAL TANK LOCOMOTIVE (6-volt Permanent Magnet Type), Reversing.
Can be run from a 6-volt accumulator or from the mains supply through the Transformer-Rectifier listed on page 42. Complete with a 6-volt Terminal Connecting Plate, Speed and Reverse Control Switch and 3 feet of flex. This model is obtainable in the goods or passenger traffic colours of the four British railway groups ... **Price 33/6**

Prices of Components that can be purchased separately:—
LOCOMOTIVE ... **Price 27/6**
TERMINAL CONNECTING PLATE ... **Price 1/3**
SPEED AND REVERSE CONTROL SWITCH ... **Price 5/3**

HORNBY LE220 ELECTRIC LOCOMOTIVE (20-volt), Automatic Reversing.
This model represents a typical electric locomotive of the pantograph collector type. The electric motor with which it is fitted can be reversed automatically by remote control. The LE220 Locomotive is available enamelled red with cream roof, cream with blue roof (as illustrated), or green with cream roof ... **Price 33/-**

HORNBY E26 SPECIAL TANK LOCOMOTIVE (6-volt).
Reversible from the cab. The design of this model is similar to that of the E220 Special Tank Locomotive, illustrated on page 8. **Price 30/-**

HORNBY LE120 ELECTRIC LOCOMOTIVE (20-volt)
This attractive locomotive is modelled on the type in use on the Swiss Federal Railways. It is fitted with an electric motor designed to run from alternating mains supply through a 20-volt Transformer. The model can be obtained enamelled in red with cream roof, green with cream roof, blue with gold roof, or cream and red roof. Reversing. **Price 20/-**

HORNBY No. LEC1 CLOCKWORK LOCOMOTIVE.
This Locomotive is similar to the above, except that it is fitted with reversing clockwork mechanism. **Price 10/6**

HORNBY COMPLETE MODEL RAILWAYS
CLOCKWORK

The Complete Model Railway Sets described on this and the opposite page are very popular, especially with the younger boys. Each Set includes a Locomotive, fitted with a speedy and powerful mechanism, various items of Rolling Stock, a set of Rails and Railway Accessories, forming a complete miniature railway that can be laid down and operated immediately.

Hornby M8 Complete Model Railway

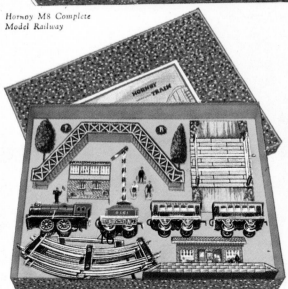

Hornby M9 Complete Model Railway

M8 COMPLETE MODEL RAILWAY

This Model Railway Set consists of a non-reversing Locomotive, Tender and two Goods Wagons, Signal, Signal Cabin, two Poplar Trees with Stands, Tunnel, Wayside Station, Footbridge and Set of Rails. The complete Set is packed in a strong carton, as illustrated.

Price 9/6

M9 COMPLETE MODEL RAILWAY

The M9 Complete Model Railway Set contains a comprehensive selection of material, consisting of an efficient non-reversing Locomotive, which may be braked from the track, Tender, and two Passenger Coaches, Signal, Station, Footbridge, Signal Cabin, Level Crossing, Guard, Porter, two Trees with Stands, two Hikers, and a Set of Rails. The complete Set is packed in a strong carton, as illustrated.

Price 12/6

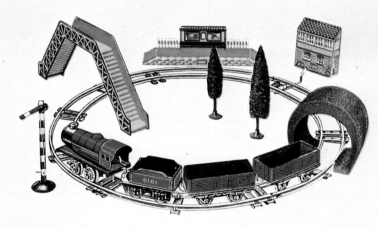

This illustration shows a suitable arrangement of the M8 Complete Model Railway Set

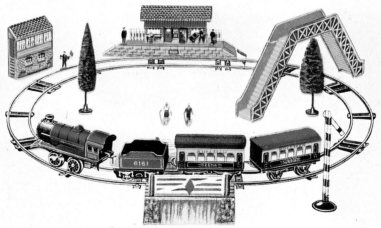

This illustration shows a suitable arrangement of the M9 Complete Model Railway Set

HORNBY COMPLETE MODEL RAILWAYS
CLOCKWORK

M10 COMPLETE MODEL RAILWAY

This is a more comprehensive Railway Set, consisting of a non-reversing Locomotive, with a reliable mechanism that can be braked from the track, Tender, two Pullman Coaches, Set of Rails, Footbridge, two Stations, Signal Cabin, two Telegraph Poles, two Signals, Loading Gauge, Tunnel, Cutting, Level Crossing, three Trees and Stands, and six Dinky Toys.

The complete Set is attractively packed in a special cabinet, as illustrated ... Price 19/6

M10 Complete Model Railway.

This illustration shows a suitable arrangement of the M10 Complete Model Railway Set.

M11 COMPLETE MODEL RAILWAY

This complete Model Railway Set is the most popular and the most comprehensive in the series. It consists of a reversing Tank Locomotive, Fibre Wagon, Timber Wagon, Open Wagon, Tunnel, Station, Signal, Level Crossing, Signal Cabin, Footbridge, one Cow, one Horse, two Trees with Stands, Guard, and a Set of Rails, including Points.

The complete Set is attractively packed in a special cabinet, as illustrated ... ... Price 25/-

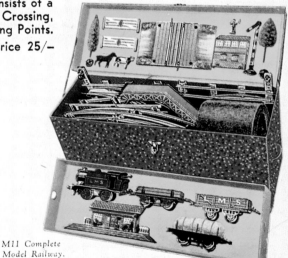

M11 Complete Model Railway.

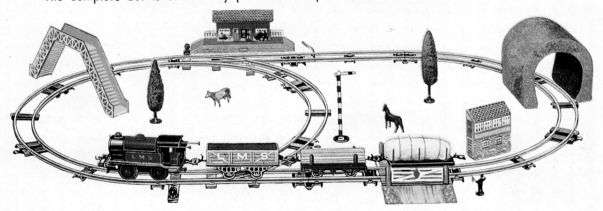

This illustration shows a suitable arrangement of the M11 Complete Model Railway Set.

THE HORNBY ELECTRIC RAILWAY SYSTEM

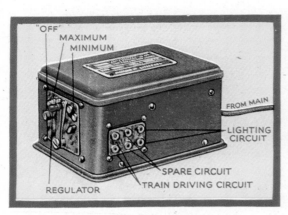

The Meccano T20A Transformer

MAINS-OPERATED TRAINS

The selection of the particular type by the individual railway owner depends on whether there is an alternating current mains supply available. Where the house lighting supply is alternating current, power can be obtained through a Meccano Transformer, which reduces the high voltage of the mains to a low voltage that is safe and economical. This is an essentially safe method of operating the miniature electric railway, for there is no direct connection between the mains supply and the railway system and therefore no risk of shock. All the Meccano Transformers are scientifically designed and perfectly constructed, and they comply fully with the requirements of the British Engineering Standards Association. To ensure absolute safety the insulation of every Meccano Transformer is tested at a pressure of 2,000 volts.

Direct current mains supplies must NOT be used to run a model electric locomotive. Any attempt to do so by direct connection is DANGEROUS owing to the risk of shock to which the operator is exposed. Therefore, where the supply is direct current, or there is no supply at all, the railway must be accumulator operated. This method is quite satisfactory provided the accumulator is kept properly charged.

MECCANO TRANSFORMERS

In order to operate a Hornby Electric Railway, the Transformer is simply plugged into a house lighting socket and the transformed current is led to the railway direct by a Terminal Connecting Plate or an EMC Combined Switch Rail. A leaflet of instructions is supplied with each of the Transformers explaining exactly how it is connected to the track.

There are two systems in use for Hornby Electric Railways, 20-volt and 6-volt.

The 20-volt system is for transformer operation from alternating current mains supplies, and it has the great advantage that the more important

Hornby Electric Trains are of two types—Mains Operated and Accumulator Operated. Mains operation is possible with all the Hornby Electric Train Sets and the chief features of these trains are set out in brief below. Full details in regard to the operation of miniature electric railways are contained in the booklet **"How to Choose and Use A Hornby Electric Railway"**, which may be obtained from any Meccano dealer, price 3d., or from Meccano Ltd., Binns Road, Liverpool 13, for 4d. post free. Every boy should have a copy of this book.

Hornby 20-volt Locomotives are fitted with automatic reversing mechanism. With these Locomotives lineside control of every movement is perfect and complete, including starting and stopping, reversing, and fine regulation of running speed. Therefore, if mains alternating current is available, the 20-volt system should be selected.

Three different Transformers are available for use with Hornby 20-volt Locomotives, and these are known respectively as the T20A, T20 and T20M. The T20A and T20 types are each fitted with a five-stud speed regulator, by means of which a train can be started or stopped, and controlled for speed. The T20M Transformer has no speed regulator, and a Resistance Controller must be used with it in order to control the speed of the train. The T20A is the ideal transformer for railway purposes for, in addition to the driving of the train, it makes possible the illumination of Hornby Accessories fitted for electric lighting.

ACCUMULATOR-OPERATED TRAINS

Where the mains supply is direct current, or there is no supply at all, the 6-volt system must be adopted, and an accumulator then forms the source of power. All Hornby 6-volt Locomotives can be run from a 6-volt accumulator, a Resistance Controller being used in conjunction with the accumulator to control the speed of the train. It sometimes happens that where an accumulator-operated 6-volt Hornby railway has been purchased, owing to the mains supply being direct current, the supply is subsequently changed over to alternating current. In that case a Meccano 6-volt Transformer can be employed, so that the railway can be run from the mains supply without the necessity of purchasing new locomotives.

Three Meccano 6-volt Transformers are available, T6A, T6 and T6M, and these resemble the corresponding 20-volt types.

Full details of all Meccano Transformers are given on page 42.

One Hornby Electric Locomotive, the EPM16 Special Tank, cannot be run from a transformer, as it requires direct current; but it can be operated from alternating current mains supply by means of the Hornby Transformer-Rectifier. This apparatus converts the high-voltage alternating current to low-voltage direct current. It is connected to the mains in a similar manner to a Transformer, with the Reverse and Resistance Control Switch made specially for this Locomotive connected between the Transformer-Rectifier and the track.

The source of power for a Hornby Electric Railway, whether Transformer, Transformer-Rectifier or accumulator, is connected to the rails by either a Terminal Connecting Plate or a Combined Switch Rail.

The Terminal Connecting Plates are separate fittings, and can be attached to the track at any point on the layout as convenient. There are two types, the TCP20, specially intended for use with T20A and T20 Transformers; and the TCP6, for use with T6A and T6 Transformers.

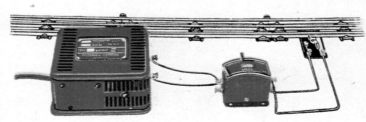

Hornby Transformer-Rectifier connected to track

The Combined Switch Rails EMC20 and EMC6, for 20-volt and 6-volt Locomotives respectively, are self-contained units consisting of a straight length of Hornby electric track fitted with a plate having terminals and a fuse, in addition to an "on-off" switch for starting and stopping a train. These fittings are specially intended for use with the Meccano T20M and T6M Transformers, which have no control gear.

Where the Hornby Transformer-Rectifier is used in conjunction with a Reverse and Resistance Control Switch for running the EPM16 Special Tank Locomotive, connection to the track should be made by a TCP6 Terminal Connecting Plate. This fitting should be used also where an accumulator is employed in conjunction with a Resistance Controller.

FITTED WITH AUTOMATIC COUPLINGS

Hopper Wagon

This wagon is unloaded by operating the handle shown. Lettered L.M.S., N.E., G.W., or S.R. ... ... Price 3/6

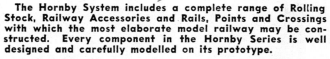

The Hornby System includes a complete range of Rolling Stock, Railway Accessories and Rails, Points and Crossings with which the most elaborate model railway may be constructed. Every component in the Hornby Series is well designed and carefully modelled on its prototype.

Hornby Rolling Stock includes almost every type in use on the big railways, and the full range is featured on this and the following pages. The Accessories are now better than ever before, while the Rails, Points and Crossings enable an endless variety of layouts to be constructed both for Electric and Clockwork trains.

Barrel Wagon

An interesting model of a type of wagon used on European railways ... ... Price 2/6

Box Car, American Type

A realistic model of the type of vehicle used in America for the conveyance of luggage and perishables.
Price 2/6

Cadbury's Chocolate Van

Fitted with opening doors.
Price 2/9

Caboose, American Type

This is a realistic model of the brake van used on the American railroads ... ... Price 2/6

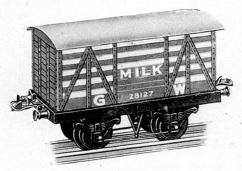

No. O Milk Traffic Van

This is a well-designed and attractively finished model. Lettered G.W. only.
Price 1/9

Tank Car, American Type

Modelled on the type of oil tank wagon used in America. Well proportioned and beautifully finished.
Price 1/9

No. 1 Milk Traffic Van

Fitted with sliding doors, and complete with four milk cans ... ... Price 2/11
Separate Milk Cans ... Price 1½d. each

49

HORNBY ROLLING STOCK
FITTED WITH AUTOMATIC COUPLINGS

MO Pullman Coach
As supplied with MO Passenger Set. Available named "Joan" or "Zena" ... ... Price 9d.

Riviera "Blue" Train Coach
"Dining Car" or "Sleeping Car". This is a beautiful model, substantially built and well finished. Suitable for 2 ft. radius rails only. Price 12/6

Continental "Mitropa" Coach No. 3
Similar in design to above. Beautifully finished in red, with white roof, and lettered "Mitropa" in gold ... ... Price 12/6

Guard's Van
Realistic model of the latest improved pattern. Obtainable in the colours of the L.M.S.R., L.N.E.R., G.W.R., or S.R. ... ... Price 2/6

No. 1 Pullman Coach
Distinctive in design and beautifully finished. Named "Cynthia", "Corsair" or "Niobe" ... ... Price 2/9

No. 1 Pullman Coach Composite
One part of this coach is designed for passenger accommodation and the other for conveyance of luggage. Named "Ansonia" or "Aurora". Price 2/9

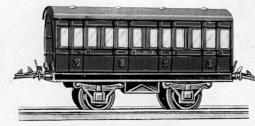

No. 1 Passenger Coach
Realistic model of the latest improved pattern. Lettered L.M.S., L.N.E.R., G.W.R., or S.R. Price 2/6

No. 2 Special Pullman Coach
As supplied with No. 2 Special Pullman and No. 3 Pullman Train Sets. This splendid Coach is perfect in detail and finish. Lettered "Loraine", "Zenobia" and "Grosvenor". Suitable for 2 ft. radius rails only ... ... Price 13/-

No. 2 Special Pullman Coach Composite
As supplied with No. 2 Special Pullman and No. 3 Pullman Train Sets. One part is designed for passenger accommodation and the other for the conveyance of luggage. Lettered "Verona", "Alberta" and "Montana". Suitable for 2-ft. radius rails only ... ... Price 14/-

No. 2 Saloon Coach
A well-proportioned model, realistically finished in the colours of the L.N.E.R. (as illustrated) or L.M.S.R. Companies. Suitable for 2 ft. radius rails only ... ... Price 9/6

M1 Pullman Coach
Named "Marjorie", "Aurelia" or "Viking". As supplied with the M1 and M2 Passenger Train Sets ... ... Price 1/-

No. O Pullman Coach
Similar to M1 Pullman Coach, illustrated above, but fitted with automatic couplings ... ... Price 1/3

No. 2 Pullman Coach
This model is substantially built and distinctive in design. Suitable for 2 ft. radius rails only ... ... Price 9/6

HORNBY ROLLING STOCK

FITTED WITH AUTOMATIC COUPLINGS

No. 2 Passenger Coach, First/Third

Available in correct colours of L.M.S.R., L.N.E.R., G.W.R., and S.R. Suitable for 2 ft. radius rails only ... Price 7/6

Gas Cylinder Wagon

Realistic in design ... ... Price 1/11

Metropolitan Coach C

As supplied with Metropolitan Clockwork Train Set ... Price 7/6

Metropolitan Coach LV

As supplied with E36 Metropolitan Electric Train Set Price 11/6

No. 2 Passenger Coach, Brake/Third

A new and attractive coach. Finished in correct colours of L.M.S., L.N.E., G.W., or Southern Railway Companies' rolling stock. Suitable for 2 ft. radius rails only ... ... Price 7/6

Brake Van

Fitted with opening doors. Obtainable with L.M.S. or G.W. lettering ... ... Price 2/11

Trolley Wagon

Trolley wagons are designed to carry exceptionally heavy loads, as their low-built construction necessitates only a minimum lift when loading. This model is fitted with four-wheel bogies, bolsters and stanchions. Suitable for 2 ft. radius rails only ... ... Price 3/11

Brake Van

Fitted with opening doors. Obtainable in N.E. or S.R. lettering ... ... Price 2/11

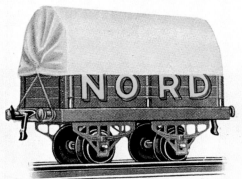

Covered Wagon (French Type)

This attractive-looking Wagon is fitted with a special frame and is supplied complete with sheet. French type, lettered "NORD" ... ... Price 2/6

Pullman Car

Imported from U.S.A. Product of Meccano factories. American Type (as illustrated). Yellow or green, with orange or red roof. Lettered "Washington" or "Madison". Price 1/6 Continental Type. "Mitropa" No. O. Red with white roof. Lettered "Mitropa" ... ... Price 1/6

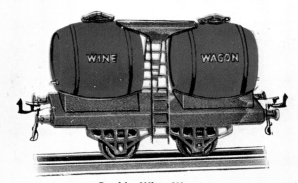

Double Wine Wagon

This interesting model represents a type of wine wagon used in France ... ... Price 4/6

HORNBY ROLLING STOCK

FITTED WITH AUTOMATIC COUPLINGS

No. 2 Lumber Wagon
Fitted with bolsters and stanchions for log transport. Suitable for 2 ft. radius rails only ... ... Price 2/11

MO Wagon
As supplied with MO Goods Train Set. Finished in red. Price 6d.

M1 Wagon
As supplied with M1 and M2 Goods Train Sets. Available lettered L.M.S., N.E., G.W., or S.R., ... Price 1/—

No. O Wagon (illustrated above)
Available lettered L.M.S., N.E., G.W., or S.R. ... Price 1/6

No. 2 Timber Wagon
Highly finished. Complete with load of timber. Suitable for 2 ft. radius rails only ... ... Price 2/6

Tarpaulin Sheets
Lettered L.M.S., G.W., N.E., or S.R. For fitting to Hornby Wagons ... ... Price 2d.

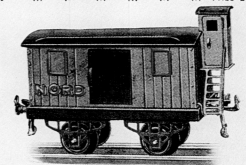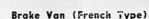

Flat Truck (complete with Cable Drum)
Available lettered L.M.S., N.E., G.W., or S.R. Price 1/9

Flat Truck (without Cable Drum)
Price 1/6

Cable Drum
British Insulated Cables Ltd. ... ... Price 3d.

Breakdown Van and Crane
Beautifully coloured and fitted with opening doors. The crane, which swivels about a pivot, is provided with a handle for hoisting loads. Suitable for 2 ft. radius rails only. Lettered L.M.S., N.E., G.W., or S.R. ... ... Price 5/11

Brake Van (French Type)
Lettered NORD only. Modelled on the type of brake van used in France. Beautifully finished ... ... Price 4/—

Meat Van
This is a very realistic model, sturdily built and well finished. Lettered L.M.S. only.
Price 1/9

Carr's Biscuit Van
Fitted with opening doors ... Price 2/9

Jacob's Biscuit Van
Fitted with opening doors ... Price 2/9

Crawford's Biscuit Van
Fitted with opening doors ... Price 2/9

HORNBY ROLLING STOCK

FITTED WITH AUTOMATIC COUPLINGS

Coal Wagon

This is similar to Hornby Wagon No. 1. It is fitted with an embossed representation of coal ... ... Price 2/3

No. 2 Luggage Van

Mounted on twin bogies, and fitted with opening doors. Suitable for 2-ft. radius rails only. Lettered L.M.S., N.E., G.W., or S.R. ... ... Price 4/6

Cement Wagon

The door at the top opens. Finished in red. Price 2/6

No. 1 Cattle Truck

Fitted with sliding doors. Realistically designed. Lettered L.M.S., N.E., G.W., or S.R. ... ... Price 2/9

No. 2 Cattle Truck

Splendid twin bogie model, fitted with double doors. Suitable for 2 ft. radius rails only. Lettered L.M.S., N.E., G.W., or S.R. ... ... Price 4/6

No. 1 Luggage Van

Realistic and highly finished. Fitted with opening doors. Lettered L.M.S., N.E., G.W., or S.R. ... ... Price 2/9

Fibre Wagon

This is an interesting model of a type of wagon used in France and other Continental countries ... ... Price 1/3

Snow Plough

Runs on specially designed heavy wheels. The plough is driven from the front axle. Price 3/9

Refrigerator Van

This is a very realistic model, fitted with opening doors. Lettered L.M.S., N.E., G.W., or S.R. ... ... Price 2/9

No. 1 Lumber Wagon

Fitted with bolsters and stanchions. Price 1/6

HORNBY ROLLING STOCK

FITTED WITH AUTOMATIC COUPLINGS

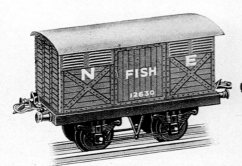

Fish Van

This is an excellent model, distinctive in design and finish. Lettered N.E. only.
Price 1/9

No. 1 Side Tipping Wagon

Robert Hudson Ltd.
Arranged to tip to either side of the track.
Price 2/-

MO Side Tipping Wagon

A new model that will tip to either side of track ... ... Price 1/-

Gunpowder Van

Fitted with opening doors. Lettered L.M.S., N.E., or S.R., and grey lettered G.W.
Price 2/9

No. 1 Banana Van

An attractive model ... ... Price 2/9

No. 1 Wagon

A well-proportioned model. Available lettered L.M.S., N.E., G.W., or S.R.
Price 1/9

Open Wagon "B"

Similar to Hornby Wagon No. 1, but fitted with , centre tarpaulin - supporting rail. Lettered L.M.S., N.E., G.W., or S.R.
Price 2/-

No. 1 Timber Wagon

Beautifully enamelled. Complete with load of timber ... ... Price 1/6

No. O Banana Van

Lettered L.M.S. only ... ... Price 1/9

MO Crane Truck

The crane revolves on its base ... Price 1/-

No. 1 Crane Truck

The crane swivels about a pivot, and is operated by a crank handle ... Price 2/11

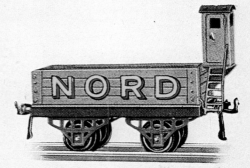

Wagon (French Type)

Lettered "NORD" only. Modelled on type of goods wagon used in France. Price 3/3

HORNBY ROLLING STOCK

FITTED WITH AUTOMATIC COUPLINGS

Milk Tank Wagon "United Dairies"

A very realistic model ... Price 4/6

Petrol Tank Wagon No. 1 "Pratts"

Realistic in design and appropriately coloured ... ... Price 2/–

Petrol Tank Wagon No. 1 "Shell"

Realistic in design and appropriately coloured ... ... Price 2/–

Petrol Tank Wagon No. 1 "B.P."

Realistic in design and appropriately coloured ... ... Price 2/–

Petrol Tank Wagon No. 1 "Redline-Glico"

Realistic in design and appropriately coloured ... ... Price 2/–

Oil Tank Wagon "Castrol"

An attractive and realistic model. Price 2/–

Oil Tank Wagon "Mobiloil"

An attractive and realistic model. Price 2/–

Bitumen Tank Wagon "Colas"

This model represents the type of wagon employed by Colas Products, Ltd. Price 3/6

MO Petrol Tank Wagon "Shell-Mex"

A new model, strongly made, and well-finished (MO Coupling) ... Price 1/–

No. O Rotary Tipping Wagon

Attractively finished. The container revolves on the base ... Price 1/6

MO Rotary Tipping Wagon

The Container revolves and tips at any angle (MO Coupling) ... Price 1/–

No. 1 Rotary Tipping Wagon

Now available finished in gold and blue. Price 2/6

HORNBY ACCESSORIES

Gauge 0, 1¼ in.

No. 1 Buffer Stops
Spring type.   Price 1/-

No. 1E Buffer Stops
As No. 1, but suitably wired for electric lighting.   Price 1/6

No. 1 Railway Station
This Station is a well-made model, richly finished in colours. By placing one or more of these stations at intervals along the track, and using Station No. 2 (illustrated below) as the main terminus, a very realistic effect is obtained.
Length 16¾ in. Width 6 in. Height 6 in.   Price 4/6

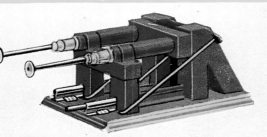

No. 2 Buffer Stops
Hydraulic type.   Price 5/6

No. 2E Buffer Stops
Similar to No. 2 Buffer Stops, but suitably wired for electric lighting.
       Price 6/-

Tunnel (Metal)
Beautifully designed and finished in colours.   Price 3/11

VIADUCT Price 6/6	VIADUCT (Electrical)	Price 7/6
VIADUCT Centre Section only	... ...	Price 4/-
VIADUCT (Electrical) Centre Section only	... ...	Price 4/6

Platelayer's Hut
This is an extremely attractive accessory, beautifully designed and finished.   Price 1/-

No. 2 Station
Built up with three detachable sections. Length 2 ft. 9 in. Breadth 6 in. Height 7 in.   Price 8/-

No. 2E Station
This Station is suitably wired for electric lighting, otherwise it is the same as the No. 2 Station, illustrated above. Price 9/3

HORNBY ACCESSORIES

Gauge 0, 1½ in.

No. 1 Goods Platform

Length 13 in. Height 6¾ in. Width 6 in. A strong and well-proportioned model. Price 7/6

No. 2 Goods Platform

Length 16¾ in. Height 6¾ in. Width 6 in. Price 10/6

No. 2E Goods Platform

This platform is suitably wired for electric lighting. Otherwise it is the same as the No. 2 Goods Platform, illustrated above. Price 11/6

Passenger Platform

Length 16¾ in. Width 3 in. This Platform may be connected to the main station or used separately. Price 2/-
The White Paled Fencing can be purchased separately. Price per length 6d.

WINDSOR

Platform Crane

Fitted with a crank handle and ratchet mechanism. Price 3/11

Island Platform

Length 32¼ in. Height 6¾ in. Width 3 in. Price 5/6
The Ramps can be purchased separately. Price per pair 1/9

E Island Platform

This platform is suitably wired for electric lighting. Otherwise it is the same as the Island Platform illustrated above. Price 6/3

HORNBY ACCESSORIES

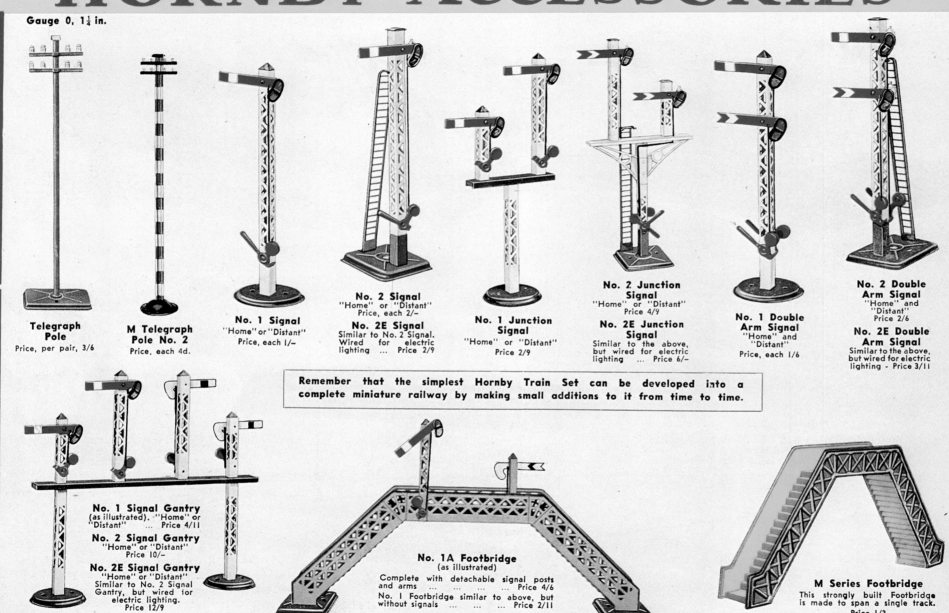

Gauge 0, 1¼ in.

Telegraph Pole
Price, per pair, 3/6

M Telegraph Pole No. 2
Price, each 4d.

No. 1 Signal
"Home" or "Distant"
Price, each 1/-

No. 2 Signal
"Home" or "Distant"
Price, each 2/-

No. 2E Signal
Similar to No. 2 Signal.
Wired for electric
lighting ... Price 2/9

No. 1 Junction Signal
"Home" or "Distant"
Price 2/9

No. 2 Junction Signal
"Home" or "Distant"
Price 4/9

No. 2E Junction Signal
Similar to the above,
but wired for electric
lighting ... Price 6/-

No. 1 Double Arm Signal
"Home" and "Distant"
Price, each 1/6

No. 2 Double Arm Signal
"Home" and "Distant"
Price 2/6

No. 2E Double Arm Signal
Similar to the above,
but wired for electric
lighting - Price 3/11

> Remember that the simplest Hornby Train Set can be developed into a complete miniature railway by making small additions to it from time to time.

No. 1 Signal Gantry
(as illustrated). "Home" or "Distant" ... Price 4/11

No. 2 Signal Gantry
"Home" or "Distant"
Price 10/-

No. 2E Signal Gantry
"Home" or "Distant"
Similar to No. 2 Signal
Gantry, but wired for
electric lighting.
Price 12/9

No. 1A Footbridge
(as illustrated)
Complete with detachable signal posts
and arms ... ... Price 4/6
No. 1 Footbridge similar to above, but
without signals ... ... Price 2/11

M Series Footbridge
This strongly built Footbridge
is made to span a single track.
Price 1/3

HORNBY ACCESSORIES

No. 1 Water Tank

Stands 6½ ins. in height. Fitted with rubber tube and spring-controlled valve, operated by a chain and lever ... Price 3/—

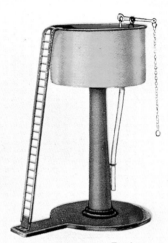

No. 2 Water Tank

Stands 8½ ins. in height. Fitted with rubber tube and spring-controlled valve, operated by a chain and lever. Price 5/9

No. 2E Water Tank

Similar to No. 2 Water Tank, but wired for electric lighting. Price 6/6

Station or Field Hoarding

This is a realistic accessory, suitable for placing on the station platform or in the fields adjacent to the track.
Price 6d.

Poster Boards

To carry Hornby Miniature Posters. Provided with lugs for attachment to Paled Fencing, etc.
Packet of 6 (3 large, 3 small) ... Price 4d.

Posters in Miniature

These posters are reproductions of familiar national advertisements. They are intended to be pasted on the Station Hoardings or the Poster Boards described above, and are beautifully printed in full colours.
Series No. 1 (packet of 51) ... ... Price 6d.
Series No. 2 (packet of 51) ... ... „ 6d.

Gauge 0, 1½ in.

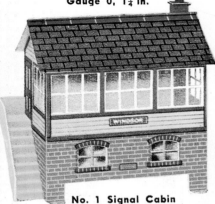

No. 1 Signal Cabin
Price 2/6

No. 2 Signal Cabin
(as illustrated) ... ... Price 3/9
Roof and back of No. 2 Signal Cabin open to allow a Hornby Control Lever Frame to be fitted inside.

No. 2E Signal Cabin
Similar to No. 2 Signal Cabin, but wired for electric lighting ... Price 4/3

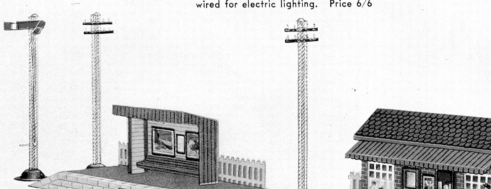

Shunter's Pole
Price 2d.

M Station Set

This realistic Station Set is composed of seven components, as illustrated. Price, complete, 3/—

The components can be purchased separately at the following prices :—

M Wayside Station ...	Price 9d. each	M Station	Price 1/— each
M Signal Box	„ 4d. „	M Telegraph Pole No. 1	„ 3d. „
M Signal	„ 4d. „		

HORNBY ACCESSORIES

Gauge 0, 1¼ in.

No. E1E Engine Shed

Similar to No. 1 Engine Shed, but suitably wired for electric lighting and provided with electrical track.
Price 15/6

No. 1 Engine Shed

This Shed will accommodate any Locomotive and Tender with an overall length not exceeding 8¾ in. It has double doors at both ends... ... ... Price 15/—

Loading Gauge
(as illustrated)
Height 7 in. Price 2/3

M Loading Gauge
Height 5½ in. Price 1/—

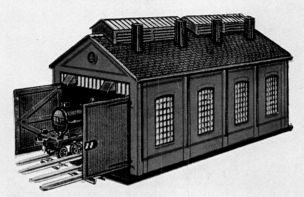

No. E2E Engine Shed

Similar to No. 2 Engine Shed, but wired for electric lighting and provided with electrical track.
Price 23/—

No. 2 Engine Shed

This realistic Engine Shed will accommodate any Locomotive and Tender with an overall length not exceeding 17½ ins. It has double doors at both ends. Price 22/6

THE HORNBY CONTROL SYSTEM

There is a certain amount of fascination about even the cheapest and simplest Miniature Railway. For a time we can take a keen interest in a single train running round a plain oval track, but presently we realise that we need something more. Then we add points and crossings and so make possible layouts with branch lines and sidings. Still later, perhaps, we add further interest by introducing a more or less complete system of signals. By this time our Railway has become a source of keen enjoyment to us and to our friends, and for a while we feel that nothing more is needed. Sooner or later, however, our thoughts turn to the Signal Cabin on a real railway and we wish that, like the signalman, we could control the operation of our railway by means of levers that would enable us to manipulate signals and points. The Hornby Control System has been devised to enable this desire to be fulfilled. Ask your dealer for the free illustrated list that tells all about the Hornby Control System.

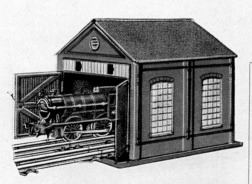

No. 1A Engine Shed

This model is more simple in design than No. 1 Engine Shed and has double doors at one end only. It will accommodate any Locomotive and Tender with an overall length not exceeding 8¾ in. ... ... Price 10/6

The more Rolling Stock and Accessories you have the better the fun

Read the 'Meccano Magazine', Price 6d., from your dealer

No. 1 Turntable, Price 2/6.   **No. 2 Turntable** (as illustrated), Price 3/9

No. E2 Turntable (Electrical)
Similar to No. 2 Turntable, but fitted with electrical rails ... Price 5/6

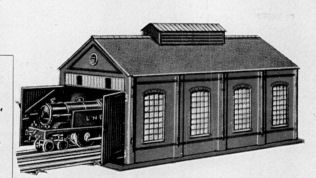

No. 2A Engine Shed

This model is more simple in design than No. 2 Engine Shed. It will accommodate any Locomotive and Tender with an overall length not exceeding 17½ in. Fitted with double doors at both ends ... Price 17/6

HORNBY ACCESSORIES

Gauge 0, 1¼ in.

No. 1 Railway Accessories
Miniature Luggage and Truck. Price 1/-

No. 2 Railway Accessories
Milk Cans and Truck   ...   .   Price 1/3

No. 4 Railway Accessories
Railway Accessories No. 4 is a composite set consisting of all the pieces contained in Railway Accessories Nos. 1, 2 and 3. Price 3/9

No. 3 Railway Accessories
Platform Machines, etc.   ...   Price 1/6

No. 1 Oil Can
This strongly made Miniature Oil Can functions perfectly   ...   .   Price 6d.

Meccano Lubricating Oil
This is the best oil obtainable for Hornby Trains, Rolling Stock, Meccano Models, Clockwork and Electric Motors, and other similar mechanisms.
Price, per bottle, 6d.

Graphite Grease
An ideal lubricant for the springs of Hornby Locomotives and Hornby Speed Boats, Meccano and Aero Clockwork Motors, and Meccano Motor Cars.
Price, per tube, 6d.

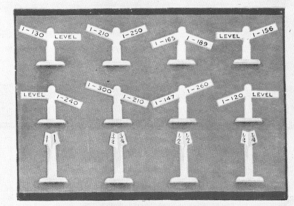

No. 5 Railway Accessories
Gradient Posts and Mile Posts   ...   Price 2/-

No. 2 Oil Can ("K" Type) Polished Copper
This Miniature Oil Can operates perfectly. The oil is ejected drop by drop by depressing the valve   ...   ...   Price 3/6

Mansell Wheels
(as illustrated)
These wheels are die-cast and are correctly designed. They may be fitted to Hornby Vans, Coaches, etc.
Price, per pair, 3d.

Die-cast Spoked Wheels
These wheels are specially suitable for fitting to Hornby Wagons, Tenders, etc.   Price, per pair, 3d.

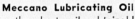

No. 8 Railway Accessories
Notice Boards   ...   .   Price 1/9

SUNDRIES
Combined Rail Gauge, Screwdriver and Spanner for Locomotives
Price 2d.

Keys for Hornby Clockwork Locomotives
M1, M3 Tank, No. O, No. 1 and LEC1 Locomotive Keys. Each 3d.
No. 1 (Special) Locomotive Key. Each 6d.
No. 2 (Special), No. 3 and Metropolitan Locomotive Keys. Each 6d.

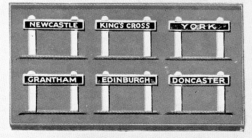

No. 7 Railway Accessories
Watchman's Hut, Brazier, Shovel and Poker   ...   Price 10d.

SUNDRIES
Fuse Wire
Fuse Wire 41 Gauge Tinned Copper
per card 2d.
Fuse Wire 32 Gauge Lead   ... per card 3d.
Fuse Wire 24 Gauge Lead   ... per card 3d.

Detachable Head Lamps for Locomotives and Tail Lamps for Coaches
Price, dozen, 1/-

No. 9 Railway Accessories
Station Name Boards   ...   ...   Price 1/9

61

HORNBY ACCESSORIES

Gauge 0, 1¼ in.

Oak Tree
Price, per doz., 2/6

Die-cast stands for above
Price, per doz., 1/-

Assorted Trees
Six Oak and six Poplar, complete with die-cast stands.
Price, per box of 1 doz.
3/-

Fencing, with four trees
Length 16¾ in. ... Price, per pair, 2/6

Hedging
Length 10¼ in. ... Price, per doz. lengths, 3/-

Poplar Tree
Price, per doz., 2/-

Die-cast stands for above
Price, per doz., 1/-

No. 1 Lamp Standard (Single)
(as illustrated). Price 3/3

No. 2 Lamp Standard (Double)
Price 3/9
Electric flashlamp bulbs may be fitted in the globes, which can be hoisted or lowered as required.

No. 1E Lamp Standard Electrical (Single)
Price 2/11

No. 2E Lamp Standard Electrical (Double)
(as illustrated) Price 3/3

The above Lamp Standards are suitably wired for electric lighting.

No. 1 Level Crossing

M Level Crossing
Suitable for single track, with rails in position.
Price 1/6

No. 1 Level Crossing
(Illustrated above). Suitable for single track, with rails in position ... ... Price 2/11

No. E1 Level Crossing (Electrical)
Similar to No. 1 Level Crossing, but fitted with electrical track ... ... Price 4/-

No. E1E Level Crossing
Similar to No. E1 Level Crossing, but suitably wired for electric lighting ... ... Price 5/3

Accessories fitted for Electric Lighting—New System

The following is a complete list of the Hornby Accessories available fitted for electric lighting on the new and simplified system adopted this season. These accessories are specially designed for lighting from the 3½-volt circuit of a Meccano T20A or T6A Transformer, and with each of these Transformers are packed for the purpose a pair of plugs, an Earthing Clip and a coil of Wire, together with full instructions. The Accessories can also be lighted from an accumulator. Each Accessory is accompanied by an Earthing Clip and Leaflet giving full instructions for use. Lamp bulbs are not provided with the Accessories.

	Price		Price		Price
No. E1E Engine Shed	15/6	No. 2E Signal	2/9	No. E2E Level Crossing	9/-
No. E2E Engine Shed	23/-	No. 2E Double Arm		No. 1E Buffer Stops	1/6
No. 2E Station ...	9/3	Signal	3/11	No. 2E Buffer Stops ...	6/-
Island Platform E	6/3	No. 2E Junction Signal	6/-	No. 2E Water Tank ...	6/6
No. 2E Goods Platform	11/6	No. 2E Signal Gantry	12/9	No. 1E Lamp Standard	2/11
No. 2E Signal Cabin ...	4/3	No. E1E Level Crossing	5/3	No. 2E Lamp Standard	3/3

The following items used in connection with the new system of Accessories lighting are available:—

Plugs for sockets of Transformers T20A and T6A ... ... Price per pair 6d.
Earthing Clips ... ... each 3d.   Connecting Wire ... Price per coil 4d.

Accessories for Lighting with Distribution Box and Flexible Leads

The old type Accessories fitted for lighting by means of a Distribution Box and Flexible Leads with plugs and sockets are still available at the following prices:—

	Price		Price		Price
No. E1E Engine Shed	18/6	No. 2E Signal... ...	4/3	No. E2E Level Crossing	11/-
No. E2E Engine Shed	26/-	No. 2E Double Arm		No. 1E Buffer Stops	1/6
No. 2E Station ...	11/6	Signal	6/6	No. 2E Buffer Stops ...	7/-
Island Platform E ...	9/-	No. 2E Junction Signal	9/-	No. 2E Water Tank ...	10/-
No. 2E Goods Platform	15/-	No. 2E Signal Gantry	18/-	No. 1E Lamp Standard	3/6
No. 2E Signal Cabin ...	5/6	No. E1E Level Crossing	7/-	No. 2E Lamp Standard	4/3

Flexible Leads, 9″, 18″ and 36″, Prices 1/4, 1/5 and 1/6 respectively.
Separate Plugs, 3d. each   Separate Sockets, 3d. each   Distribution Box, Price 2/6

No. 2 Level Crossing

No. 2 Level Crossing
(Illustrated above). Suitable for a double track, with rails in position. Measures 13¼ × 10¼ ins. Price 5/6

No. E2 Level Crossing (Electrical)
Similar to the No. 2 Level Crossing, but fitted with electrical track ... ... Price 7/6

No. E2E Level Crossing
Similar to No. E2 Level Crossing, but suitably wired for electric lighting ... ... Price 9/-

HORNBY ACCESSORIES

Gauge 0, 1¼ in.

No. 1 Tunnel

Two No. 1 and one No. 2 Cuttings are illustrated here.

No. 3 Tunnel

No. O Tunnel (Straight)
Base measurements: Length 6 in., width 6 in.
Price 1/3

No. 1 Tunnel (Straight)
Base measurements: Length 7¾ in., width 6¼ in. (as illustrated) ... ... Price 1/9

No. 2 Tunnel (Straight)
Base measurements: Length 15⅝ in., width 9½ in.
Price 3/6

Tunnel Ends
Tunnels of varying lengths can be made with cardboard or other suitable material and then fitted to the Tunnel Ends ... Price, per pair, 1/6

No. 4 Cutting

No. O Cutting
This is a double cutting, mounted on a base over which the railway track can be laid. Base measurements: 8 in. × 8 in. ... ... Price 1/9

No. 4 Cutting
This double cutting (illustrated above) is similar in design to Cutting No. O. The base measurements are: Length 15⅝ in., width 15 in. ... ... Price 6/-

No. 1 Cutting (end section)
(as illustrated)
Base measurements: Length 7¾ in., width 6 in. ... Price, per pair, 3/-

No. 2 Cutting (centre section, straight)
(as illustrated)
The addition of these Centre Sections enables a Hornby Railway Cutting to be extended to any length. They are intended to be used in conjunction with the End Sections (Cutting No. 1, see illustration above), between which they are fitted. Base measurements: Length 10¼ in., width 6 in. ... ... Price 2/-

No. 3 Cutting (centre section, curved)
This is used for curved track in the same manner as the straight Centre Section, described above, is used for a straight track. It is suitable for both 1 ft. and 2 ft. radius track ... ... Price 2/-

No. 3 Tunnel (Curved)
Base measurements: Length 15 in., width 9⅝ in.
For 1 ft. or 2 ft. radius track ... Price 4/-

No. 4 Tunnel (Curved)
Base measurements: Length 20 in., width 9⅝ in.
For 2 ft. radius track only ... Price 4/9

Train Name Boards
These Name Boards are for No. 2 Special Pullman Coaches and add greatly to the realistic appearance of the coaches. Details are as follows:—

No. 1. The Flying Scotsman.	No. 10. King's Cross, Edinburgh and Aberdeen.
No. 2. The Scarborough Flier.	No. 11. London (Euston) and Liverpool (Lime Street).
No. 3. The Royal Scot.	
No. 4. The Merseyside Express	No. 12. London (Euston) and Glasgow (Central).
No. 5. The Golden Arrow.	No. 13. Victoria and Dover.
No. 6. Bournemouth Belle.	No. 14. Waterloo, Salisbury and Exeter.
No. 7. Cornish Riviera Express.	
No. 8. Torbay Limited Express.	No. 15. Paddington, Exeter and Plymouth.
No. 9. King's Cross, York and Edinburgh.	No. 16. Paddington and Bristol.

Price, per packet of four of a kind, 4d.

Clips for Train Name Boards
These Clips are for use with coaches that are not fitted with brackets to take the Name Boards. There are two types: No. 2S, for No. 2 Special Pullman and No. 2 Special Pullman Composite Coaches, and No. 2 for No. 2 Pullman, Saloon and Metropolitan Coaches.

Price, per packet of 12, 1/- (either kind).

No. 5 Tunnel

No. 5 Tunnel (left-hand, curved)
(as illustrated)
This Tunnel is in the form of a small hill, through which the track runs obliquely. For 2 ft. radius track. Base measurements: 15⅝ in. × 14¾ in. Length of track 17¼ in. ... ... Price 6/9

No. 6 Tunnel (right-hand, curved)
Similar to No. 5 Tunnel, but with track in the reverse position. For 2 ft. radius track only. Base measurements: 15⅝ in. × 14¾ in. Length of track 17¼ in.
Price 6/9

HORNBY RAILS POINTS & CROSSINGS

Straight Rails

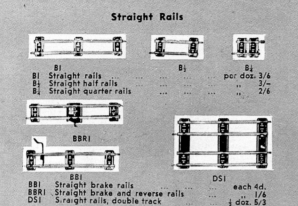

B1	Straight rails				per doz. 3/6
B½	Straight half rails				" 3/-
B¼	Straight quarter rails				" 2/6

BB1	Straight brake rails				each 4d.
BBR1	Straight brake and reverse rails				1/6
DS1	Straight rails, double track				½ doz. 5/3

Double Symmetrical Points
For 1 ft. and 2 ft. Radius Curves

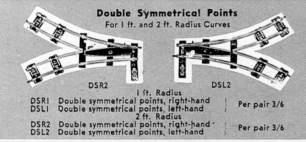

DSR2   DSL2
1 ft. Radius

DSR1	Double symmetrical points, right-hand	Per pair 3/6
DSL1	Double symmetrical points, left-hand	
	2 ft. Radius	
DSR2	Double symmetrical points, right-hand	Per pair 3/6
DSL2	Double symmetrical points, left-hand	

Points
For 1 ft. and 2 ft. Radius Curves

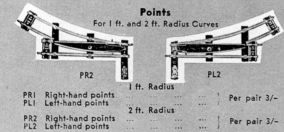

PR2   PL2
1 ft. Radius

PR1	Right-hand points			Per pair 3/-
PL1	Left-hand points			
	2 ft. Radius			
PR2	Right-hand points			Per pair 3/-
PL2	Left-hand points			

Parallel Points
For 1 ft. and 2 ft. Radius Curves

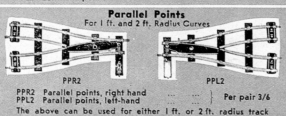

PPR2   PPL2

| PPR2 | Parallel points, right hand | Per pair 3/6 |
| PPL2 | Parallel points, left-hand | |

The above can be used for either 1 ft. or 2 ft. radius track

RAILS FOR CLOCKWORK & STEAM TRAINS
Gauge O, 1¼ in.

The addition of extra rails to a Hornby Railway System greatly enhances the fun and realism. There is practically no limit to the number of rail formations that can be built with Hornby Rails, Points and Crossings.

The Hornby Railway System is constructed to Gauge O, and in this gauge the track is 1¼ in. wide, the measurement being made between the insides of the heads of the rails. Hornby clockwork-type track is suitable for use with all Gauge O clockwork or steam locomotives and rolling stock.

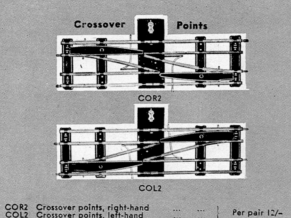

Crossover   Points

COR2

COL2

| COR2 | Crossover points, right-hand | | | | Per pair 12/- |
| COL2 | Crossover points, left-hand | | | | |

BRAKING AND REVERSING FROM THE TRACK

The MB9 Curved Brake Rail can only be used to brake the MO (non-reversing) Locomotive. The BB1 Straight Brake Rail can only be used to brake the M1, M3 Tank, and No. O Locomotives. Their reversing gear must be operated by means of the lever in the cab. The AB2 Curved Brake Rail can only be used to brake or reverse the No. 1 Locomotives, both tender and tank. The BBR1 Brake and Reverse Rail is intended for braking or reversing the No. 1 Special, No. 2 Special, and No. 3C Locomotives.

Rails for MO Trains

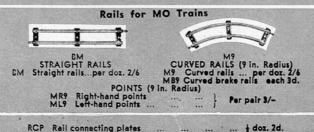

BM   M9

BM	STRAIGHT RAILS			CURVED RAILS (9 in. Radius)	
BM	Straight rails...per doz. 2/6		M9	Curved rails ... per doz. 2/6	
			MB9	Curved brake rails	each 3d.
	POINTS (9 in. Radius)				
MR9	Right-hand points			Per pair 3/-	
ML9	Left-hand points				

| RCP | Rail connecting plates | | | | ½ doz. 2d. |

Curved Rails
For 1 ft. and 2 ft. Radius Curves

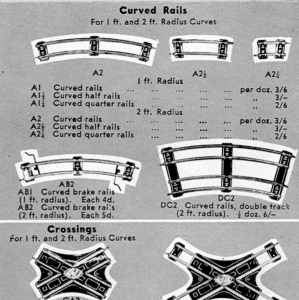

A2   A2½   A2¼
1 ft. Radius

A1	Curved rails			per doz. 3/6
A1½	Curved half rails			" 3/-
A1¼	Curved quarter rails			" 2/6
	2 ft. Radius			
A2	Curved rails			per doz. 3/6
A2½	Curved half rails			" 3/-
A2¼	Curved quarter rails			" 2/6

AB2

DC2

AB1	Curved brake rails (1 ft. radius).	Each 4d.
AB2	Curved brake rails (2 ft. radius).	Each 5d.
DC2	Curved rails, double track (2 ft. radius).	½ doz. 6/-

Crossings
For 1 ft. and 2 ft. Radius Curves

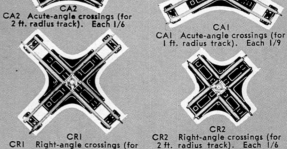

CA2	Acute-angle crossings (for 2 ft. radius track). Each 1/6
CA1	Acute-angle crossings (for 1 ft. radius track). Each 1/9
CR1	Right-angle crossings (for 1 ft. radius track). Each 1/9
CR2	Right-angle crossings (for 2 ft. radius track). Each 1/6

Points on Solid Base
For 2 ft. Radius Curve only

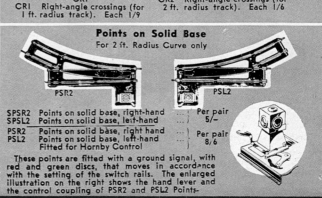

PSR2   PSL2

SPSR2	Points on solid base, right-hand	Per pair 5/-
SPSL2	Points on solid base, left-hand	
PSR2	Points on solid base, right hand	Per pair 8/6
PSL2	Points on solid base, left-hand	

Fitted for Hornby Control

These points are fitted with a ground signal, with red and green discs, that moves in accordance with the setting of the switch rails. The enlarged illustration on the right shows the hand lever and the control coupling of PSR2 and PSL2 Points.

HORNBY RAILS POINTS & CROSSINGS

Straight Rails

EB1 Straight rails. Per doz. 5/-

EB½ Straight quarter rails ... Per doz. 4/-

EB½ Straight half rails. Per doz. 4/6

EDS1 Straight rails, double track, ½ doz. 8/6

Switch Rails

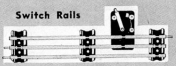

EMC20 Switch rails (20-volt) ... ... each 1/3
EMC6 Switch rails (6-volt) 1/3

Crossings

ECA Acute-angle crossings. Each 2/9

ECR Right-angle crossings. Each 2/9

ECA and ECR crossings are used as illustrated for 2 ft. radius layouts. For 1 ft. radius layouts an EB½ Straight quarter rail must be added to each arm.

Points

For 1 ft. and 2 ft. Radius Curves

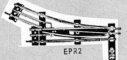

EPR2 EPL2

1 ft. Radius

EPR1 Right-hand points ... ... } per pair 5/9
EPL1 Left-hand points ... ...

2 ft. Radius

EPR2 Right-hand points ... ... } per pair 6/6
EPL2 Left-hand points ... ...

RAILS FOR ELECTRIC TRAINS
Gauge O, 1¼ in.

Hornby Rails, Points and Crossings are designed to meet the most exacting requirements of model railway enthusiasts. They make possible an endless number of realistic and railway-like layouts. Only the finest materials are used in their manufacture. Their adaptability is well shown in the booklets "How to Plan your Hornby Railway," and "Hornby Layouts— One Hundred Suggestions," each of which is obtainable from your dealer, price 3d., or direct from Meccano Ltd., Binns Road, Liverpool 13, price 4d., post free.

It should be noted that Hornby Electric track is designed on the "all-level" system, and can be used with all Gauge O electric trains that operate on this system.

Crossover Points

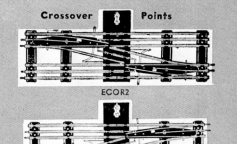

ECOR2

ECOL2

ECOR2 Crossover points, right-hand ... ... } per pair 24/-
ECOL2 Crossover points, left-hand ...

Centre Rails for Converting Ordinary Track to Electrical

ICR Insulators for insulating centre rails. Per doz. 3d.

CCR Clips for fixing centre rails. Per doz. 6d.

CURVED RAILS, 1 ft. Radius

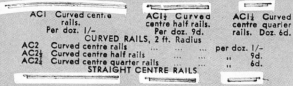

AC1 Curved centre rails. Per doz. 1/-

AC1½ Curved centre half rails. Per doz. 9d.

AC1¼ Curved centre quarter rails. Doz. 6d.

CURVED RAILS, 2 ft. Radius

AC2 Curved centre rails ... ... per doz. 1/-
AC2½ Curved centre half rails ... ... " 9d.
AC2¼ Curved centre quarter rails ... ... " 6d.

STRAIGHT CENTRE RAILS

BC1 Straight centre rails. Per doz. 1/-

BC½ Straight centre half rails. Per doz. 9d.

BC¼ Straight centre quarter rails. Doz. 6d.

Curved Rails

For 1 ft. and 2 ft. Radius Curves

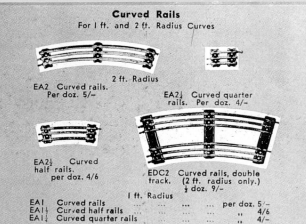

2 ft. Radius

EA2 Curved rails. Per doz. 5/-

EA2¼ Curved quarter rails. Per doz. 4/-

EA2½ Curved half rails. per doz. 4/6

EDC2 Curved rails, double track. (2 ft. radius only.) ½ doz. 9/-

1 ft. Radius

EA1 Curved rails ... ... per doz. 5/-
EA1½ Curved half rails ... ... " 4/6
EA1¼ Curved quarter rails ... ... " 4/-

Double Symmetrical Points

For 1 ft. and 2 ft. Radius Curves

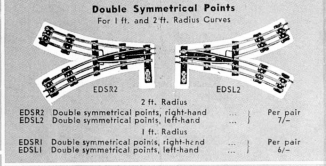

EDSR2 EDSL2

2 ft. Radius

EDSR2 Double symmetrical points, right-hand } Per pair 7/-
EDSL2 Double symmetrical points, left-hand

1 ft. Radius

EDSR1 Double symmetrical points, right-hand } Per pair 6/-
EDSL1 Double symmetrical points, left-hand

Terminal Connecting Plates

TCP20 Terminal connecting plates (20-volt). Ea. 1/3

TCP6 Terminal connecting plates (6-volt). Ea. 1/3

Parallel Points

EPPR2 EPPL2

EPPR2 Parallel points, right-hand ... } Per pair 7/-
EPPL2 Parallel points, left-hand ...

The Parallel Points can be used for either 1 ft. or 2 ft. radius track.

MECCANO OUTFITS

MECCANO. The famous Meccano Engineering Constructional Toy grows in popularity every year with boys all over the world. Hundreds of fascinating models that actually work, ranging from the simplest types to huge cranes, bridges and engines of all kinds, can be built from the accurately-made and beautifully-finished Meccano parts. There are more than 300 of these, every one a real engineering part in miniature. Building with Meccano is the greatest fun and there is nothing difficult about it. Included in every Outfit is a splendidly-illustrated Manual of Instructions, together with a screwdriver and a spanner, which are the only tools needed. Any boy can start building at once.

Boys who already have Red-Green Meccano Outfits (numbered OO-7) should note that they can obtain Connecting Outfits to bring their existing Outfits into line with the contents of the Blue-Gold Outfits (lettered B-L).

DINKY BUILDER. This is the most fascinating building toy ever produced for young children to play with. The beautiful enamelled parts make it delightful and easy for boys or girls to build real-looking Coaches, Carts and vehicles of all kinds, Garages, Towers and Bridges—hundreds of toys, each one a strong and perfect plaything.

AEROPLANE OUTFITS. These are the finest constructional Outfits of their kind in existence. Building aeroplanes is fine fun, and at the same time it teaches the principles of aeroplane construction, with which every boy should be familiar.

MOTOR CAR OUTFITS. The cars built with these Outfits are not only wonderfully realistic in appearance, but are capable of making long runs at high speed. The Outfits have become firm favourites on account of the splendid fun of building the models.

HORNBY SPEED BOATS AND RACING BOATS. These magnificent model boats are the finest of their kind ever produced. For value and efficiency they have no equal. They are steady in the water, they steer well, and they are so fast that they win all the races on the local ponds!

KEMEX CHEMICAL AND ELEKTRON ELECTRICAL OUTFITS. Every boy who is keen on exploring the wonders of science should obtain one of these fine Outfits. They contain all the necessary apparatus and materials for carrying out a large number of interesting experiments.

DINKY TOYS. Dinky Toys are rapidly taking a place in the forefront of Meccano products. There are now more than 200 of these delightful miniatures, each one unique in its realism and perfection of finish. Many of them can be used with splendid effect with Hornby Railway layouts, and with models built with Dinky Builder Outfits.

All Meccano Products are manufactured by Meccano Limited, Liverpool, and are constructed throughout by expert craftsmen from the finest materials that can be obtained.

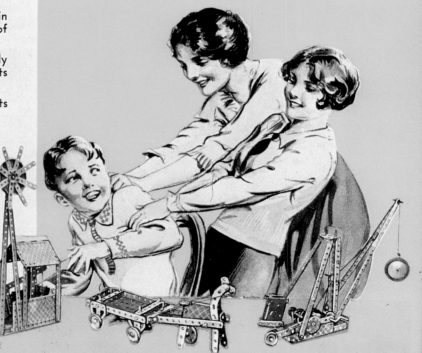

MECCANO OUTFIT "A"

BUILDS 98 MODELS

This is an excellent Outfit with which to commence the Meccano hobby. A special Manual of Instructions is included showing how 98 interesting models can be constructed. This fine range includes Ships, Steam Engine, Cranes, Trolleys, Horses and Carts, Scales, Swing, etc., each capable of providing hours of fun. A special page of working models fitted with the *Magic* Motor (see page 42) is also included. Keen model-builders will derive great pleasure from building additional models of their own creation.

Price 5/-

An Aa Accessory Outfit, costing 2/6, will convert an A into a B Outfit.

MECCANO IS REAL ENGINEERING IN MINIATURE

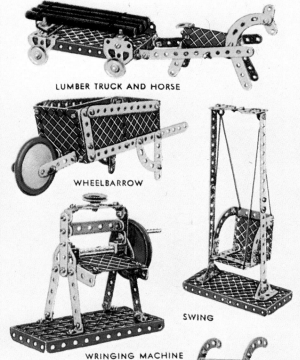

LUMBER TRUCK AND HORSE

WHEELBARROW

WRINGING MACHINE

SWING

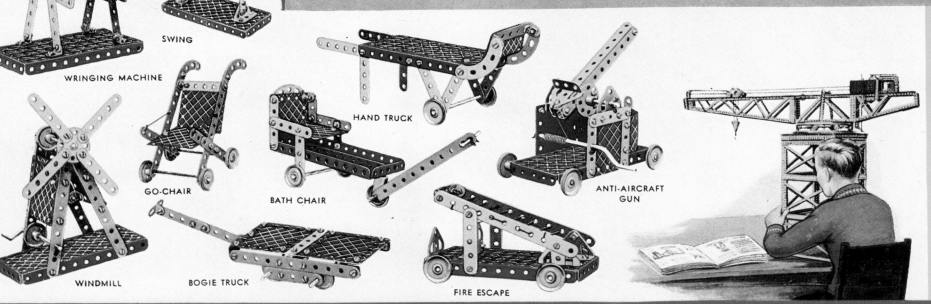

WINDMILL

GO-CHAIR

BATH CHAIR

BOGIE TRUCK

HAND TRUCK

ANTI-AIRCRAFT GUN

FIRE ESCAPE

MECCANO OUTFIT "B"

BUILDS 219 MODELS

The B Outfit contains a splendid assortment of Meccano Strips, Rods, Wheels, Plates, Nuts, Bolts, etc., and a special Manual of Instructions giving examples of 219 models that can be built with the Outfit. The models illustrated include Motor Cycle and Sidecar, Clock, Wrestlers, Flyboats, Signals, Furniture, Arc Lamp and a variety of others, amongst which are ten of extra special interest showing how the *Magic* Motor, described on page 42, can be fitted to increase the fun and realism. Everything necessary for building the models is included.

Price 7/6

A Ba Accessory Outfit, costing 3/–, will convert a B into a C Outfit.

MECCANO IS THE FINEST HOBBY IN THE WORLD

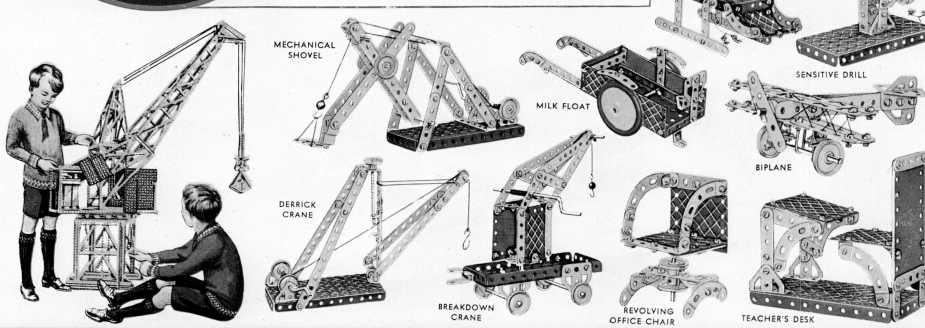

HAWKER'S CART

DENTIST'S CHAIR

SENSITIVE DRILL

MECHANICAL SHOVEL

MILK FLOAT

BIPLANE

DERRICK CRANE

BREAKDOWN CRANE

REVOLVING OFFICE CHAIR

TEACHER'S DESK

MECCANO OUTFIT "C"

CENTRIFUGAL GOVERNOR

BUILDS 330 MODELS

This popular Outfit contains a large number and an excellent variety of Meccano parts with which a fine range of models can be built, including Sports Car and Sports Coupé, Cranes, Seaplanes, Paddle Steamer, etc. A big, fully illustrated Manual of Instructions is included, giving examples of 330 models, an interesting selection of which are fitted with the *Magic* Motor described on page 42. In addition, inventive boys can build scores of others to their own ideas.

Price 10/-

A Ca Accessory Outfit, costing 5/6, will convert a C into a D Outfit.

THE WORLD'S HAPPIEST BOYS ARE MECCANO BOYS

EXTENDED ASH TIP

WINDMILL PUMP

ELEVATED JIB CRANE

MOBILE CRANE

TELEPHONE

CART

SPORTS COUPÉ

GIANT FOUNDRY LADLE

MECHANICAL SHOVEL

MECCANO OUTFIT "D"

BUILDS 360 MODELS

The fortunate possessor of an Outfit D is able to build models of a more complicated and interesting type, including large Cranes, Pit-head Gear, Motor Wagons, Roundabouts, Aeroplane, Turn-table, Mechanical Hammer, etc., all designed on correct engineering principles. Full instructions for building 360 models are included with the Outfit. The illustrations show clearly the design of each model.

Price 15/-

A Da Accessory Outfit (5/6) converts a D into an E Outfit.

MECCANO IS A THOUSAND TOYS IN ONE

SEWING MACHINE

FOOTBRIDGE

ANTI-AIRCRAFT GUN

COASTER

TURNTABLE

HAY TEDDER

TIPPING MOTOR WAGON

PIT-HEAD GEAR

MECCANO OUTFIT "E"

BUILDS 393 MODELS

This fine Outfit contains a good range of parts by means of which a splendid selection of realistic models can be built, including Roundabout, Embossing Machine, Fire Escape, Windmill, Cranes, etc. The illustrated Manual included with the Outfit gives full instructions for building 393 models, the construction of which is full of interest.

Price 20/-

An Ea Accessory Outfit (11/-) converts an E into an F Outfit.

BOYHOOD'S BEST DAYS—BUILDING WITH MECCANO

MONOPLANE

RAILWAY BRIDGE

LAWN MARKER

STAMPING MILL

TRAVELLING JIB CRANE

WINDMILL

ELECTRIC TRUCK

STEAM LORRY

MECCANO OUTFITS F, G, H, K & L

The splendid Outfits F to L, illustrated on this page, contain a wide range of Meccano parts with which, in addition to building the models in the Manuals of Instructions, an inventive boy can construct a number of large and elaborate models of his own design.

OUTFIT G BUILDS 501 MODELS

Model-building possibilities are very greatly increased with this Outfit, which contains a splendid selection of Meccano parts. 501 examples of real engineering models are illustrated in the Manuals of Instructions, including Windmill, Girder Crane, Elliptical Lathe, Coal Tipper, Steam Wagon, Power Press, etc. They provide hours of fascination and enjoyment ... ... Price 55/-
A Ga Accessory Outfit, costing 17/6, converts a G into an H Outfit.

Outfit F

OUTFIT F BUILDS 435 MODELS

This excellent Outfit contains many Meccano parts of an advanced engineering type. The Cranes, Bridges, etc., that it builds are of a higher standard, and, in addition, such excellent models as the Tower Wagon, Vertical Steam Engine and Railway Breakdown Crane can be constructed. Manuals of Instructions, showing how to build 435 models, are included.   Price 30/-
An Fa Accessory Outfit, costing 26/6, converts an F into a G Outfit.

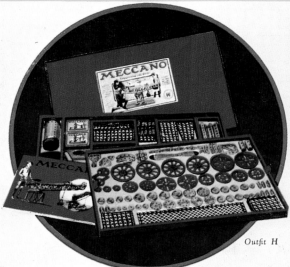

Outfit H

OUTFIT H BUILDS 547 MODELS

The H Outfit is supplied either in a stout carton or in a handsome enamelled cabinet. The number of Meccano parts contained in each type of Outfit is the same. The Manuals included give examples of 547 models that can be constructed.
Price (packed in strong carton) 72/6
Price (packed in enamelled cabinet, fitted with lock and key) 97/6
An Ha Accessory Outfit, costing 60/-, converts an H into a K Outfit.

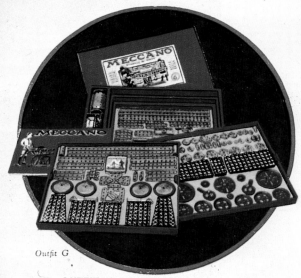

Outfit G

Outfit K

OUTFIT K BUILDS 592 MODELS

The K Outfit is supplied either in a strong carton or in a handsome enamelled cabinet with lock and key. Realistic working models of many of the world's most famous engineering masterpieces can be built with this Outfit. The Manuals of Instructions included give examples of 592 splendid models that can be constructed.
Price (packed in strong carton) 132/6
Price (packed in enamelled cabinet, fitted with lock and key) 157/6
A Ka Accessory Outfit, costing 225/-, converts a K into an L Outfit.

OUTFIT L BUILDS 635 MODELS

This is a complete and comprehensive Outfit, containing all the Meccano parts necessary to build each of the models featured in all the Manuals of Instructions. It is an ideal present for a boy interested in mechanics.
Price (packed in beautifully enamelled cabinet fitted with lock and key) 400/-

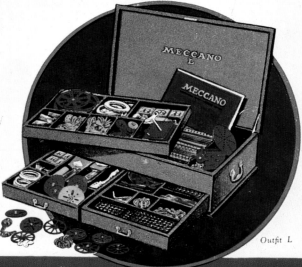

Outfit L

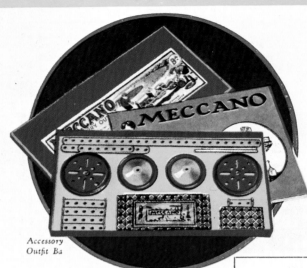

Accessory Outfit Ba

Each complete Meccano Outfit can be converted into the one next higher by means of a Meccano Accessory Outfit. Thus, a boy who commences with one of the small Outfits can build up his equipment by easy stages until he is the possessor of an L Outfit.

The A Outfit can be converted into a B by adding to it an Aa Accessory Outfit. A Ba Accessory Outfit would then convert the B Outfit into a C, and so on.

PRICES OF MECCANO ACCESSORY OUTFITS

				Price						Price
Aa converts A Outfit into B				2/6	Fa converts F Outfit into G					26/6
Ba	,,	B	,,	,,	C	3/-	Ga	,,	G	,,	,,	H		17/6
Ca	,,	C	,,	,,	D	5/6	*Ha	,,	H	,,	,,	K		60/-
Da	,,	D	,,	,,	E	5/6	†Ka	,,	K	,,	,,	L		225/-
Ea	,,	E	,,	,,	F	11/-	* Carton. † Cabinet.				

MECCANO LIGHTING SET

It is great fun to illuminate your Meccano models by electric light, and a special Meccano Lighting Set can be obtained from your dealer for this purpose. This consists of two spot lights, one stand lamp, two special brackets, and two pea lamps, operated from a 4-volt flashlamp battery (not included in the set). The stand lamp is used for decorative purposes, and the spot lights can be used as car headlamps, floodlights on cranes, and in countless other attractive ways.

Price 3/-

Accessory Outfit Ga

MECCANO CONNECTING OUTFITS

Owners of the old style Red-Green numerical Outfits can convert them into Outfits in the new Blue-Gold alphabetical series by means of these Connecting Outfits. Details are as follows:—

No. OOB Outfit converts a	No. OO Outfit (Red-Green)	into an Outfit	B	...	...	Price 4/-
No. OC	,,	,,	No. O	,,	,,	,,	,,	C	...	...	,, 5/6
No. 1D	,,	,,	No. 1	,,	,,	,,	,,	D	...	...	,, 5/9
No. 2E	,,	,,	No. 2	,,	,,	,,	,,	E	...	...	,, 6/-
No. 3F	,,	,,	No. 3	,,	,,	,,	,,	F	...	...	,, 6/6
No. 4H	,,	,,	No. 4	,,	,,	,,	,,	H	...	...	,, 23/6
No. 5K	,,	,,	No. 5	,,	,,	,,	,,	K	...	...	,, 66/-
No. 6K	,,	,,	No. 6	,,	,,	,,	,,	K	...	...	,, 10/-
No. 7L	,,	,,	No. 7	,,	,,	,,	,,	L	...	...	,, 17/6

MECCANO-RED-GREEN OUTFITS

No. OOO Outfit

BUILDS 162 MODELS

This Outfit contains a good selection of Meccano red-green parts and is specially suitable for the younger model-building enthusiasts.

Price 2/6

IMPORTANT.—An Accessory Outfit to convert a No. OOO Outfit into a No. OO is not supplied, but the extra parts required, and a No. OO Manual, can be obtained from any Meccano dealer.

No. OO Outfit

BUILDS 189 MODELS

This is an excellent Outfit with which to commence the Meccano hobby. A special Manual of Instructions is included showing how 189 interesting models can be constructed. This fine range includes Trucks, Barrows, Cranes and many others ... Price 3/6

X Series Outfits and Motor

No. X1 Outfit builds 70 models	...	...	...	Price 1/-
No. X2 Outfit builds 96 models	...	...	...	Price 1/6
No. X1a Accessory Outfit. Converts No. X1 Outfit into No. X2	...	...	Price 9d.
X Series Clockwork Motor	...	...	Price 2/-

No. OO Outfit

No. OOO Outfit

MECCANO PARTS AND ACCESSORIES

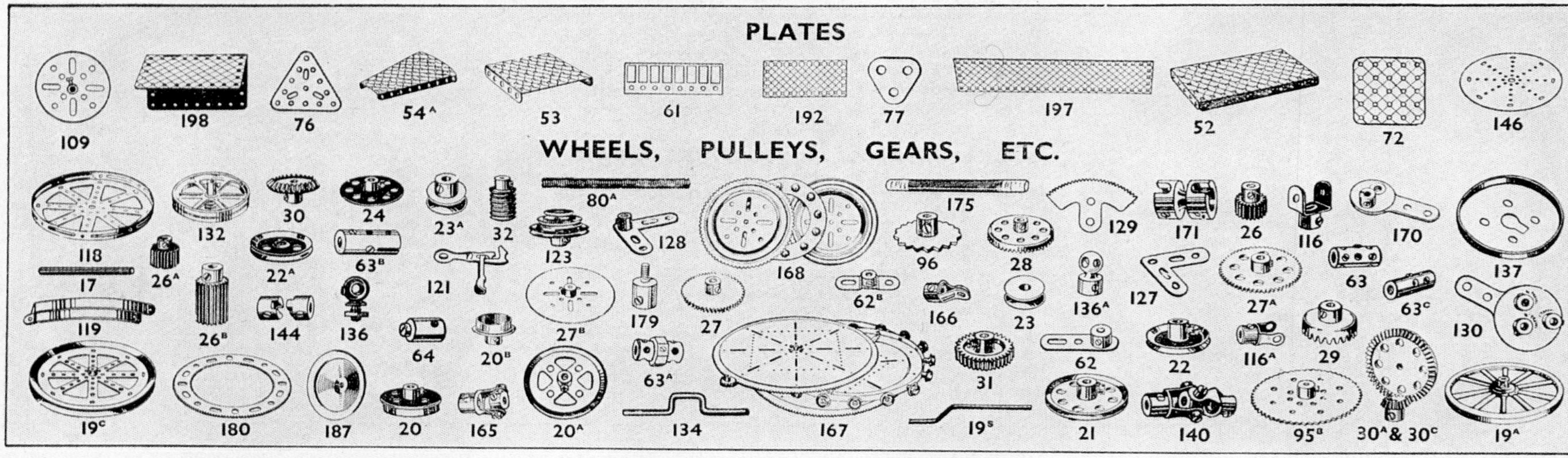

PLATES
109
198
76
54A
53
61
192
77
197
52
72
146
WHEELS, PULLEYS, GEARS, ETC.
118
132
30
24
23A
32
80A
123
128
168
175
96
28
129
171
26
116
170
137
17
26A
22A
63B
121
27B
179
27
62B
166
23
136A
127
27A
63
63C
119
26B
144
136
64
20B
63A
62
22
116A
29
130
19C
180
187
20
165
20A
134
167
19S
31
21
140
95B
30A & 30C
19A

Perforated Strips.

No.			s.	d.	No.			s.	d.
1	12½″	½ doz.	1	0	3	3½″	½ doz.	0	4
1a	9½″	,,	0	9	4	3″	,,	0	3
1b	7½″	,,	0	8	5	2½″	,,	0	3
2	5½″	,,	0	6	6	2″	,,	0	3
2a	4½″	,,	0	5	6a	1½″	,,	0	3

Angle Girders.

No.			s.	d.	No.			s.	d.
7	24½″	each	0	8	9a	4½″	½ doz.	0	10
7a	18½″	,,	0	6	9b	3½″	,,	0	8
8	12½″	½ doz.	1	6	9c	3″	,,	0	8
8a	9½″	,,	1	3	9d	2½″	,,	0	7
8b	7½″	,,	1	2	9e	2″	,,	0	6
9	5½″	,,	1	0	9f	1½″	,,	0	6

No.	Description		s.	d.
10	Flat Brackets	doz.	0	1
11	Double Brackets	,,	0	3
12	Angle Brackets ½″×½″	,,	0	2
12a	,, ,, 1″×1″	,,	0	6
12b	,, ,, 1″×½″	,,	0	4
12c	Obtuse Angle Brackets ½″×½″ ...	,,	0	2

Axle Rods

No.			s.	d.	No.			s.	d.
13	11½″	each	0	2	16	3½″	2 for	0	1
13a	8″	,,	0	2	16a	2½″	,,	0	1
14	6½″	,,	0	1	16b	3″	,,	0	1
15	5″	,,	0	1	17	2″	3 for	0	1
15a	4½″	2 for	0	1	18a	1½″	,,	0	1
15b	4″	,,	0	1	18b	1″	,,	0	1

No.	Description		s.	d.
19	Crank Handles, Large 5″... ...	each	0	2
19s	,, ,, Small 3½″ ...	,,	0	1
19a	Wheels, 3″ diam., with set screws	,,	0	6
20	Flanged Wheels, 1⅛″ diam. ...	,,	0	5
20b	,, ,, ¾″ ,, ...	,,	0	3

Pulley Wheels.

No.	Description		s.	d.
19b	3″ dia., with centre boss & set screw	each	0	4
19c	6″ ,, ,, ,, ,, ,,	,,	1	9
20a	2″ ,, ,, ,, ,, ,,	,,	0	4
21	1½″ ,, ,, ,, ,, ,,	,,	0	4
22	1″ ,, ,, ,, ,, ,,	,,	0	3
23a	½″ ,, ,, ,, grub screw	,,	0	3

Pulley Wheels.

No.	Description	each	s.	d.
22a	1 dia., without centre boss & grub screw		0	2
23	½″ ,, ,, ,, ,, ,,	,,	0	2
24	Bush Wheels	,,	0	4
25	Pinion Wheels, ¾″ diam., ¼″ face...	,,	0	5
25a	,, ,, ¾″ ,, ½″ ,, ...	,,	0	7
25b	,, ,, ¾″ ,, ¾″ ,, ...	,,	0	9
26	,, ,, ½″ ,, ¼″ ,, ...	,,	0	4
26a	,, ,, ½″ ,, ½″ ,, ...	,,	0	5
26b	,, ,, ½″ ,, ¾″ ,, ...	,,	0	6

Gear Wheels

No.	Description		s.	d.
27	50 teeth to gear with ¾″ pinion ...	each	0	5
27a	57 ,, ,, ,, ½″ ,, ...	,,	0	6
27b	133 ,, ,, ,, ½″ ,, (3½″ diam.)	,,	1	3
27c	95 ,, ,, ,, ½″ pinion (2½″ diam.)	,,	0	10
28	Contrate Wheels, 1½″ diam. ...	,,	0	9
29	,, ,, ¾″ ,, ...	,,	0	6
30	Bevel Gears, ⅞″, 26 teeth ...	,,	0	7
30a	,, ,, ½″, 16 ,, (Can only be	,,	0	6
30c	,, ,, 1½″. 48 ,, used together)	,,	1	6
31	Gear Wheels, 1″, 38 teeth ...	,,	0	10
32	Worms	,,	0	4
34	Spanners	,,	0	1
34b	Box Spanners	,,	0	4
35	Spring Clips	box doz.	0	2
35f	,, ,, ...	box of 50	0	7
36	Screwdrivers	each	0	3
36a	,, Extra Long	,,	0	6
36b	,, Special	,,	1	0
37	Nuts and Bolts, 7/32″ ...	box doz.	0	3
37a	Nuts	box doz.	0	2
37af	,, ...	box of 50	0	7
37b	Bolts, 7/32″	box doz.	0	2
37bf	Bolts, 7/32″	box of 50	0	7
37f	Nuts and Bolts, 7/32″ ...	box of 50	1	0
37g	,, ,, ,, ...	box of 144	2	9
38	Washers	doz.	0	1
38f	,, ...	box of 50	0	3
40	Hanks of Cord	2 for	0	3
41	Propeller Blades	pair	0	4

No.	Description.		s.	d.
43	Springs	each	0	2
44	Cranked Bent Strips	,,	0	1
45	Double ,, ,, ...	,,	0	1

Double Angle Strips.

No.			s.	d.	No.			s.	d.
46	2½″×1″	½ doz.	0	6	48a	2½″×½″	½ doz.	0	5
47	2½″×1½″	,,	0	9	48b	3½″×½″	,,	0	6
47a	3″×1½″	,,	0	10	48c	4½″×½″	,,	0	9
48	1½″×½″	,,	0	4	48d	5½″×½″	,,	0	9

No.	Description.		s.	d.
50a	Eye Pieces, with boss	each	0	4
51	Flanged Plates, 2½″×1½″ ...	,,	0	2
52	,, ,, 5½″×2½″ ...	,,	0	5
52a	Flat Plates, 5½″×3½″	,,	0	5
53	Flanged Plates, 3½″×2½″	,,	0	3
53a	Flat Plates, 4½″×2½″	,,	0	3
54a	Flanged Sector Plates, 4½″ long ...	,,	0	3
55	Perforated Strips, slotted, 5½″ long	doz.	1	6
55a	,, ,, ,, 2″ ,,	,,	0	9
57	Hooks	2 for	0	1
57a	,, Scientific	each	0	1
57b	,, Loaded, Large	,,	0	2
57c	,, Loaded, Small	,,	0	1
58	Spring Cord	40″ Length	0	9
58a	Coupling Screws for Spring Cord	doz.	0	6
58b	Hooks for Spring Cord	,,	0	6
59	Collars with Grub Screws... ...	each	0	1
61	Windmill Sails	4 for	0	6
62	Cranks	each	0	3
62a	Threaded Cranks	,,	0	4
62b	Double Arm Cranks	,,	0	3
63	Couplings	,,	0	6
63a	Octagonal Couplings	,,	0	8
63b	Strip Couplings	,,	0	7
63c	Threaded Couplings	,,	0	6
64	,, Bosses	,,	0	2
65	Centre Forks	,,	0	1
66	Weights, 50 grammes	,,	0	9
67	Weights, 25 grammes	each	0	6
68	Woodscrews, ½″	doz.	0	3
69	Set Screws	,,	0	3
69a	Grub Screws, 5/32″	,,	0	4
69b	,, ,, 7/32″	,,	0	5

No.	Description.		s.	d.
70	Flat Plates, 5½″×2½″	each	0	4
72	,, ,, 2½″×2½″	,,	0	2
73	,, ,, 3″×1½″	2 for	0	3
76	Triangular Plates, 2½″	each	0	2
77	,, ,, 1″	,,	0	1

Screwed Rods.

No.			s.	d.	No.			s.	d.
78	11½″	each	0	6	80a	3½″	each	0	3
79	8″	,,	0	5	80b	4½″	,,	0	3
79a	6″	,,	0	4	81	2″	doz.	0	6
80	5″	,,	0	3	82	1″	,,	0	4

No.	Description.		s.	d.
89	5½″ Curved Strips, 10″ radius ...	each	0	2
89a	3″ ,, ,, cranked, 1¾″ radius, 4 to circle	,,	0	2
89b	4″ Curved Strips, cranked, 4½″ radius, 8 to circle	,,	0	2
90	2½″ Curved Strips, 2⅜″ radius ...	,,	0	1
90a	2½″ ,, ,, cranked, 1⅜″ radius, 4 to circle	,,	0	1
94	Sprocket Chain	40″ length	0	6
95	Sprocket Wheels, 36 teeth, 2″ diam.	each	0	5
95a	,, ,, 28 ,, 1½″ ,,	,,	0	4
95b	,, ,, 56 ,, 3″ ,,	,,	0	6
96	,, ,, 18 ,, 1″ ,,	,,	0	3
96a	,, ,, 14 ,, ¾″ ,,	,,	0	3

Braced Girders.

No.			s.	d.	No.			s.	d.
97	3½″ long	½ doz.	0	9	99a	9½″ long	½ doz.	2	0
97a	3″ ,,	,,	0	8	99b	7½″ ,,	,,	2	0
98	2½″ ,,	,,	0	8	100	5½″ ,,	,,	1	0
99	12½″ ,,	,,	2	6	100a	4½″ ,,	,,	0	10

No.	Description.		s.	d.
101	Healds, for looms	doz.	0	3
102	Single Bent Strips	each	0	1

Flat Girders.

No.			s.	d.	No.			s.	d.
103	5½″ long	½ doz.	0	10	103e	3″ long	½ doz.	0	6
103a	9½″ ,,	,,	1	2	103f	2½″ ,,	,,	0	5
103b	12½″ ,,	,,	1	3	103g	2″ ,,	,,	0	4
103c	4½″ ,,	,,	0	9	103h	1½″ ,,	,,	0	4
103d	3½″ ,,	,,	0	7	103k	7½″ ,,	,,	1	0

No.	Description.		s.	d.
104	Shuttles, for looms	each	5	0
105	Reed Hooks, for looms	,,	0	4

MECCANO PARTS AND ACCESSORIES

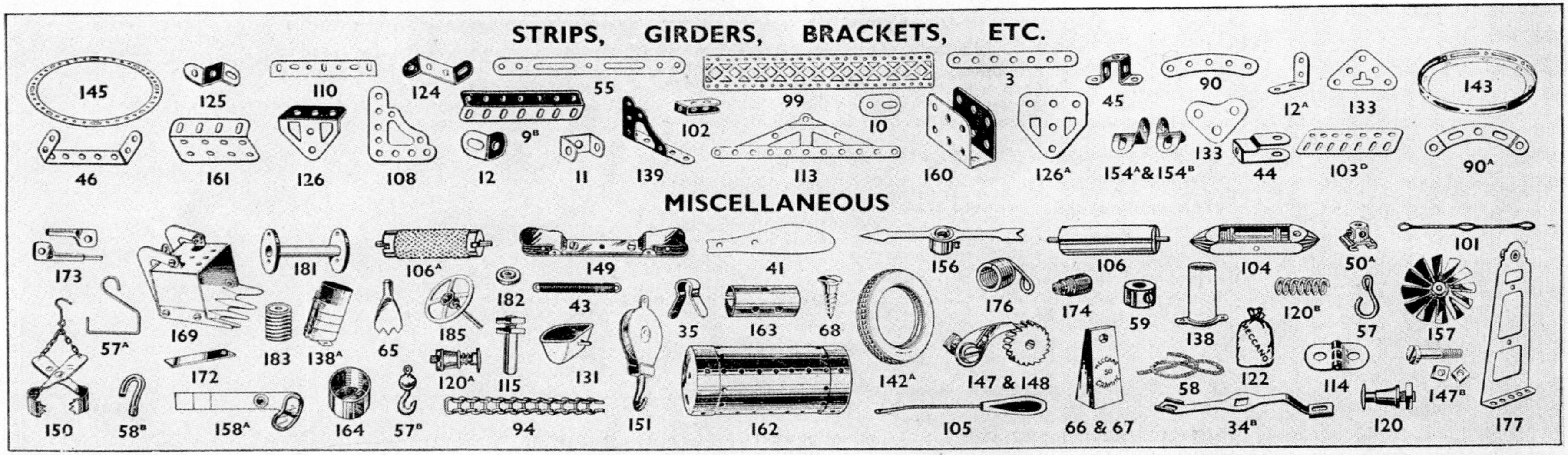

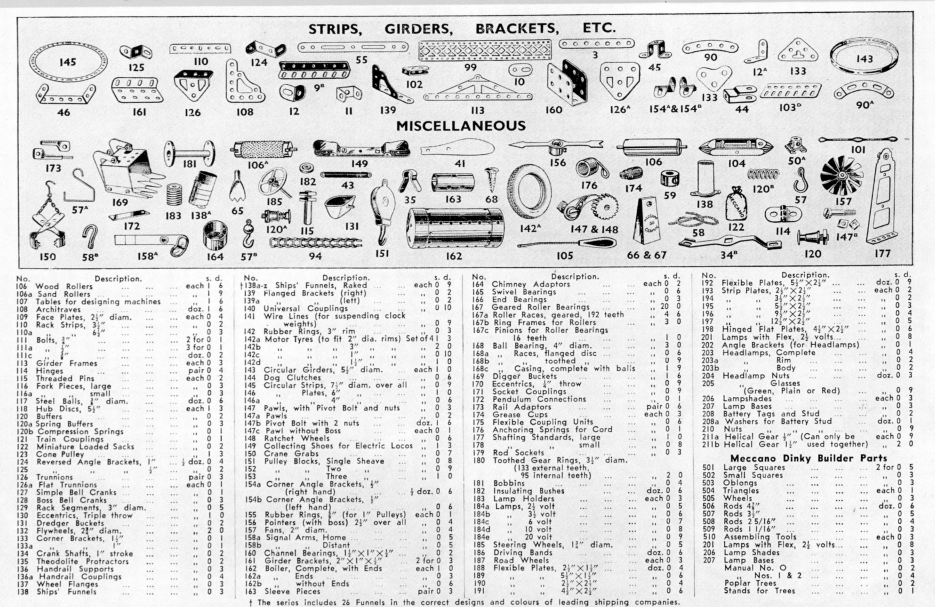

No.	Description.		s.	d.
106	Wood Rollers	each	1	6
106a	Sand Rollers	,,	1	9
107	Tables for designing machines	,,	1	6
108	Architraves	doz.	1	6
109	Face Plates, 2½″ diam.	each	0	4
110	Rack Strips, 3½″	,,	0	2
110a	,, ,, 6½″	,,	0	3
111	Bolts, ¾″	2 for	0	1
111a	,, ½″	3 for	0	1
111c	,, ⅜″	doz.	0	2
113	Girder Frames	each	0	3
114	Hinges	pair	0	4
115	Threaded Pins	each	0	2
116	Fork Pieces, large	,,	0	3
116a	,, ,, small	,,	0	3
117	Steel Balls, ⅜″ diam.	doz.	0	6
118	Hub Discs, 5½″	each	1	3
120	Buffers	,,	0	2
120a	Spring Buffers	,,	0	3
120b	Compression Springs	,,	0	1
121	Train Couplings	,,	0	1
122	Miniature Loaded Sacks	,,	0	2
123	Cone Pulley	,,	1	3
124	Reversed Angle Brackets, 1″	½ doz.	0	4
125	,, ,, ,, ½″	,,	0	2
126	Trunnions	pair	0	3
126a	Flat Trunnions	each	0	1
127	Simple Bell Cranks	,,	0	1
128	Boss Bell Cranks	,,	0	3
129	Rack Segments, 3″ diam.	,,	0	5
130	Eccentrics, Triple throw	,,	1	0
131	Dredger Buckets	,,	0	2
132	Flywheels, 2¾″ diam.	,,	2	0
133	Corner Brackets, 1½″	,,	0	1
133a	,, ,, 1″	,,	0	1
134	Crank Shafts, 1″ stroke	,,	0	2
135	Theodolite Protractors	,,	0	2
136	Handrail Supports	,,	0	3
136a	Handrail Couplings	,,	0	4
137	Wheel Flanges	,,	0	3
138	Ships' Funnels	,,	0	3

No.	Description.		s.	d.
†138a-z	Ships' Funnels, Raked	each	0	9
139	Flanged Brackets (right)	,,	0	2
139a	,, ,, (left)	,,	0	2
140	Universal Couplings	,,	0	10
141	Wire Lines (for suspending clock weights)	,,	0	9
142	Rubber Rings, 3″ rim	,,	0	3
142a	Motor Tyres (to fit 2″ dia. rims)	Set of 4	1	3
142b	,, ,, ,, 3″ ,, ,,	,,	2	0
142c	,, ,, ,, 1″ ,, ,,	,,	0	10
142d	,, ,, ,, 1½″ ,, ,,	,,	1	0
143	Circular Girders, 5½″ diam.	each	1	0
144	Dog Clutches	,,	0	6
145	Circular Strips, 7½″ diam. over all	,,	0	9
146	,, Plates, 6″ ,,	,,	1	0
146a	,, ,, 4″ ,,	,,	0	6
147	Pawls, with Pivot Bolt and nuts	,,	0	3
147a	Pawls	,,	0	2
147b	Pivot Bolt with 2 nuts	doz.	1	6
147c	Pawl without Boss	each	0	1
148	Ratchet Wheels	,,	0	6
149	Collecting Shoes for Electric Locos	,,	1	3
150	Crane Grabs	,,	0	7
151	Pulley Blocks, Single Sheave	,,	0	8
152	,, ,, Two ,,	,,	0	9
153	,, ,, Three ,,	,,	1	0
154a	Corner Angle Brackets, ½″ (right hand)	½ doz.	0	6
154b	Corner Angle Brackets, ½″ (left hand)	,,	0	6
155	Rubber Rings, ⅝″ (for 1″ Pulleys)	each	0	1
156	Pointers (with boss) 2½″ over all	,,	0	4
157	Fans, 2″ diam.	,,	0	4
158a	Signal Arms, Home	,,	0	5
158b	,, ,, Distant	,,	0	5
160	Channel Bearings, 1½″×1″×½″	,,	0	2
161	Girder Brackets, 2″×1″×½″	2 for	0	3
162	Boiler, Complete, with Ends	each	1	0
162a	,, Ends	,,	0	3
162b	,, without Ends	,,	0	6
163	Sleeve Pieces	pair	0	3

No.	Description.		s.	d.
164	Chimney Adaptors	each	0	2
165	Swivel Bearings	,,	0	6
166	End Bearings	,,	0	3
167	Geared Roller Bearings	,,	20	0
167a	Roller Races, geared, 192 teeth	,,	4	6
167b	Ring Frames for Rollers	,,	3	0
167c	Pinions for Roller Bearings 16 teeth	,,	1	0
168	Ball Bearing, 4″ diam.	,,	3	0
168a	,, Races, flanged disc	,,	0	6
168b	,, ,, toothed ,,	,,	0	9
168c	,, Casing, complete with balls	,,	1	9
169	Digger Buckets	,,	1	6
170	Eccentrics, ¼″ throw	,,	0	9
171	Socket Couplings	,,	0	9
172	Pendulum Connections	,,	0	1
173	Rail Adaptors	pair	0	6
174	Grease Cups	each	0	3
175	Flexible Coupling Units	,,	0	6
176	Anchoring Springs for Cord	,,	0	1
177	Shafting Standards, large	,,	1	0
178	,, ,, small	,,	0	8
179	Rod Sockets	,,	0	3
180	Toothed Gear Rings, 3½″ diam. (133 external teeth, 95 internal teeth)	,,	2	0
181	Bobbins	,,	0	4
182	Insulating Bushes	doz.	0	6
183	Lamp Holders	each	0	3
184a	Lamps, 2½ volt	,,	0	5
184b	,, 3½ volt	,,	0	6
184c	,, 6 volt	,,	0	7
184d	,, 10 volt	,,	0	8
184e	,, 20 volt	,,	0	9
185	Steering Wheels, 1¾″ diam.	,,	0	5
186	Driving Bands	doz.	0	6
187	Road Wheels	each	0	3
188	Flexible Plates, 2½″×1½″	doz.	0	4
189	,, ,, 5½″×1½″	,,	0	6
190	,, ,, 2½″×2½″	,,	0	4
191	,, ,, 4½″×2½″	,,	0	6

No.	Description.		s.	d.
192	Flexible Plates, 5½″×2½″	doz.	0	9
193	Strip Plates, 2½″×2½″	each	0	2
194	,, ,, 3½″×2½″	,,	0	2
195	,, ,, 5½″×2½″	,,	0	3
196	,, ,, 9½″×2½″	,,	0	4
197	,, ,, 12½″×2½″	,,	0	5
198	Hinged Flat Plates, 4½″×2½″	,,	0	6
201	Lamps with Flex, 2½ volts	,,	0	8
202	Angle Brackets (for Headlamps)	,,	0	1
203	Headlamps, Complete	,,	0	4
203a	,, Rim	,,	0	2
203b	,, Body	,,	0	2
204	Headlamp Nuts	doz.	0	3
205	,, Glasses (Green, Plain or Red)	,,	0	9
206	Lampshades	each	0	3
207	Lamp Bases	,,	0	3
208	Battery Tags and Stud	,,	0	2
208a	Washers for Battery Stud	doz.	0	1
210	Nuts ,, ,, ,,	,,	0	9
211a	Helical Gear ½″ (Can only be	each	0	9
211b	Helical Gear 1½″ used together)	,,	2	0

Meccano Dinky Builder Parts

No.	Description.		s.	d.
501	Large Squares	2 for	0	5
502	Small Squares	,,	0	3
503	Oblongs	,,	0	3
504	Triangles	each	0	1
505	Wheels	,,	0	3
506	Rods 4⅞″	doz.	0	6
507	Rods 3½″	,,	0	5
508	Rods 2 5/16″	,,	0	4
509	Rods 1 1/16″	,,	0	3
510	Assembling Tools	each	0	3
201	Lamps with Flex, 2½ volts	,,	0	8
206	Lamp Shades	,,	0	3
207	Lamp Bases	,,	0	3
	Manual No. O	,,	0	2
	,, Nos. 1 & 2	,,	0	4
	Poplar Trees	,,	0	2
	Stands for Trees	,,	0	1

† The series includes 26 Funnels in the correct designs and colours of leading shipping companies.

MECCANO POWER UNITS

RUN YOUR MECCANO MODELS WITH THE MECCANO POWER UNITS

If you want to obtain the fullest enjoyment from the Meccano hobby you must operate your models by means of one of the Meccano power units described on this and the next page. You push over the control lever of the Clockwork or Electric Motor and immediately your Crane, Motor Car, Ship Coaler or Windmill commences to work in exactly the same manner as its prototype in real life.

The side plates and bases of each Motor are pierced with the standard Meccano equidistant holes, which makes it easy to build the Motor into any Meccano model in the exact position required.

MECCANO CLOCKWORK MOTORS

These are the finest clockwork motors obtainable for model driving. They have exceptional power and length of run and their gears are cut with such precision as to make them perfectly smooth and steady in operation.

THE MECCANO *MAGIC* MOTOR. The Meccano *Magic* Motor is well designed, strongly constructed, and fitted with a powerful spring giving a long and steady run. Each *Magic* Motor is supplied with a separate ½" Pulley Wheel and three pairs of driving bands of different lengths, so that it is a simple matter to fit the Motor in models of various types to set them in motion.

This splendid Motor is capable of driving most of the models that can be built with Meccano A and B Outfits, and many of the lighter models illustrated in the Manuals for the C, D and E Outfits. It is non-reversing. Price 2/-

No. 1 CLOCKWORK MOTOR. An efficient and long-running Motor fitted with a brake lever by means of which it can be started and stopped. It is non-reversing. Price 5/-

No. 1A CLOCKWORK MOTOR. This Motor is more powerful than the No. 1 Motor and is fitted with reversing motion. It has brake and reverse levers. Price 7/6

No. 2 CLOCKWORK MOTOR. This is a Motor of super quality. Brake and reverse levers enable it to be started, stopped or reversed, as required. Price 9/-

MECCANO ELECTRIC MOTORS

The four Meccano Electric Motors listed below have been designed specially to provide smooth-running power units for the operation of Meccano models. They are operated from the mains—where the supply is Alternating Current—through a Meccano Transformer. The 6-volt Motors can be run also from a 6-volt accumulator. They cannot be run satisfactorily from dry cells.

Each Motor is a highly efficient power unit and, with ordinary care, will give long and excellent service.

No. E1 ELECTRIC MOTOR (6-VOLT). Non-reversing... Price 9/-
No. E6 ELECTRIC MOTOR (6-VOLT). Reversing ... „ 15/6
No. E120 ELECTRIC MOTOR (20-VOLT). Non-reversing... „ 10/-
No. E20B ELECTRIC MOTOR (20-VOLT). Reversing ... „ 18/6

MECCANO TRANSFORMERS

Meccano Transformers provide a convenient and safe means of driving 6-volt or 20-volt Electric Motors and Train Sets from the mains supply where this is alternating current.

All Meccano Transformers, and the Hornby Transformer-Rectifier, are available for the following Alternating Current Supplies:—100/110 volts, 50 cycles; 200/225 volts, 50 cycles; 225/250 volts, 50 cycles. They can be specially wound for other supplies.

In ordering a Transformer or a Transformer-Rectifier the voltage and frequency of the supply must be stated. These particulars are given on the supply meter.

No. T6A TRANSFORMER (Output 40 VA at 9/3½ volts) for 6-volt Electric Motors or 6-volt Trains. Fitted with speed regulator and separate circuit for supplying current for eighteen 3½-volt lamps. Price 22/6

No. T6 TRANSFORMER (Output 25 VA at 9 volts) for 6-volt Electric Motors or 6-volt Trains. Fitted with speed regulator. Price 17/6

No. T6M TRANSFORMER (Output 25 VA at 9 volts) for 6-volt Electric Motors or 6-volt Trains. This is similar to No. T6, but it is not fitted with a speed regulator. Price 12/6

No. TR6 TRANSFORMER-RECTIFIER (Output 6 volts at 1½ Amps.) for use with Hornby No. EPM16 Special Tank Locomotive (6-volt, Permanent Magnet). Price 29/6

No. T20A TRANSFORMER (Output 35 VA at 20/3½ volts) for 20-volt Electric Motors or 20-volt Trains. Fitted with speed regulator and separate circuit for lighting up to fourteen 3½-volt lamps. Price 22/6

No. T20 TRANSFORMER (Output 20 VA at 20 volts) for 20-volt Electric Motors or 20-volt Trains. Fitted with speed regulator. Price 17/6

No. T20M TRANSFORMER (Output 20 VA at 20 volts) for 20-volt Electric Motors or 20-volt Trains. This is similar to No. T20, but is not fitted with speed regulator. Price 12/6

RESISTANCE CONTROLLERS

Where a Meccano 6-volt Electric Motor or Hornby 6-volt Train is operated from an accumulator or from a Meccano No. T6M Transformer; or a Meccano 20-volt Electric Motor or Hornby 20-volt Train from a Meccano T20M Transformer, a variable resistance is required to control and regulate the speed. For this purpose a Meccano Resistance Controller should be used.

MECCANO RESISTANCE CONTROLLER, 6-volt or 20-volt. Price 3/9

No. 1 CLOCKWORK MOTOR

No. 2 CLOCKWORK MOTOR

MECCANO MAGIC MOTOR

No. E1 ELECTRIC MOTOR (6 volt)

No. E6 ELECTRIC MOTOR (6 volt)

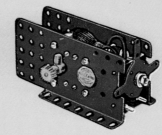

No. E20B ELECTRIC MOTOR (20-volt)

RESISTANCE CONTROLLER

MECCANO DINKY BUILDER OUTFITS

No. O Dinky Builder Outfit

A delightful Hobby for Boys and Girls

This is one of the most fascinating building systems ever devised for young children to play with. The beautifully enamelled parts enable boys or girls to build very real looking Coaches, Aeroplane Hangars, Garages, Towers, Bridges, Wheel Toys, Windmills—hundreds of toys, each one a real strong plaything.

There are three Outfits in the series, each of which is supplied in two colour combinations—bright red and emerald green; salmon pink and light green.

No. O Dinky Builder Outfit

This is an excellent Outfit, containing a good assortment of Dinky Builder parts, including two road wheels, with which a splendid range of models can be built. The Instruction Folder included gives examples of 40 models.   Price 2/6

No. 1 Dinky Builder Outfit

This splendid Outfit contains a varied selection of parts, including two trees on die-cast stands that lend the correct atmosphere to models of farm buildings, churches, etc. A further attraction is a set of four road wheels for constructing miniature wheel toys. The Instruction Folder shows a total of 70 fine models that any boy or girl can build.   Price 4/11

No. 2 Dinky Builder Outfit

The parts in this fine Outfit enable all the No. O and No. 1 Outfits models to be built, and also make possible the construction of seven groups of realistic miniature modern furniture. Full instructions for building the complete range of models are given in the Instruction Folder.   Price 7/11

Dinky Builder "A"

The Dinky Builder "A" packet contains a useful assortment of Dinky Builder parts. Boys and girls who own No. O, No. 1 or No. 2 Outfits should supplement them by purchasing one or more of these packets, which will increase the scope and enable bigger and better models to be built.   Price 1/-

No. 1 Dinky Builder Outfit

HIGH BACK CHAIR
Built with No. O Outfit

DUST CART
Built with No. O Outfit

PORTER'S TRUCK
Built with No. O Outfit

GARAGE
Built with No. 1 Outfit

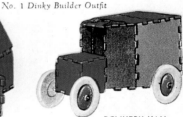

DELIVERY VAN
Built with No. 1 Outfit

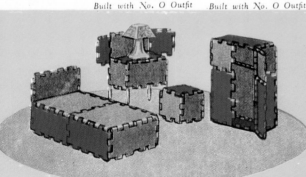

Suite of Bedroom Furniture made with No. 2 Outfit

No. 2 Dinky Builder Outfit

Group of Office Furniture made with No. 2 Outfit

Dinky Builder Parts can be purchased separately. See Price List on Page 40 (column 4).

MOTOR CAR CONSTRUCTOR OUTFIT No 1

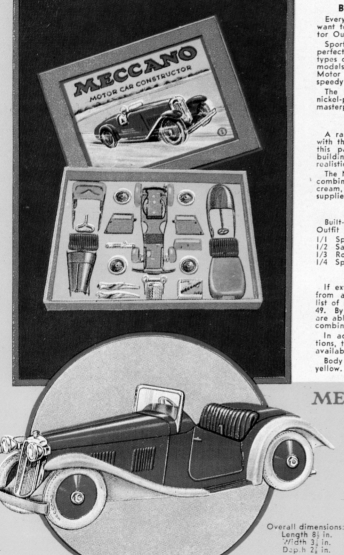

BUILD YOUR OWN MOTOR CARS

Every boy who is keen on model-building will want to possess one of the fine Motor Car Constructor Outfits described on this and the opposite page.

Sports four-seaters, coupés, speed cars, and other perfect miniature reproductions of many different types of car can be built with these Outfits. All the models are driven by means of a powerful Clockwork Motor (included in each Outfit), giving a long, speedy and realistic run on each winding.

The motor car parts are finished in rich enamel, nickel-plate and chromium, the complete Outfits being masterpieces of miniature automobile craftsmanship.

MOTOR CAR OUTFIT No. 1

A range of superb motor car models can be built with this Outfit. Look at the examples illustrated on this page, and think of the fun you could have building these and other types equally graceful and realistic.

The No. 1 Outfit is available in four different colour combinations—red and light blue, light blue and cream, green and yellow, and cream and red. It is supplied complete with powerful Clockwork Motor.

Price 10/-

Built-up models of motor cars made with No. 1 Outfit are available at the following prices:—

1/1 Sports Tourer (with hood)	... ...	9/6
1/2 Saloon Coupé	... ...	10/-
1/3 Road Racer	... ...	9/-
1/4 Sports Tourer	... ...	9/-

CHOICE RANGE OF COLOURS

If extra parts are required they can be purchased from any Meccano dealer. A complete illustrated list of No. 1 Motor Car Outfit parts is given on page 49. By adding separate parts in various colours you are able to construct models in a number of pleasing combinations, thus adding considerably to the interest.

In addition to the four standard colour combinations, the following No. 1 Motor Car Outfit parts are available in the colours indicated:—

Body Sections: orange, yellow. Wheels: orange, yellow. Wings: orange, green.

MECCANO TWO-SEATER SPORTS CAR

Non-Constructional

This realistic model of a two-seater sports car is beautifully made and finished. It is fitted with a strong clockwork motor that gives a long and steady run on each winding.

The model faithfully resembles the modern type of sports two-seater car. It is available in three different colours— red, blue and cream. Non-constructional.

Price 6/6

Overall dimensions:
Length 8½ in.
Width 3½ in.
Depth 2½ in.

Model of a Sports Tourer built with No. 1 Outfit.

Model of a Road Racer built with No. 1 Outfit.

Model of a Sports Tourer built with No. 1 Outfit

Model of a Saloon Coupé built with No. 1 Outfit.

IMPORTANT.—It should be noted that the No. 1 Motor Car Outfit parts cannot be used in conjunction with those of the No. 2 Outfit.

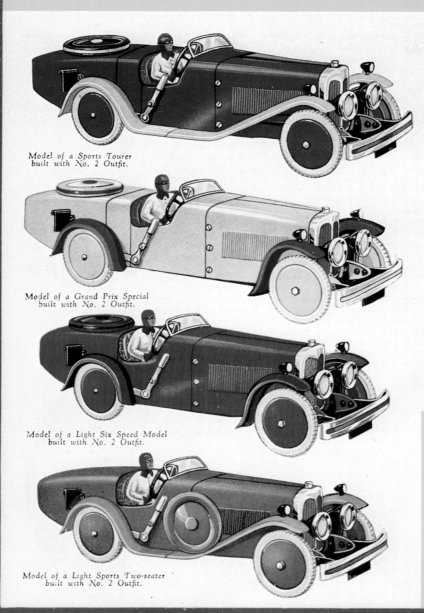

Model of a Sports Tourer
built with No. 2 Outfit.

Model of a Grand Prix Special
built with No. 2 Outfit.

Model of a Light Six Speed Model
built with No. 2 Outfit.

Model of a Light Sports Two-seater
built with No. 2 Outfit.

PERFECTLY-DESIGNED MODELS

Larger models of a superior type can be built with the No. 2 Motor Car Outfit. They are all perfectly designed, beautifully finished and the most attractive examples of constructional engineering ever produced. Their handsome and realistic appearance can be judged from the illustrations on this page.

No. 2 Outfit is available in four different colour combinations—red and light blue, light blue and cream, green and yellow, and cream and red. A powerful Clockwork Motor that gives a run of 150 feet on one winding is included.

Price 20/-

Built-up models of any of the Motor Cars that can be made with No. 2 Outfit are available.

Price 20/- each

CHOICE RANGE OF COLOURS

Extra parts in any of the colours mentioned above can be purchased from any Meccano dealer. See list of parts on page 49.

In addition to the four standard colour combinations the following No. 2 Outfit parts are available in the colours indicated:—

Body Sections: orange, yellow. Wheels: orange, yellow. Wings: orange, green.

MOTOR CAR LIGHTING SET

This Lighting Set enables the headlamps of Motor Car models built with the No. 2 Motor Car Outfit to be electrically lighted.

Price 2/6

The Lighting Set contains everything necessary for equipping No. 2 Motor Car models with electric lighting, excepting a dry battery. This should be of the 3-volt type, size $1\frac{1}{2}$ in. $\times$ $2\frac{1}{2}$ in. $\times\frac{3}{4}$ in., and can be obtained from any dealer in electrical supplies.

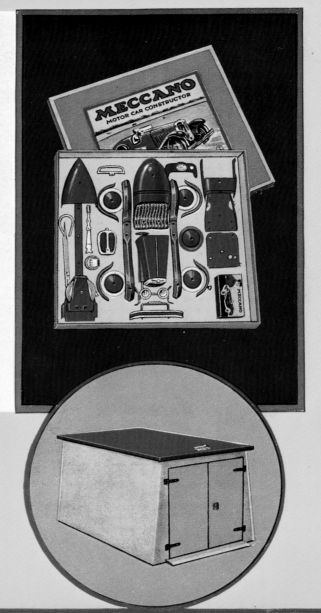

MECCANO GARAGE

The Meccano Motor Car Garage provides accommodation for any Meccano model motor car or other car of suitable size. It is strongly built, with imitation rough-cast finish, and adds the final touch of realism.

Inside dimensions: Height 5 in. Length 13 in. Width $7\frac{1}{2}$ in.

Price 5/6

MECCANO AEROPLANE

BUILD REALISTIC MODELS OF THE WORLD'S AIRCRAFT

The Aeroplane Constructor Outfits described on this and the following page contain all the parts necessary for building model aeroplanes, each one a joy to look at and to play with. A large number of different models can be built by varying the positions of the parts, which are all interchangeable on the famous Meccano principle. The parts in the Nos. 1 and 2 and the No. 1 Special and No. 2 Special Outfits can be used in conjunction with the standard Meccano parts.

No. OO Aeroplane Outfit

This excellent Outfit contains a good selection of Aeroplane Parts, with which models of realistic appearance can be built. It is an ideal present for young boys who are keen on aeroplanes. There are three colour schemes from which to choose. Price 3/3

No. O Aeroplane Outfit

With the parts contained in this Outfit an interesting range of aeroplane models can be built, including high and low wing monoplanes, seaplanes and standard light biplanes. There are three colour schemes from which to choose. Price 4/6

No. O1P Aeroplane Hangar Outfit

This novel Outfit consists of the complete range of No. O Aeroplane Outfit parts packed in a No. O1 Aeroplane Hangar instead of in a carton. Price 8/9

NOTE.—The parts in the No. OO, No. O and No. O1P Outfits are smaller than those in the other Outfits in the series and are not intended for use with these Outfits.

No. 1 Aeroplane Outfit

Magnificent models of high and low wing monoplanes and interesting model biplanes representing standard types can be built with this Outfit. The biplanes include models based on the single-seater fighter type of military aircraft, and on the popular light aeroplane. There are three colour schemes from which to choose. Price 7/6
Meccano Aeroplane Constructor Accessory Outfit No. 1a, costing 6/-, will convert a No. 1 Outfit into a No. 2.

No. 2 Aeroplane Outfit

A much wider range of models can be built with this Outfit, including triple-engined monoplanes and biplanes, and a racing seaplane of the type that was used in the Schneider Trophy Contests. A particularly interesting model is that of a giant Italian bombing machine, and there are also models of amphibians. The Manual of Instructions included in the No. 2 Outfit gives full details of how to build these wonderful models. There are three colour schemes from which to choose. Price 12/6

AEROPLANE HANGARS

These splendid hangars, with double doors, have been specially designed to house model aeroplanes.

No. O1 Aeroplane Hangar

Will accommodate one model made with the No. OO, No. O or No. O1P Outfits. Length 11½ in. Depth 10¼ in. Height 4¼ in. Price 4/6

No. O2 Aeroplane Hangar

Will accommodate two models made with the No. OO, No. O or No. O1P Outfits. Length 21½ in. Depth 11 in. Height 6½ in. Price 5/11

No. 1 and No. 2 Aeroplane Outfit separate parts are listed on page 48.

Model of a High Wing Monoplane built with No. O Aeroplane Outfit.

Model of a Standard Light Biplane built with No. 1 Aeroplane Outfit.

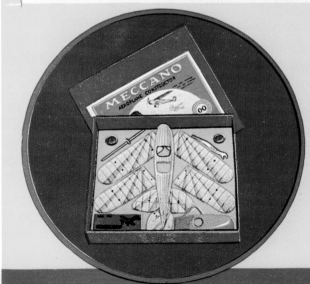

No. OO AEROPLANE OUTFIT

No. O AEROPLANE OUTFIT

No. 1 AEROPLANE OUTFIT

CONSTRUCTOR OUTFITS

Model of a Single-engined Commercial Biplane built with No. 1 Special Aeroplane Outfit.

Model of a High Wing Air Liner built with No. 2 Special Aeroplane Outfit.

SPECIAL AEROPLANE OUTFITS

The Special Aeroplane Constructor Outfits have been designed to enable more realistic models of the latest types of aircraft to be built. They contain many new and improved parts.

A specially prepared Manual of Instructions is included with each of the Special Aeroplane Outfits. In addition to photographs of 44 Meccano model aeroplanes and their prototypes, this contains a section devoted to flying a real aeroplane, and explains how all the most difficult "stunts" are done.

No. 1 Special Aeroplane Outfit

The parts in this super Aeroplane Outfit will build over 20 realistic models of different types of aircraft. The range of special parts includes mainplanes fitted with ailerons, tail planes with elevators, movable rudder, radial engine cowling, etc.

The Outfit is available in three different colour combinations—red and cream, blue and white, and green and cream. Price 12/6

A No. 1a Special Aeroplane Accessory Outfit, Price 10/-, will convert a No. 1 Special Aeroplane Constructor Outfit into a No. 2 Special.

No. 2 Special Aeroplane Outfit

This is the finest and most attractive Aeroplane Constructor Outfit on the market. It contains a big range of aircraft parts, with which numerous models of practically any type of machine can be built—44 examples are shown in the Manual of Instructions. All the parts that are special features of the No. 1 Outfit are included, also a number of other parts of special design. As in the case of the No. 1 Special Outfit, the No. 2 is available in three different colour schemes—red and cream, blue and white, and green and cream. Price 21/-

No. 1 Special and No. 2 Special Aeroplane Outfit separate parts are listed on page 48.

RUN YOUR AEROPLANE MODELS WITH A MECCANO AERO MOTOR

No. 1 Aero Clockwork Motor

This long-running Motor is specially designed to fit into the fuselage of Aeroplane models made with No. 1, No. 2, No. 1 Special or No. 2 Special Aeroplane Outfits. It will rotate the propeller at high speed, thus greatly adding to the realism of a model.

Price 1/9

No. 2 Aero Clockwork Motor

This is a more powerful Motor. In addition to rotating the propeller it also drives the landing wheels of No. 1, No. 2, No. 1 Special or No. 2 Special Aeroplane Outfit models, making the machines taxi along the floor in a most realistic manner. An Adjustable Tail Wheel is supplied with the Motor.

Price 3/6

All Aeroplane Constructor Outfits are available in three different colour combinations—red and cream, blue and white, and cream and green.

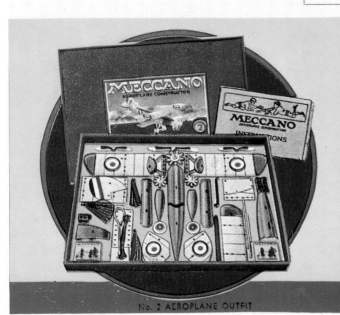

NO. 2 AEROPLANE OUTFIT

NO. 1 SPECIAL AEROPLANE OUTFIT

NO. 2 SPECIAL AEROPLANE OUTFIT

AEROPLANE CONSTRUCTOR PARTS

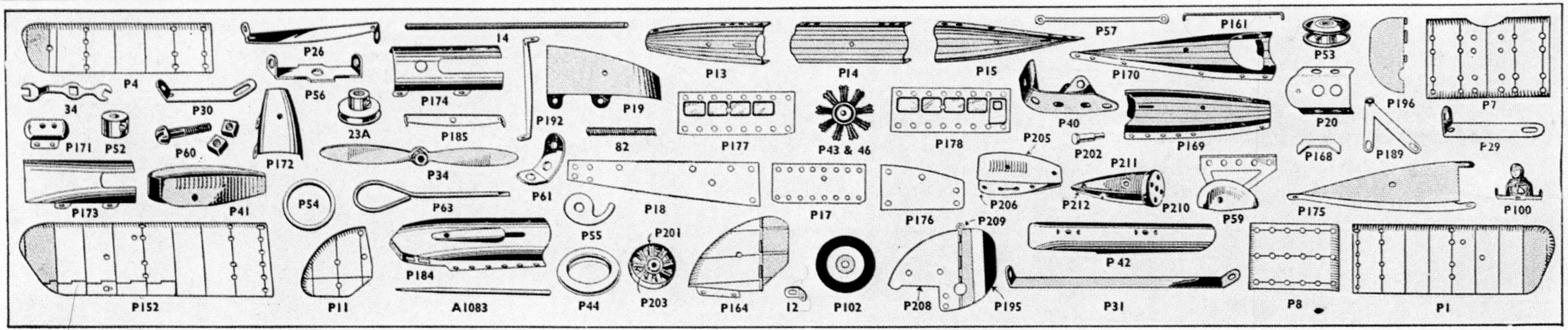

Nos. 1 and 2 AEROPLANE OUTFIT PARTS

No.	Description.		s.	d.
P1	Mainplane—Large, R.H. ...	each	0	4
P2	,, ,, L.H. ...	,,	0	4
P3	,, Small, R.H. ...	,,	0	3
P4	,, ,, L.H. ...	,,	0	3
P7	Centre Section Plane ...	,,	0	2
P8	Extension Plane	pair	0	3
P10	Tail Plane—R.H.	each	0	1
P11	,, ,, L.H.	,,	0	1
P13	Fuselage Top—Front	,,	0	2
P14	,, ,, Middle	,,	0	2
P15	,, ,, Rear	,,	0	2
P16	,, Side—Front	,,	0	1
P17	,, ,, Middle	,,	0	1
P18	,, ,, Rear	,,	0	1
P19	,, Underside	,,	0	1
P20	,, Front	,,	0	1
P24	Interplane Strut—Staggered—R.H.	doz.	0	6
P25	Interplane Strut—Staggered—L.H.	doz.	0	6
P26	,, ,, —Angled—R.H.	,,	0	6
P27	,, ,, — ,, —L.H.	,,	0	6
P28	,, ,, —Straight ...	,,	0	6
P29	Centre Section Strut—Straight	,,	0	6
P30	Float and Centre Section Strut—Angled	,,	0	6
P31	Wing Stay	,,	0	6
P32	Rudder and Fin, Military ...	each	0	3
P34	Propeller—Large	,,	0	3
P35	,, Small	,,	0	3
P40	Base for Engine Casing ...	,,	0	1
P41	Top for Engine Casing ...	,,	0	2
P42	Float, complete	,,	0	4
P43	Radial Engine, small	,,	0	3
P44	Tyre for Aeroplane Landing Wheel	pair	0	3
P46	Radial Engine, Large	each	0	5
P52	Collar	,,	0	1
P53	Aeroplane Landing Wheel ...	,,	0	2
P54	Rubber Driving Band	doz.	0	6
P55	Tail Skid	,,	0	6
P56	Rear Bracket for Propeller Shaft	2 for	0	1
P57	Tie Rod for Floats	each	0	1
P58	Undercarriage piece and wheel shield—R.H.	,,	0	4
P59	Undercarriage piece and wheel shield—L.H.	,,	0	4
P60	Pivot Bolt with two nuts ...	,,	0	1
P61	Engine Bracket	pair	0	1
P62	Axle Rod, 3¼" long	2 for	0	1
P63	Screwdriver	each	0	2
P64	Rudder and Fin, Civil	,,	0	3
P65	Adjustable Tail Wheel	,,	0	3
P75	Manual No. 1	each	0	3
P76	Manual No. 2	,,	0	6
P100	Pilot	,,	0	4
*P101	Identification Markings, Large	Packet of 4 (2 Large 2 Small)	0	3
*P102	Identification Markings, Small			
12	Angle Brackets, ½" × ½"	doz.	0	2
14	Axle Rod—6½" long	each	0	1
16a	,, ,, —2½" ,, ...	2 for	0	1
23a	Fast Pulley—½" diam.	each	0	3
34	Spanner	,,	0	1
82	Screwed Rod, 1"	doz.	0	4
537a	Nuts	,,	0	2
537b	Bolts 7/32" long	,,	0	2
540	Hank of Cord	2 for	0	3
611c	Bolts ⅜" long	doz.	0	2

Nos. 1 and 2 SPECIAL AEROPLANE OUTFIT PARTS

No.	Description.		s.	d.
P3	Mainplane—Small—R.H.	each	0	3
P4	,, ,, L.H.	,,	0	3
P7	Centre Section Plane	,,	0	2
P8	Extension Plane	pair	0	3
P14	Fuselage Top—Middle	each	0	2
P15	,, ,, Rear	,,	0	2
P18	Fuselage Side—Rear	,,	0	1
P24	Interplane Strut—Staggered—R.H.	doz.	0	6
P25	,, ,, — ,, —L.H.	,,	0	6
P26	,, ,, —Angled—R.H.	,,	0	6
P27	,, ,, — ,, —L.H.	,,	0	6
P28	Interplane Strut—Straight ...	,,	0	6
P29	Centre Section Strut—Straight...	,,	0	6
P30	Float and Centre Section Strut—Angled	,,	0	6
P31	Wing Stay	,,	0	6
P42	Float, complete	each	0	4
P44	Tyre for Aeroplane Landing Wheel	pair	0	3
P52	Collar	each	0	1
P53	Aeroplane Landing Wheel ...	,,	0	2
P54	Rubber Driving Band	doz.	0	6
P55	Tail Skid	,,	0	6
P56	Rear Bracket for Propeller Shaft	2 for	0	1
P57	Tie Rod for Floats	each	0	1
P58	Undercarriage piece and wheel shield—R.H.	,,	0	4
P59	Undercarriage piece and wheel shield—L.H.	each	0	4
P60	Pivot Bolt with two nuts	,,	0	1
P62	Axle Rod, 3¼" long	2 for	0	1
P63	Screwdriver	each	0	2
P65	Adjustable Tail Wheel	,,	0	3
P100	Pilot	,,	0	4
*P101	Identification Markings, Large	Packet of 4 (2 Large 2 Small)	0	3
*P102	Identification Markings, Small			
P151	Mainplane Top, Right Hand ...	each	0	6
P152	,, ,, Left Hand ...	,,	0	6
P155	,, Bottom, Right Hand	,,	0	6
P156	,, ,, Left Hand	,,	0	6
P161	Aileron Connecting Wire, Medium	doz.	0	3
P162	Aileron Connecting Wire, Short	,,	0	3
P163	Aileron Connecting Wire, Long	,,	0	3
P164	Tail Plane and Elevator Right Hand	each	0	4
P165	Tail Plane and Elevator Left Hand	,,	0	4
P168	Elevator Coupling Piece ...	,,	0	1
P169	Fuselage Top, Front	each	0	4
P170	,, ,, Rear with cockpit	,,	0	3
P171	,, Front	,,	0	1
P172	,, Underside Front ...	,,	0	2
P173	,, ,, Middle ...	,,	0	3
P174	,, ,, Extension ...	,,	0	2
P175	,, ,, Rear	,,	0	3
P176	,, Side Front	,,	0	1
P177	Fuselage Side Middle Left Hand Front	,,	0	5
P178	Fuselage Side Middle Left Hand Rear	,,	0	5
P179	Fuselage Side Middle Right Hand	,,	0	5
P184	Cabin Head	,,	0	4
P185	Interplane Strut Staggered Right Hand Pierced	doz.	0	6
P186	Interplane Strut Staggered Left Hand Pierced	,,	0	6
P187	Interplane Strut Straight Pierced	,,	0	6
P188	V Type Cross Strut Right Hand	each	0	1
P189	,, ,, ,, Left Hand	,,	0	1
P190	Cross Strut Staggered Right Hand	doz.	0	6
P191	,, ,, ,, Left Hand	,,	0	6
P192	Cross Strut Angled Right Hand	,,	0	6
P193	,, ,, ,, Left Hand...	,,	0	6
P194	Strut for Nacelle	pair	0	1
P195	Rudder, Military	each	0	4
P196	Rudder, Civil	each	0	1
P198	Propeller, Large	,,	0	4
P199	Propeller, Small	,,	0	4
P201	Townend Ring	,,	0	2
P202	Axis Pin for Propeller and Radial Engine	,,	0	1
P203	Small Radial Engine	,,	0	4
P205	Engine Casing Top	,,	0	3
P206	,, ,, Bottom	,,	0	4
P207	Screwed Rod 1-9/32"	doz.	0	4
P208	Fin	each	0	2
P209	Rudder Pin	doz.	0	1
P210	Nacelle Front	each	0	2
P211	,, Side	,,	0	2
P212	,, Side with Pin ...	,,	0	3
P225	Manual No. 1-2, Special	,,	1	6
12	Angle Bracket, ½" × ½"	doz.	0	2
14	Axle Rod—6½" long	each	0	1
16a	,, ,, —2½" ,, ...	2 for	0	1
23a	Fast Pulley—½" diam.	each	0	3
34	Spanner	,,	0	1
38	Washers	doz.	0	1
537a	Nuts	,,	0	2
537b	Bolts, 7/32" long	,,	0	2
540	Hank of Cord	2 for	0	3
611c	Bolts ⅜" long	doz.	0	2
A1083	Drift	each	0	1

* The Aero Identification Markings included in the series represent the national markings of 16 different countries.

MOTOR CAR CONSTRUCTOR PARTS

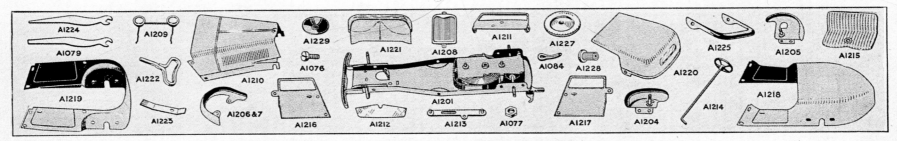

No. 1 MOTOR CAR OUTFIT PARTS

No.	Description.	s. d.	No.	Description.	s. d.	No.	Description.	s. d.	No.	Description.	s. d.
A1201	Chassis Frame complete with mechanism	each 4 0	A1210	Bonnet	each 0 5	A1218	Sports Body	each 0 8	A1226	Manual No. 1	each 0 3
A1204	Front Mudguard, Right	,, 0 3	A1211	Dashboard and Windscreen Frame	,, 0 3	A1219	Saloon Body	,, 0 6	A1227	Wheel, Bush and Tyre	,, 0 2
A1205	,, Left	,, 0 3	A1212	Windscreen	,, 0 1	A1220	Saloon Roof with window	,, 0 7	A1229	Wheel Disc	set of 4 0 2
A1206	Rear Mudguard, Right	,, 0 2	A1213	Track Rod	,, 0 2	A1221	Tonneau Cover	,, 0 3	A1230	Spanner	each 0 1
A1207	,, Left	,, 0 2	A1214	Steering Wheel and Column	,, 0 2	A1222	Winding Key	,, 0 2	A1076	Bolts, 5/32" 6BA	doz. 0 2
A1208	Radiator	,, 0 3	A1215	Seat	,, 0 2	A1223	Spring for Track Rod	doz. 0 6	A1077	Nuts, Hexagon	,, 0 2
A1209	Headlamps, Set	,, 0 4	A1216	Door, Right	,, 0 2	A1224	Combined Spanner and Drift	each 0 1	A1084	Split Pins	doz. 0 1
			A1217	,, Left	,, 0 2	A1225	Folded Hood	,, 0 2			

No. 2 MOTOR CAR OUTFIT PARTS

No.	Description.	s. d.	No.	Description.	s. d.	No.	Description.	s. d.	No.	Description.	s. d.
A1000	Radiator, Parallel sides	each 0 7	A1025	Bracket, Lower Front Mudguard	pair 0 1	A1050	Clockwork Motor with Key	each 4 0	A1074	Driving Pinion	each 0 3
A1001	,, Curved ,,	,, 0 7	A1026	,, Upper ,, R.H.	each 0 1	A1051	Headlamp	,, 0 4	A1075	Stub Axle, L.H.	,, 0 2
A1004	Clamping Plate for Radiator, parallel sides	,, 0 1	A1027	Tie Rod, Front Mudguard	,, 0 1	A1052	Sidelamp	,, 0 2	A1076	Bolts, 5/32" 6BA	doz. 0 2
A1005	Clamping Plate for Radiator, curved sides	,, 0 1	A1028	Bracket, Upper Front Mudguard L.H.	,, 0 1	A1055	Wheel, Disc, Front	pair 0 7	A1077	Nuts, Hexagon	,, 0 2
A1006	Clamping Plate Nut	doz. 0 6	A1029	Steering Wheel and Column	,, 0 4	A1056	Bolt, for fixing Imitation Spare Wheel Cover	doz. 0 6	A1078	Screwdriver	each 0 2
A1008	Bonnet	each 0 5	A1031	Sleeve for Steering Column	doz. 0 6	A1057	Wheel, Disc, Rear	pair 0 7	A1079	Spanner	,, 0 1
A1010	Windscreen	,, 0 5	A1032	Bracket for Steering Column	each 0 1	A1058	Tyres	pair 0 7	A1080	Winding Key	,, 0 4
A1012	Dash	,, 0 6	A1034	Track Rod	,, 0 1	A1059	Grub Screw for Disc Wheel, Rear	doz. 0 4	A1082	Bolts, ¼" 6BA	doz. 0 2
A1014	Body, Centre Section	,, 0 2	A1035	Stud for Track Rod	pair 0 1	A1060	Imitation Spare Wheel Cover	each 0 3	A1083	Drift	each 0 1
A1015	,, Rear Section rounded	,, 0 10	A1037	Collar	each 0 1	A1061	Number Plate, Rear	,, 0 1	A1085	Bolts (6BA 5/16") for fixing Brake	doz. 0 5
A1016	,, ,, tapered	,, 0 10	A1038	Stud for Bell Crank	,, 0 1	A1063	Undershield, Rear	,, 0 2	A1086	Bell Crank and Nut Block	each 0 1
A1020	Mudguard, Front	,, 0 2	A1039	Bumper	,, 0 6	A1064	,, Front	,, 0 2	A1087	Nut for fixing Driver	doz. 0 2
A1021	,, and Running Board, Front	,, 0 2	A1040	Bracket for Bumper with front number plate	,, 0 2	A1065	Frame Side Member	pair 0 5	A1088	Bolt	,, 0 2
A1022	,, Rear	,, 0 2	A1041	Brake Lever and Rod	,, 0 5	A1066	Front Cross Member	each 0 1	A1090	Manual No. 2	each 0 3
A1023	,, and Running Board, Rear	,, 0 2	A1043	Expanding Brake Drum	,, 0 2	A1069	Screw for Stub Axle	doz. 0 6	A1091	Lamps with Flex, for Lighting Set	pair 1 4
A1024	Bracket, Rear Mudguard	pair 0 1	A1044	Distance Bush for Brake Lever	,, 0 1	A1070	Rear Axle	each 0 1	A1092	Switch, for Lighting Set	each 0 8
			A1045	Seat	,, 0 5	A1071	Pivot for Stub Axle	,, 0 1	A1093	Battery Clip, for Lighting Set	,, 0 6
			A1046	Instrument Board	,, 0 4	A1072	Stub Axle, R.H.	,, 0 2	A1100	Driver	,, 0 6
						A1073	Axle Bracket	pair 0 1			

MECCANO ELEKTRON ELECTRICAL OUTFITS

No. 1
Elektron
Outfit.

No. 2
Elektron
Outfit.

A Fascinating Hobby of Endless Variety

In these days of radio, X-rays and electric trams and trains, every boy should have a knowledge of electricity. The only way to gain this knowledge is by means of experiments, and the Meccano Elektron Outfits have been produced specially for this purpose. They provide the necessary material for carrying out a series of fascinating experiments in magnetism, frictional electricity and current electricity.

Each Outfit is packed in a handsome box, and includes a Manual, splendidly illustrated, giving full directions and explaining every experiment in simple language.

No. 1 Meccano Elektron Outfit
MAGNETISM AND STATIC ELECTRICITY

The No. 1 Outfit contains two powerful Bar Magnets, a Horse-shoe Magnet, and a reliable Magnetic Compass, together with everything necessary for the carrying out of a series of fascinating magnetic experiments. In addition there are materials for experiments in frictional or static electricity, and for the construction of an Electric Compass, two forms of Electroscope, and an Electrophorus.

Price 6/6

No. 2 Meccano Elektron Outfit
CURRENT ELECTRICITY

This splendid Outfit provides all that is necessary for a series of attractive experiments with electric currents. It contains the parts required to make a powerful Bichromate Cell, and to build an extensive range of electrical devices, including Electro-Magnets, a real Electric Bell, and a Buzzer for use in an electric telegraph system. A Shocking Coil that will give hours of fun, and two different types of working Electric Motors also can be constructed from the contents of this Outfit.

Price 17/6

A complete illustrated list of Meccano Elektron parts is given on the opposite page.

THE "MECCANO MAGAZINE"
The World's Best Magazine for Boys

The "Meccano Magazine" contains splendid articles on a large variety of subjects of interest to boys. These include stories of Famous Engineers and Inventors, descriptions of Wonderful Machinery, Bridges, Ships and Aeroplanes, and special articles for owners of Elektron and Kemex Outfits and other Meccano Products.

The "Meccano Magazine" is published on the first day of each month, price 6d., and is obtainable from any Meccano dealer or newsagent. If you have any difficulty in obtaining a copy, write to the Editor of the "Meccano Magazine", Binns Road, Liverpool 13.

HOURS OF
FUN—
ENDLESS
THRILLS

MECCANO ELEKTRON OUTFIT PARTS

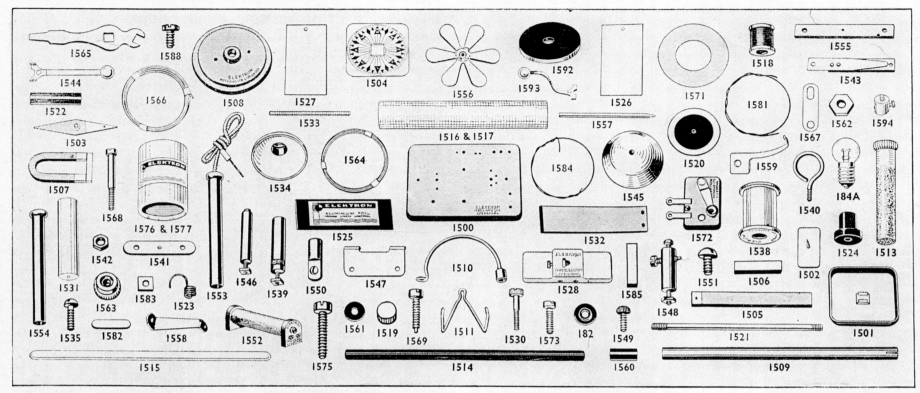

Below is a list giving the numbers and prices of the parts included in Elektron Electrical Outfits. Owners of these Outfits who wish to extend their range of electrical experiments can obtain any of these parts separately from their dealers, or direct from Meccano Limited. The numbers given in the list should always be quoted when ordering.

No.	Description	s. d.	No.	Description	s. d.	No.	Description	s. d.	No.	Description	s. d.
1500	Universal Base	each 0 6	1523	Electroscope Hook	each 0 1	1549	Bell Contact Locking Screw ...	each 0 1	1572	Switch	each 0 9
1501	Compass Box	,, 0 2	1524	Ebonite Bush	,, 0 2	1550	Armature Support	,, 0 2	1573	6 B.A. Bolt, ¼"	doz. 0 6
1502	,, Mount and Pivot ...	,, 0 1	1525	Sheet of Aluminium Foil ...	,, 0 1	1551	,, Screw	doz. 0 3	1575	6 B.A. Bolt, ¾"	,, 0 6
1503	,, Needle and Cup ...	,, 0 3	1526	Copper Plate, 2"×1" ...	doz. 0 6	1552	Wound Bobbin for Shocking Coil	each 2 0	1576	Container of Copper Sulphate ...	each 0 3
1504	,, Chart	,, 0 1	1527	Zinc ,, ,, ...	,, 0 6	1553	Shocking Coil Handle ...	,, 0 6	1577	Container of Bichromate of Potash	,, 0 4
1505	Bar Magnet	,, 0 5	1528	Cell Mounting	each 0 4	1554	,, Slide ...	,, 0 3	1581	Resistance Wire, 6" ...	doz. 0 3
1506	,, Keeper	,, 0 1	1530	,, Bolt	,, 0 1	1555	Magnet Yoke, Large ...	,, 0 1	1582	Steel Piece	,, 0 3
1507	Horseshoe Magnet and Keeper ...	,, 0 6	1531	Zinc Rod	,, 0 3	1556	Armature and Commutator ...	,, 0 6	1583	6 B.A. Square Nut	,, 0 3
1508	Circular Base	,, 0 3	1532	Carbon Plate	,, 0 3	1557	,, Shaft ...	,, 0 1	1584	26G. Copper Wire, 6" length	each 0 1
1509	Erinoid Tube for Stand Bracket ...	,, 0 3	1533	Threaded Rod	doz. 0 6	1558	Bearing Bracket	,, 0 1	1585	Horseshoe Magnet Keeper ...	each 0 1
1510	Stand Bracket	,, 0 3	1534	Lampholder	each 0 3	1559	Commutator Contact Brush ...	,, 0 1	1586	26G. S.C.C. Copper Wire ...	reel 2 0
1511	Stirrup	,, 0 1	1535	Lampholder Screw	doz. 0 6	1560	Erinoid Sleeve, 11/16" long ...	,, 0 1	1587	23G. S.C.C. Copper Wire ...	,, 1 9
1512	Sifter Box and Lid	,, 0 3	1538	Magnet Coil	each 0 9	1561	Insulating Washer	doz. 0 1	1588	Screw for Bell Hammer and Bell	
1513	Tube of Iron Filings	,, 0 1	1539	,, Core (complete) ...	,, 0 2	1562	6 B.A. Hex. Nut	,, 0 3		Armature	doz. 0 3
1514	Ebonite Rod	,, 0 2	1540	,, Hook	,, 0 1	1563	Terminals	each 0 1	1589	Instruction Book No. 1 ...	each 1 0
1515	Glass	,, 0 2	1541	,, Yoke, Small ...	,, 0 2	1564	10 yd. Coil No. 35G. E.S.C.C.		1590	,, ,, No. 2 ...	,, 1 0
1516	Square of Flannel	,, 0 2	1542	,, Hook Nut ...	doz. 0 6		Copper Wire	,, 0 3	1591	Terminal Screw for Coils ...	doz. 0 6
1517	,, Silk	,, 0 2	1543	Bell Armature (complete) ...	each 0 6	1565	Spanner, Screwdriver	,, 0 3	1592	Ebonite Disc in Holder ...	each 0 7
1518	Reel of Silk Thread	,, 0 1	1544	,, Rod and Hammer ...	,, 0 2	1566	Connection Wire ...	coil 0 3	1593	Sparking Rod	,, 0 1
1519	Cork	doz. 0 1	1545	Gong	,, 0 6	1567	Connecting Link ...	each 0 1	1594	Brass Holder for Ebonite Rod ...	,, 0 2
1520	Electroscope Plate	each 0 3	1546	,, Pillar (with Nut and Screw)	,, 0 3	1568	6 B.A. 1" Special Bolt	,, 0 3	182	Insulating Bush, 6 B.A. ...	doz. 0 6
1521	,, Rod	,, 0 2	1547	Angle Yoke	,, 0 2	1569	,, Contact Screw ...	,, 0 2	184a	Flashlamp Bulb, 2½ volt ...	each 0 5
1522	Erinoid Sleeve, 1½" long ...	,, 0 1	1548	Bell Contact Pillar (complete) ...	,, 0 6	1571	Coloured Ring	dcz. 0 3			

MECCANO KEMEX CHEMICAL OUTFITS

Hundreds of Interesting Experiments

The contents of the Kemex Chemical Outfits will provide many hours of fascinating fun. With the apparatus and materials contained in them a boy can make inks and soaps; dye wool, cotton and silk, and bleach fabrics that are already dyed; test foodstuffs for impurities; analyse air and water; grow crystals; write with electricity; make invisible inks and a chemical garden; and perform a host of other interesting chemical experiments.

The No. O, No. 1, No. 2L and No. 3L Kemex Outfits each contain a Spirit Lamp for use as a source of heat. In the No. 2B and No. 3B Outfits a Bunsen Burner is included instead of a Spirit Lamp.

No. O KEMEX OUTFIT
75 EXPERIMENTS

The apparatus provided in the No. O Outfit includes Test Tubes, Test Tube Brush, Delivery Tubes and Corks, Spirit Lamp, and a variety of chemicals with which 75 interesting experiments can be carried out. Price 5/-

No. 1 KEMEX OUTFIT
130 EXPERIMENTS

This Outfit includes the whole of the contents of the No. O Outfit, together with further chemicals that increase the number of experiments that can be performed to 130. The additional apparatus includes a Test Tube Holder, Glass Stirring Rod, Funnel and Filter Papers. Price 7/6

No. 2L KEMEX OUTFIT
250 EXPERIMENTS

This Outfit includes the whole of the contents of the No. 1 Outfit, and further chemicals that increase the range of experiments up to 250. The additional apparatus includes a porcelain Evaporating Dish, Special Test Tubes to withstand high temperatures, a handsome Test Tube Stand, and an Evaporating Stand including a Ring, with Wire Gauze. Price 15/-

No. 2B KEMEX OUTFIT

Similar to the No. 2L Outfit, except that a highly efficient Bunsen Burner, with rubber tubing, is included in place of the Spirit Lamp. Price 15/-

No. 3L KEMEX OUTFIT
350-400 EXPERIMENTS

This is a splendid complete Outfit that provides a boy with all he requires to carry out between 350 and 400 experiments, and thus enables him to acquire a sound knowledge of the fascinating principles of chemistry. The Outfit includes the contents of the No. 2 Outfit, with additional chemicals and apparatus. The latter includes a gas-generating apparatus, consisting of a large Wide-necked Flask with Thistle Funnel and Delivery Tubes, and a Blowpipe and a Charcoal Block. Price 25/-

No. 3B KEMEX OUTFIT

Similar to the No. 3L Outfit, except that a highly efficient Bunsen Burner, with rubber tubing, is included in place of the Spirit Lamp. Price 25/-

A complete illustrated list of Kemex Parts is given on the next page.

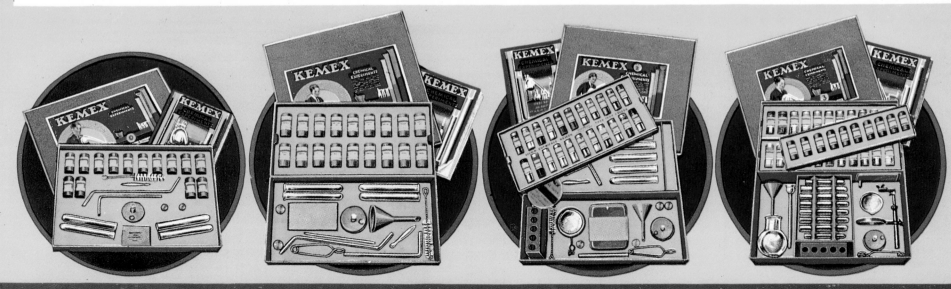

KEMEX CHEMICAL OUTFIT PARTS

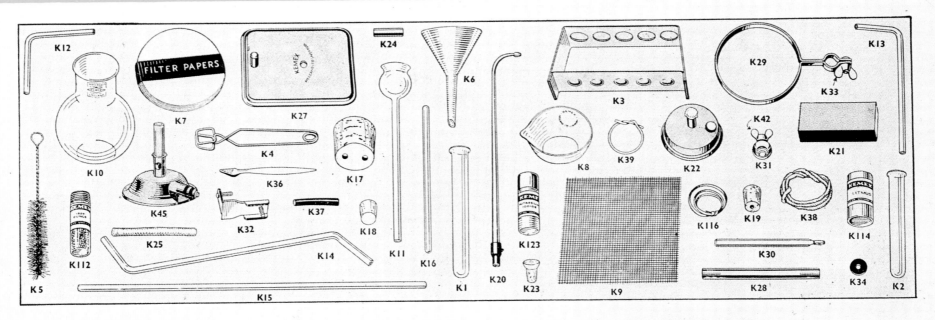

Owners of Kemex Chemical Outfits will be keenly desirous of continuing their fascinating experiments, and can do so readily by increasing their stock of apparatus. Any Kemex part or chemical included in the following list or illustrated above can be obtained separately from Meccano dealers, or ordered direct from Meccano Ltd. When ordering, the distinguishing number of the part or chemical required should be stated in addition to the name.

No.	Description.		s. d.
K1	Test Tube, 5″×⅝″	each	0 1
K2	,, ,, Heat Resisting, 4″×½″	,,	0 1
K3	,, ,, Stand	,,	1 0
K4	,, ,, Holder	,,	0 3
K5	,, ,, Brush	,,	0 2
K6	Funnel	,,	0 6
K7	Filter Paper, 3½″ diameter	doz.	0 1
K8	Evaporating Dish	each	0 6
K9	Gauze Square	,,	0 2
K10	Flask, Wide-necked	,,	1 3
K11	Thistle Funnel	,,	0 4
K12	Right Angle Delivery Tube, Small	,,	0 1
K13	,, ,, ,, ,, Large	,,	0 1
K14	Double Angle Delivery Tube	,,	0 2
K15	Glass Tube, 12″	,,	0 1
K16	,, Rod	,,	0 1
K17	Cork, Large, Double Bore	,,	0 3
K18	,, Small	doz.	0 4
K19	,, ,, Bored	,,	0 6
K20	Blowpipe	each	1 4
K21	Charcoal Block	,,	0 6

No.	Description.		s. d.
K22	Spirit Lamp, Complete	each	0 6
K23	,, ,, Stopper	,,	0 1
K24	,, ,, Wick Holder	,,	0 1
K25	,, ,, Wick	doz.	0 4
K26	Universal Stand, Complete	each	3 6
K27	,, ,, Base	,,	0 8
K28	,, ,, Pillar	,,	0 8
K29	,, ,, Ring	,,	0 5
K30	,, ,, Pillar Extension	,,	0 6
K31	,, ,, Clamp	,,	0 5
K32	,, ,, Top Bracket	,,	0 4
K33	,, ,, Wing Nut	,,	0 2
K34	,, ,, Washer	,,	0 1
K35	Evaporating Stand	,,	1 9
K36	Scoop	,,	0 1
K37	Rubber Connection Tube	,,	0 1
K38	Asbestos Fibre	yard	0 1
K39	Nickel Chrome Wire	per foot	0 1
K40	Instruction Manual, No. 1	each	0 9
K41	Instruction Manual, No. 2-3	,,	1 0
K42	Universal Stand, Wing Screw	,,	0 3

No.	Description.		s. d.
K43	Glass Container with Screw Cap	each	0 2
K44	,, ,, Cork	,,	0 2
K45	Bunsen Burner (with tubing)	,,	1 6
K46	Instruction Manual, No. O		0 6
K47	Rubber Tubing	yard	0 6
K100	Aluminium Sulphate	each	0 2
K101	Ammonium Chloride	,,	0 2
K102	Calcium Carbonate (Marble)	,,	0 2
K103	,, Oxide (Lime)	,,	0 2
K104	Charcoal	,,	0 2
K105	Cobalt Chloride	,,	0 5
K106	Congo Red	,,	0 3
K107	Copper Oxide	,,	0 2
K108	,, Sulphate	,,	0 2
K109	,, Turnings	,,	0 2
K110	Ferrous Ammonium Sulphate	,,	0 2
K111	Iron Alum	,,	0 2
K112	,, Filings	,,	0 2
K113	Lead Nitrate	,,	0 2
K114	Litmus	,,	0 5

No.	Description.		s. d.
K115	Logwood	each	0 2
K116	Magnesium Ribbon	yard	0 1
K117	,, Sulphate	each	0 2
K118	Manganese Dioxide	,,	0 2
K119	,, Sulphate	,,	0 2
K120	Nickel Ammonium Sulphate	,,	0 2
K121	Phenolphthalein Solution	,,	0 5
K122	Potassium Chlorate	,,	0 2
K123	,, Iod'de Solution	,,	0 5
K124	,, Nitrate	,,	0 2
K125	Sodium Bisulphate	,,	0 2
K126	,, Bisulphite	,,	0 2
K127	,, Borate (Borax)	,,	0 2
K128	,, Ferrocyanide	,,	0 2
K129	,, Thiocyanate	,,	0 5
K130	Strontium Nitrate	,,	0 2
K131	Sulphur	,,	0 2
K132	Tannic Acid (Tannin)	,,	0 3
K133	Tartaric Acid	,,	0 2
K134	Zinc, Granulated	,,	0 2

NOTE—Kemex Parts Nos. K100 to K134, with the exception of K105, K121, K123, K125 and K129 (which are supplied only **in glass containers**) are packed in cardboard containers.

HORNBY SPEED BOATS

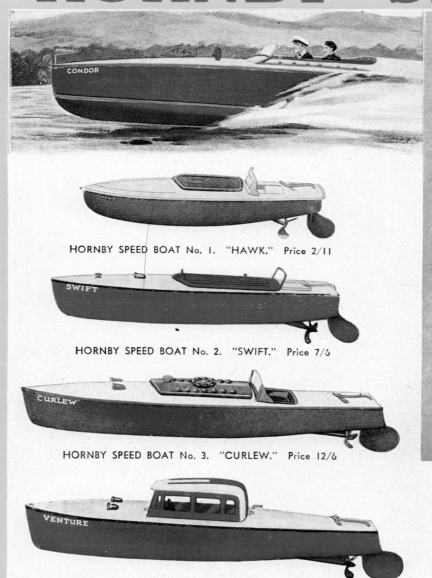

HORNBY SPEED BOAT No. 1. "HAWK." Price 2/11

HORNBY SPEED BOAT No. 2. "SWIFT." Price 7/6

HORNBY SPEED BOAT No. 3. "CURLEW." Price 12/6

HORNBY LIMOUSINE BOAT No. 4. "VENTURE." Price 15/6

EXCEPTIONAL PERFORMANCE — BEAUTIFUL FINISH

If you want to experience the joy and thrills of running a boat of outstanding performance and remarkable efficiency, get a Hornby Speed Boat—the best that you can buy. There are five splendid models from which to choose, all beautifully finished in attractive colours. Each one follows closely the design and general characteristics of a famous speed boat prototype.

Hornby Speed Boats have established a very high standard of excellence in model boat production. Every line and every feature emphasise their excellent qualities, speed and reliability. The special design of the propeller and the unique methods employed in the construction of the hull give each model exceptional speed and length of run.

HORNBY SPEED BOAT No. 1. "HAWK."
Price 2/11

For value and efficiency this model has no equal. It gives an excellent performance, travelling over 100 feet on one winding, and it is finished in three different colour combinations—red and cream, blue and white, and green and ivory. Dimensions: Length 9¼ in. Beam 3 in.

HORNBY SPEED BOAT No. 2. "SWIFT."
Price 7/6

The exceptionally fine performance of Hornby Speed Boat No. 2 makes it one of the most popular of the Hornby models. It will travel over 300 feet on one winding. Finished in three different colour combinations—red and cream, blue and white, and yellow and white. Dimensions: Length 12½ in. Beam 3 in.

HORNBY SPEED BOAT No. 3.
Price 12/6

Hornby Speed Boat No. 3 is a great favourite with boys. It will travel over 500 feet on one winding. Available with three different names and in three different colour combinations, as follows:— "CONDOR" (red and cream), "GANNET" (blue and white), "CURLEW" (green and ivory). Dimensions: Length 16½ in. Beam 3½ in.

HORNBY LIMOUSINE BOAT No. 4.
"VENTURE." Price 15/6

Hornby Limousine Boat No. 4 is a magnificent model. It will travel over 500 feet on one winding. Finished in three different colour combinations—red and cream, blue and white, and green and ivory. Dimensions: Length 16½ in. Beam 3½ in.

HORNBY CABIN CRUISER No. 5. "VIKING."
Price 16/6

The perfect design and handsome appearance of Hornby Cabin Cruiser No. 5 makes it a model of outstanding merit. It will travel over 500 feet on one winding. Finished in three different colour combinations—red and cream, blue and white, and green and ivory. Dimensions: Length 16½ in. Beam 3½ in.

PENNANTS

PENNANTS for Hornby Speed Boats Nos. 3 and 4 may be purchased separately. They add the final touch of realism to these boats. Price 2d. each.

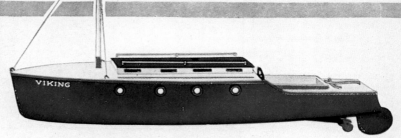

HORNBY CABIN CRUISER No. 5. "VIKING." Price 16/6

HORNBY RACING BOATS

PERFECT DESIGN — REMARKABLE EFFICIENCY

The series of Hornby Racing Boats is composed of three exceptionally fine models that are considerably faster than the corresponding standard Hornby Speed Boats. They are "quick off the mark", and they maintain a high rate of speed throughout the whole length of their run. They steer well—a very important feature in any racing boat—and they possess the good quality of being very steady in the water.

Every minute spent in playing with a Hornby Racing Boat is brimful of thrills and enjoyment—nothing could possibly give you greater pleasure or more fun. You are certain to be proud of your model when you have tested it and discovered its splendid qualities.

Each model is available in a pleasing colour combination that gives it an exceedingly attractive appearance. Details of the three boats in the series are given below.

HORNBY RACING BOAT No. 1.
"RACER I."   Price 4/6

This attractive model will travel over 120 feet at high speed on one winding. It is tastefully finished in cream and green. Dimensions: Length 8½ in. Beam 2½ in.

HORNBY RACING BOAT No. 2.
"RACER II."   Price 8/6

This popular and efficient model travels over 200 feet at high speed on one winding. It is beautifully finished in blue and cream. Dimensions: Length 12½ in. Beam 3 in.

HORNBY RACING BOAT No. 3.
"RACER III."   Price 14/6

This is one of the finest examples of model craftsmanship ever produced. It will travel over 300 feet at high speed on one winding. There are two cockpits, each of which is provided with a windscreen, and a dummy steering wheel is fitted in the forward one. The powerful clockwork motor is easily accessible for oiling by the removal of the hatch fitted with quick-release handles. Finished in red and cream. Dimensions: Length 16½ in. Beam 3½ in.

The Hornby Speed and Racing Boat Clockwork Motors and Propellers and Shafts are available separately for boys who prefer to build their own Speed Boats. The prices are as follows:—

Hornby Speed Boat No. 1 and Hornby Water Toy Motor	...	Price 1/9	Propeller and Shaft	Price 4d.
Hornby Speed Boat No. 2 Motor	...	Price 3/-	Propeller and Shaft	Price 6d.
Hornby Speed Boats Nos. 3, 4 and 5 Motor	...	Price 4/-	Propeller and Shaft	Price 6d.
Hornby Racing Boat No. 1 Motor	...	Price 2/3	Propeller and Shaft	Price 4d.
Hornby Racing Boat No. 2 Motor	...	Price 3/6	Propeller and Shaft	Price 5d.
Hornby Racing Boat No. 3 Motor	...	Price 5/-	Propeller and Shaft	Price 6d.

HORNBY WATER TOY
(DUCK)

RICHLY FINISHED   STRONGLY MADE

This novel boat, which travels over 100 feet on one winding, is particularly suitable for young children. The deck carries a realistically moulded model of a Duck, as shown in the illustration below. Dimensions: Length 9¼ in. Beam 3 in.

Price 2/6

HORNBY RACING BOAT No. 1. "RACER I."   Price 4/6
Travels over 120 feet at high speed on one winding.

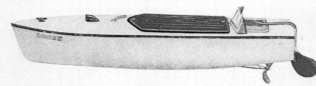

HORNBY RACING BOAT No. 2. "RACER II."   Price 8/6
Travels over 200 feet at high speed on one winding.

HORNBY WATER TOY (DUCK).   Price 2/6

Every owner of a Hornby Speed Boat or Hornby Racing Boat should join the Hornby Speed Boat Club. This may be done by purchasing the badge, illustrated above, from any Meccano dealer, price 6d.

HORNBY RACING BOAT No. 3. "RACER III."   Price 14/6
Travels over 300 feet at high speed on one winding.

MECCANO 200 VARIETIES DINKY TOYS

A FASCINATING COLLECTING HOBBY

Dinky Toys are the most realistic and the most attractive models in miniature ever produced, unique in their perfection of finish. Already they include railway officials and passengers, trains, motor vehicles of every well-known type, aeroplanes, warships and famous liners. Many other models of equal interest are in preparation. Ask your dealer for the latest list.

Station Staff
Dinky Toys No. 1

No. 1a Station Master	each 3d.	No. 1d Driver	each 3d.
No. 1b Guard	,, 3d.	No. 1e Porter with Bags	,, 3d.
No. 1c Ticket Collector	,, 3d.	No. 1f Porter	,, 3d.

Price of complete set 1/6

Farmyard Animals
Dinky Toys No. 2

No. 2a Horses (2)	each 3½d.	No. 2c Pig	each 2d.
No. 2b Cows (2)	,, 3½d.	No. 2d Sheep	,, 2d.

Price of complete set 1/6

Passengers
Dinky Toys No. 3

No. 3a Woman & Child	each 3d.	No. 3d Female Hiker	each 3d.
No. 3b Business Man	,, 3d.	No. 3e Newsboy	,, 3d.
No. 3c Male Hiker	,, 3d.	No. 3f Woman	,, 3d.

Price of complete set 1/6

Train and Hotel Staff
Dinky Toys No. 5

No. 5a Pullman Car Conductor		each 3d.
No. 5b Pullman Car Waiters (2)		,, 3d.
No. 5c Hotel Porters (2)		,, 3d.

Price of complete set 1/3

Shepherd Set
Dinky Toys No. 6

No. 6a Shepherd		each 3d.
No. 6b Dog		,, 2d.
No. 2d Sheep (4)		,, 2d.

Price of complete set 1/-

Engineering Staff
Dinky Toys No. 4

No. 4a Electrician	each 3d.	No. 4d Greaser	each 3d.
No. 4b Fitters (2)	,, 3d.	No. 4e Engine Room	
No. 4c Storekeeper	,, 3d.	Attendant	,, 3d.

Price of complete set 1/6

Passenger Train Set
Dinky Toys No. 17

No. 17a Locomotive	each 9d.	No. 20a Coach	each 7d.
No. 17b Tender	,, 5d.	No. 20b Guard's Van	,, 7d.

Price of complete set 2/9

Hall's Distemper Advertisement
Dinky Toys No. 13

This miniature of a well-known line-side advertisement is intended to be placed in the fields adjoining the railway track. Price 9d.

Goods Train Set
Dinky Toys No. 13

No. 21a Tank Locomotive		each 9d.
No. 21b Wagons (3)		,, 4d.

Price of complete set 1/9

Mixed Goods Train Set
Dinky Toys No. 19

No. 21a Tank Locomotive	each 9d.	No. 21d Patrol Tank Wagon	each 6d.
No. 21b Wagon	,, 4d.	No. 21e Lumber Wagon	,, 5d.

Price of complete set 1/11

G.W.R. Rail Car
Dinky Toys No. 26

Assorted Colours

Price 6d. each

Passenger Train Set
Dinky Toys No. 20

No. 21a Tank Locomotive	each 9d.	No. 20b Guard's Van	each 7d.
No. 20a Coaches (2)	,, 7d.		

Price of complete set 2/6

MECCANO DINKY TOYS

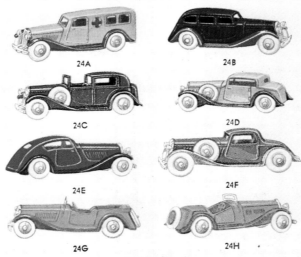

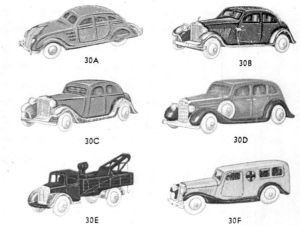

Commercial Motor Vehicles
Dinky Toys No. 25
Fitted with rubber tyres and silver-plated radiators.

No. 25a Wagon ... ... each 9d.	No. 25e Tipping Wagon each 9d.
No. 25b Covered Van ... „ 9d.	No. 25f Market Gardener's
No. 25c Flat Truck ... „ 9d.	Van ... ... „ 9d.
No. 25d Petrol Tank Wagon „ 9d.	

Price of complete set 4/6

Motor Cars
Dinky Toys No. 24
Fitted with rubber tyres and silver-plated radiators.

No. 24a Ambulance ...	each 9d.	No. 24f Sportsman's Coupé	each 9d.
No. 24b Limousine ...	„ 9d.		
No. 24c Town Sedan	„ 9d.	No. 24g Sports Tourer	
No. 24d Vogue Saloon	„ 9d.	(4 seater)	„ 9d.
No. 24e Super Streamline		No. 24h Sports Tourer	
Saloon ...	„ 9d.	(2 seater)	„ 9d.

Price of complete set 6/-

Motor Vehicles
Dinky Toys No. 30
Fitted with rubber tyres and silver-plated radiators.

No. 30a Chrysler "Airflow"	No. 30d, Vauxhall Car	each 9d.
Saloon Car each 9d.	No. 30e Breakdown Car	„ 9d.
No. 30b Rolls-Royce Car „ 9d.	No. 30f Ambulance	„ 9d.
No. 30c Daimler Car „ 9d.		

Price of complete set 4/6

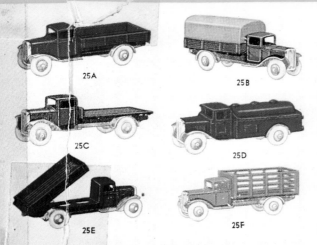

Holland Coachcraft Van
Dinky Toys No. 31
Assorted colours. Fitted with
rubber tyres. Price 6d. each

Meccano Dinky Toys No. 23
Racing Car
Assorted Colours. Fitted with
rubber tyres. Price 6d. each

Hotchkiss Racing Car
Dinky Toys No. 23b
Assorted colours. Fitted with
rubber tyres. Price 6d. each

28A

Delivery Vans
Dinky Toys No. 28/1

No. 28a Hornby Trains Van... each 6d.	
No. 28b Pickford's Removal	
Van ... ... „ 6d.	
No. 28c Manchester Guardian	
Van ... ... „ 6d.	
No. 28e Firestone Tyres Van „ 6d.	
No. 28f Palethorpe's Sausage	
Van ... ... „ 6d.	
No. 28n Atco Lawn Mowers Van „ 6d.	

Price of complete set 3/-

Delivery Vans
Dinky Toys No. 28/2

No. 28d Oxo Van ... ... each 6d.	
No. 28g Kodak Cameras Van „ 6d.	
No. 28h Dunlop Tyres Van „ 6d.	
No. 28k Marsh & Baxter's	
Sausage Van ... „ 6d.	
No. 28m Wakefield's Castrol Oil	
Van ... ... „ 6d.	
No. 28p Crawford's Biscuit Van „ 6d.	

Price of complete set 3/-

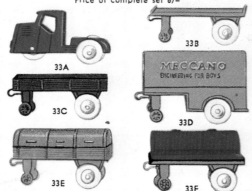

Mechanical Horse and Five Assorted Trailers
Dinky Toys No. 33
Fitted with rubber tyres.

No. 33a Mechanical Horse each 6d.	No. 33d Box Van ... each 8d.
No. 33b Flat Truck ... „ 6d.	No. 33e Dust Wagon „ 8d.
No. 33c Open Wagon „ 6d.	No. 33f Petrol Tank ... „ 8d.

Price of complete set 3/6

Motor Truck
Dinky Toys No. 22c
Rubber tyres. Price 6d. each

Tractor
Dinky Toys No. 22e
Price 9d. each

Tank
Dinky Toys No. 22f
Price 9d. each

Streamline Tourer
Dinky Toys No. 22g
Rubber tyres. Price 6d. each

Streamline Saloon
Dinky Toys No. 22h
Rubber tyres. Price 6d. each

Trailer for use with
No. 25 Series
Dinky Toys No. 25g
Fitted with rubber tyres.
Price 7d. each

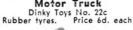

MECCANO DINKY TOYS

Aeroplanes
Dinky Toys No. 60

No. 60a Imperial Airways Liner	... each 9d.
No. 60b D.H. "Leopard Moth"	... 6d.
No. 60c Percival "Gull"	... 6d.
No. 60d Low Wing Monoplane	... 6d.
No. 60e General "Monospar"	... 6d.
No. 60f Cierva "Autogiro"	... 6d.
Price of complete set 3/-	

Garage
Dinky Toys No. 45
Fitted with opening double doors. Will accommodate any two Dinky Toys motor cars.   Price 1/6 each

Pillar Letter Box—G.P.O.
Dinky Toys No. 12a
Price 3d. each

Petrol Station
Dinky Toys No. 48
Accurate reproduction of a filling station.   Price 1/6 each

R.A.C. Hut, Motor Cycle Patrol and Guides
Dinky Toys No. 43

No. 43a R.A.C. Hut	... each 6d.
No. 43b R.A.C. Motor Cycle Patrol	... " 9d.
No. 43c R.A.C. Guide directing traffic	... " 3d.
No. 43d R.A.C. Guide at salute	... " 3d.
Price of complete set 1/9	

Petrol Pumps   Dinky Toys No. 49
Scale models fitted with rubber hose pipes.

No. 49a Bowser Pump ea. 4d.	No. 49d Shell Pump ea. 4d.
No. 49b Wayne Pump " 4d.	No. 49e Oil Bin
No. 49c Theo Pump " 4d.	(Pratts) " 3d.
Price of complete set 1/6	

Robot Traffic Signals
Dinky Toys No. 47a
(Four-way)
Price 3d. each
No. 47b
(Three-way)
Price 3d. each
No. 47c
(Two-way)
Price 3d. each

Motor Bus
Dinky Toys No. 29
Assorted colours.
Price 4d. each

Pillar Letter Box Air Mail
Dinky Toys No. 12b
Price 3d. each

Tram Car
Dinky Toys No. 27
Assorted colours.
Price 3d. each

D.H. "Comet" Aeroplane
Dinky Toys No. 60g
Scale model of plane used by C. W. A. Scott and T. C. Black in their record Australian flight.   Price 6d. each

Beacon
Dinky Toys No. 47d
Realistic model of the Belisha Safety Beacon.
Price 1d. each

A.A. Hut, Motor Cycle Patrol and Guides
Dinky Toys No. 44

No. 44a A.A. Hut	... each 8d.
No. 44b A.A. Motor Cycle Patrol	... " 9d.
No. 44c A.A. Guide directing traffic	... " 3d.
No. 44d A.A. Guide at salute	... " 3d.
Price of complete set 1/11	

Cunard White Star Liner "Queen Mary"
Dinky Toys No. 52b
A Scale Model of Britain's largest ocean liner.   Price 1/- each
Dinky Toys No. 52a
Exactly as No. 52b, but fitted with roller wheels.   Price 1/- each

Ships of the British Navy   Dinky Toys No. 50

No. 50a Battle Cruiser "Hood"	... each 9d.	No. 50e Cruiser "Delhi"	... each 4d.
No. 50b Battleships, "Nelson" Class (2)	... " 6d.	No. 50f Destroyers, "Broke" Class (3)	... 1d.
No. 50c Cruiser "Effingham"	... " 4d.	No. 50g Submarine, "K" Class	... 1d.
No. 50d Cruiser "York"	... " 4d.	No. 50h Destroyers, "Amazon" Class (3)	... 1d.
		No. 50k Submarine, "X" Class	... 1d.
Price of complete set 3/6			

Famous Liners
Dinky Toys No. 51

No. 51b "Europa"	... each 9d.	No. 51e "Strathaird"	... each 6d.
No. 51c "Rex"	... " 9d.	No. 51f "Queen of Bermuda"	... " 6d.
No. 51d "Empress of Britain"	... " 8d.	No. 51g "Britannic"	... " 6d.
Price of complete set 3/6			

"Normandie"
Dinky Toys No. 52c
A scale model of the French Line's new giant steamship. Made in France by Meccano (France) Ltd.   Price 1/6 each

ALL ARTICLES ILLUSTRATED IN THIS BOOK ARE MANUFACTURED BY MECCANO LIMITED.
Published by MECCANO LIMITED, BINNS ROAD, LIVERPOOL 13
7/835/65

Fig. 40

A fascinating building hobby

FOR BOYS AND GIRLS

Dinky Builder Outfits are great favourites with boys and girls. The parts contained in them provide a most fascinating constructional hobby, specially designed for the younger children. These brightly coloured parts are fitted together in a most simple and ingenious manner without the use of any nuts and bolts.

There are four Outfits in the series, Nos. 0, 1, 2 and 3, in all of which the parts are beautifully enamelled in striking colours, giving a distinction to the models that is outstandingly attractive.

No. 0 DINKY BUILDER OUTFIT

This is an excellent Outfit with which a splendid range of models can be built. The Instruction Folder included gives examples of 40 delightful models.   Price 2/6

No. 1 DINKY BUILDER OUTFIT

This fine Outfit contains a varied selection of parts, including a set of four road wheels for constructing miniature wheeled toys, many examples of which are illustrated in the Instruction Manual. These instructions show a total of 56 fine models that any boy or girl can build.   Price 4/11

No. 2 DINKY BUILDER OUTFIT

The No. 2 Dinky Builder Outfit contains a comprehensive selection of parts with which all the No. 0 and No. 1 Outfits models can be built. In addition, the parts in this fine Outfit make possible the construction of six groups of miniature model furniture. Full instructions are given in the Instruction Manual included in the Outfit.   Price 7/9

DINKY BUILDER "A"

The Dinky Builder "A" packet contains a useful assortment of Dinky Builder Parts with which Outfits No. 0, No. 1, No. 2 and No. 3 may be supplemented.   Price 1/-

No. 2 Dinky Builder Outfit

Garage

No. 3 DINKY BUILDER OUTFIT

This is the largest Outfit in the series, and its model-building possibilities are almost limitless It is the ideal gift for young boys and girls.

The parts contained in this Outfit can be used over and over again to make hundreds of different models, including Towers, Bridges, Buildings of all types, Furniture, Aeroplanes, etc. Complete instructions are provided.   Price 10/9

DINKY BUILDER

Manufactured by Meccano Limited, Binns Road, Liverpool 13

Chemistry and Electrical Sets

In the 1930s, chemical and electrical sets were enjoying a great vogue, and at least three manufacturers were producing both types in this country alone. A typical chemistry set contained phials of chemicals, test tubes, a funnel, a flask and a Bunsen burner. Electrical sets were more diverse, some being merely lighting outfits, while others contained apparatus to carry out experiments in magnetism and static electricity. These sets were designed principally to enable the more visually exciting experiments to be carried out.

Meccano Ltd entered this field in the spring of 1933 with an announcement of their 'Kemex' chemistry and 'Elektron' electrical outfits. For several months, whole-page advertisements appeared in the *Meccano Magazine*, and in September 1933, a series of articles began. Initially there were three Kemex outfits, numbered 1 to 3. Later a smaller set No. 0, was added to the range. Each set contained a spirit lamp, chemicals and test tubes, and the larger sets included test tube stands, gas-generating apparatus, evaporating dishes and other items. After 1936, sets 2 and 3 could be obtained with a Bunsen burner instead of a spirit lamp. No accessory outfits were available in the Kemex series for converting a set to the next highest, although this system was available for Elektron.

From the start, Meccano Ltd adopted a serious attitude towards these sets and stressed their educational value. To quote from the first article about Kemex sets: 'If the contents of a Kemex Outfit are simply tumbled out on a table and a few disconnected experiments made, the real interest of the outfit is missed and its owner soon becomes tired of it'. The article went on to explain how a 'bit of method' could make for greater interest and safety.

Unlike other manufacturers, whose chemistry sets contained apparatus almost identical to that found in school laboratories, Meccano Ltd designed special equipment. Their test tube stand and other items were of metal painted in the same colours as Meccano. Glassware, however, closely resembled existing school apparatus and was probably obtained from an outside contractor. Chemicals and apparatus had part numbers, and each item could be bought separately from Meccano dealers. Articles about chemistry continued in the *Meccano Magazine* until about the middle of 1934, augmenting the information in the instruction manuals supplied with each outfit.

Elektron Outfits only came in two sizes, numbered 1 and 2, with a conversion set also available. The smaller set enabled experiments to be made in magnetism and static electricity while the larger set added experiments in current electricity. Apparatus contained in Elektron outfits was divided into two types: parts similar to those found in a physics laboratory and others resembling standard Meccano accessory parts. In the former category were magnets, copper sheets and chemicals while the Meccano-like parts included lamps, brackets, coils, and 6BA nuts and bolts. The *Meccano Magazine* ran a parallel series of articles on electrical experiments during the same period as those on chemistry.

It would appear that Kemex and Elektron sets were not particularly successful. They strongly featured in the Magazine for a year or so and thereafter only in occasional advertisements. Perhaps there was strong competition from longer-established chemistry and electrical sets, or maybe interest in these hobbies had waned by the late 1930s.

Hornby Speed Boats

As manufacturers of the highest grade of clockwork motors for toy trains, and possessors of machinery to fabricate tinplate, the decision by Meccano Ltd to manufacture model boats was not surprising. In August 1932, the first Speed Boat was announced. Available in green, red or blue, and named *Hornby*, it was a 16″ model of an open-cockpit speed boat and cost 12/6d. The following Spring, a whole range of new speed boats was announced. The original speed boat became No. 3, and two similar but smaller boats joined the range. The upper end of the series consisted of two special boats, a limousine and a cabin cruiser, all based on the No. 3 boat but with more elaborate superstructures.

Meccano Ltd gave considerable publicity to Hornby Speed Boats in the Summer of 1933. One *Meccano Magazine* carried a centre-page advertisement, an article, and a full-colour picture of all five boats on the back page. The powerful clockwork motor in the larger boats gave a run of five hundred feet, which certainly beat its contemporaries. The colourful two-tone finish, which did not seem to be affected by water, equalled the high-grade stove enamelling on all Meccano's pre-war products.

In 1934, the range was further extended to include Hornby Racing Boats which had higher-geared motors with rather shorter lengths of run. A cheap boat selling at 2/11d was also introduced together with a model duck – a really beautiful piece

Built with Outfit No. 13

Fig. 41

Fig. 42

Fig. 43

BAYKO
Building Outfit
13
FOR BOYS & GIRLS OF ALL AGES

BAYKO Building Outfit

of tinplate art – as a toy for younger children. During the years up to 1939, the range remained unchanged except that motors, shafts, and propellers for Hornby Speed Boats could be purchased separately, and pennants and stands were also available.

Unlike many of the products in this review, Hornby Speed Boats *did* return after the war, albeit with plastic instead of tinplate bodies. The first three post-war boats were announced in July 1960, and represented a river launch, a patrol launch, and an RAF launch. The bodies were detailed plastic mouldings, 10″ long, with clockwork motors which gave a 130-ft run. In 1963, a larger boat joined the range, powered by an electric motor, driven by two dry cells. Only two Hornby Speed Boats appeared in the 1963 catalogues, the electric launch and the clockwork RAF launch. The clockwork boat disappeared after the take-over of Meccano Ltd by the Lines Bros group, but the electric launch was advertised up to 1969.

Dinky Builder

This was a simple but attractive constructional toy which also appeared in Meccano Ltd's pre- and post-war product range (Fig. 40). First introduced for the 1934 Christmas season, Dinky Builder consisted essentially of square, oblong and triangular metal pieces fitted together with rods which had to be pushed into hinges on the sides of the metal pieces. There were two sets, each finished in pink and green. Set No. 1, for general construction, included wheeled toys, whilst Set No. 2 was specifically intended for making pieces of modern furniture. The former set, in addition to standard pieces, included blue wheels with white-metal tyres, while the latter included a standard lamp for lighting from a flashlight battery.

By 1937, the range of sets had extended to include No. 0 (a smaller set) and No. 3, the largest in the series. Wheels were now included with all sets, and squares were obtainable to represent windows. The series remained unaltered from this point until the outbreak of World War 2.

Dinky Builder returned soon after the war, and the 1948 catalogue showed two sets now finished in blue and yellow, but substantially the same as the pre-war No. 1 and No. 2 sets. Windows and doors were painted on some pieces, and later a sheet of flags and clock faces, etc was also included for application to the appropriate models.

Although not advertised after 1965, Dinky Builder sets could be found in small out-of-the-way shops until comparatively recently. They have a special charm of their own, and represent tinplate toys of a bye-gone era.

Bayko Building Sets

The well-known Bayko Sets (Fig. 41) were a well-established series taken over by Meccano Ltd in 1960 from the Plimpton Engineering Company. At the time there were four standard sets plus a large super outfit. Meccano Ltd renumbered the former and withdrew the latter.

Bayko consisted of plastic pieces representing bricks, windows, pillars and doors. Models were made by inserting rods into a flat, perforated base and sliding the plastic pieces between the rods. The buildings were completed by various styles of roofs and chimneys.

In August 1962, the four standard Bayko sets, 11, 12, 13 (Fig. 43) and 14 were joined by a fifth which included new parts such as pantile roofs, dormer windows and a shop front. Accessory outfits were available to convert sets to the next larger in the series in the usual Meccano manner. The Company pointed out that in addition to being a constructional hobby in itself, Bayko made excellent lineside effects for model railways. Bayko was listed by Meccano Ltd up to 1967, and stocks remained in some shops for a year or two after that.

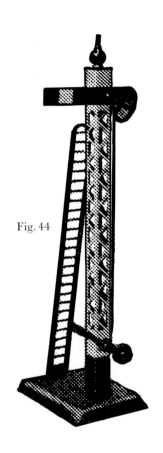

Fig. 44

THE DETAILS OF THE BEGINNINGS of Hornby Trains are shrouded in a certain amount of mystery. Some historians claim that Hornby Trains existed prior to or possibly during World War 1. (The topic of Raylo Trains, catalogued as a railway game by Meccano around 1915, will be dealt with in Volume 5.) It must be noted however, that memories of long-ago childhood tend to be unreliable, and that all tin trains, in this country at least, were referred to by some parents as 'Hornby Trains'. Certainly no advertising material so far unearthed is dated before 1920, and I feel that I can do no better than begin with Frank Hornby's own account of the birth of Hornby Trains which appeared in an article in *Meccano Magazine* for June 1932.

During World War 1, Meccano's factory was mainly employed on Government work, as were most engineering firms during both wars. Some Meccano was made however, between 1914 and 1918, and in the last year of the War, a new part called an Architrave (a type of corner bracket) was added to the system. Using this new part for cab sides, and special parts for boiler and chimney, Hornby had a small Meccano locomotive made up (Fig. 45). This led to the idea of constructional model trains being considered as a post-war venture, and in 1920, after spending two years catching up with demands for Meccano, the first Hornby Train was marketed.

It is interesting to speculate why these early trains were constructional; in fact, almost special-purpose Meccano sets. At that time, competitors' trains, either wholly or partly made in Germany, were of the familiar tin printed type assembled by tabs through slots, and strengthened with solder in some cases. Trains of this kind were eventually produced by Meccano Ltd, but it seems that Frank Hornby was firmly committed to the Meccano principle, and it was, therefore, quite natural for him to produce trains which could be taken to pieces and re-assembled. Actually, one or two Meccano parts were used, but the 0–4–0 locomotive, tender and open wagon which formed the first train sets (Fig. 46) were, for the most part,

constructed of large components, assembled with ordinary Meccano Nuts and Bolts. Separate parts were available to replace any that might become damaged or lost.

The locomotive was supplied in black, red, green or blue, but was not lettered in the style of any railway company. Instead, the loco cab side had a brass plate which bore the number '2710' and a motif on the tender incorporated Meccano's trade mark 'M Ld L'. The wagons had white-metal letters attached to their sides by clips denoting LNWR, GN, MR, CR or LBSC. A rather strange feature was that buffers and couplings were provided between engine and tender. A familiar-style oval of tinplate track completed the set, which was packed in an imitation leatherette box.

To quote Mr Hornby: 'The success of these first Hornby trains was immediate, and indeed it surpassed all expectations. The reason for this was that the army of Meccano boys had complete faith in anything turned out by the Meccano factory, and consequently Hornby Trains were purchased without hesitation.' These were proud words, and in my opinion, true words.

Within two years, considerable expansion had taken place in the Hornby Series. Modifications to the original engine included the removal of the buffers between engine and tender. This was now known as the No. 1 Locomotive, (Figs. 47 & 48) as a larger example, described as the No. 2, (Figs. 49 & 50) had made its appearance. This was a 4–4–0, finished in the same styles as the No. 1, but numbered 2711. To complement the larger engine, bogie Pullman Coaches finished in green and cream were added to the system, together with smaller four-wheeled coaches. Shortly after this, 'Zulu' trains were introduced (Fig. 51 & 52). No one is *quite* sure why they were so named, but the official explanation given at the time was that the name was derived from a well-known Great Western Railway train. 'Zulu' trains, finished in overall black, were cheaper, non-reversing, non-constructional versions of Hornby No. 1 Sets.

The little Meccano locomotive from which a great industry grew—the production of Hornby Trains. The earliest Hornby locomotives, tenders and trucks were built up from standard units and could be taken to pieces and re-built in a similar manner to Meccano models.

Fig. 45

Fig. 47

Fig. 48

Fig. 46

Fig. 49

Fig. 50

Fig. 51

Fig. 52

Fig. 53

Fig. 54

In 1923, the grouping of the real railways took place, and in that year the Hornby 4–4–4 Tank engine appeared (Fig. 54). This seems to have been the first Hornby engine to be painted in the colours of an actual railway, and the example shown in contemporary catalogues carried the legend 'LM & SR' and the number '1019' on its side tanks.

Hornby's next productions were rolling stock and accessories. There were bogie vans, timber and trolley wagons; and in the four-wheeled range items that were to become firm favourites over the next decade, included a brake van, various other vans and special-purpose vehicles such as gas cylinder wagons and petrol tankers. Accessories included a Station called the 'Windsor' station (for obviously patriotic rather than regional reasons), signals, signal cabins, metal tunnels, and platform accessories such as milk cans and luggage.

In 1925, the coloured *Hornby Book of Trains* was first produced, and this became a yearly catalogue, issued in almost every year up to 1940. These are now eagerly sought, as they provide the Hornby historian with a wealth of information.

The year brought other changes to the Hornby system. In the article referred to previously Hornby wrote: '. . . we found that the building of locomotives and rolling stock on the Meccano constructional plan was proving a handicap to the development of more realistic and true-to-type models. After careful consideration, therefore, we decided to abandon the constructional plan, and since 1925 all Hornby locomotives and rolling stock have been built from specially-made components, assembled into a complete unit.' This fundamental change must have caused Hornby and his staff much heart-searching, but Meccano products have never stood still and the change was inevitable in the interests of progress.

The 1925 catalogue listed some trains which have since caused considerable interest, and controversy. Known as the '00' series they were, nevertheless, Gauge '0' clockwork trains of simple design (Fig. 53), closely resembling toy trains of German manufacture. Did Mr Hornby do a quiet deal with a German manufacturer for the finished trains or perhaps the unassembled parts? Was it significant that the catalogue page on which they appeared did not say 'British and guaranteed', while every other page did? Those who could answer these questions have passed away long ago, leaving historians to conjecture. Some would claim that many other items were

THE
HORNBY ELECTRIC TRAIN
~ The Latest Hornby Thrill

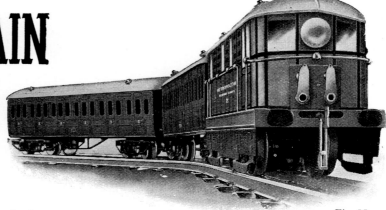

Fig. 55

THE Hornby Electric Train is modelled from the rolling-stock of the Metropolitan Railway, and is most realistic in appearance. Both Loco and Coaches are fitted with electric lights, which may be switched on and off at will. The finish and workmanship are of the highest quality.

Any boy can fit up the track and operate the train. It is designed to run from the ordinary town current of 100 to 240 volts, either alternating or direct. It is connected to the house supply by inserting the adapter, which is included in the set, to the nearest lamp socket. The current is converted to the correct pressure through a 60-watt lamp of the same voltage as the supply. (The lamp is not included in the set. Everything else necessary is provided) Full instructions accompany each set, and there are no difficulties or dangers.

Loco, Coaches and rails are fully covered by our usual guarantee.

What fun it is to sit by the regulator and with a touch of the finger send this superb model electric train gliding along the track—to stop it— to start it up gradually—to watch it accelerate !

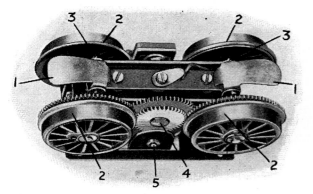

2. THE LOCOMOTIVE

The Hornby Electric Locomotive is an exceptionally powerful model, and will start on, and climb a steep gradient. It measures 9¾″ in length from buffer to buffer, and weighs 1 lb. 14 ozs. The motor is the most efficient ever fitted to a model loco. The field winding is 150 yards in length and consists of D.S. Covered wire, which eliminates any possibility of insulation breakdown.

We illustrate below the 4-wheeled motor bogie. The collecting shoes (1), wheel flanges (2), and rails should be kept clean and free from oil, to ensure good contact. The axles (3), gear bearings (4), and both ends of the armature shaft (5) should be lubricated with a little light oil, but not too freely.

THE SET contains Electric Loco, two Metropolitan Passenger Coaches, and Electric Rails to form a circle 4 ft. in diameter, together with a rheostat, with adapter and length of flex, and rail terminal plate. The Loco is fitted with reversing gear.

Complete set, in strong box .. Price £5/10/-
Hornby Electric Loco .. .. Price 52/6   Hornby Coach, Metropolitan .. Price 18/-
Rheostat, with adapter and length of flex, Price 16/-

FROM ALL MECCANO DEALERS.

Fig. 56
ROLLING STOCK AND ACCESSORIES FOR TRAINS
HORNBY SERIES
GAUGE 0

RAILWAY STATION
Excellent model, beautifully designed and finished. Dimensions: Length, 2ft. 9ins. ;
Breadth, 6ins. ; Height, 7ins. ... ... Price 12/6

L.M.S. BRAKE VAN Finished in colours. Opening doors Price 4/-	***REFRIGERATOR VAN** Enamelled in white. Opening doors ... ... Price 4/-	***GUNPOWDER VAN** Finished in Red. Opening doors Price 4/-	**L.N.E.R. BRAKE VAN** Finished in colours. Opening doors ... ... Price 4/-

***MILK TRAFFIC VAN** Fitted with sliding door, and complete with milk cans ... Price 4/6	***No. 2 CATTLE TRUCK** Splendid model, fitted with double doors. Suitable for 2ft. radius rails only ... Price 6/6	***No. 1 CATTLE TRUCK** Fitted with sliding door. Very realistic design ... Price 4/-

CARR'S BISCUIT VAN Finished in dark blue. Opening doors ... ... Price 4/-	**JACOB'S BISCUIT VAN** Finished in crimson lake. Lettered in gold and black. Opening doors ... ... Price 4/-	**CRAWFORD'S BISCUIT VAN** Finished in red. Opening doors Price 4/-

***No. 1 LUGGAGE VAN** Representative colours. Opening doors, Price 4/-	***No. 2 LUGGAGE VAN** Finished in colour. Fitted with double doors. Suitable for 2ft. radius rails only ... Price 6/6	**SECCOTINE VAN** Finished in blue. Opening doors Price 4/-

Lettered L.M.S. or L.N.E.R.

'made out', possibly in *other* countries and, of course, in recent times, items made abroad are stamped or labelled with the name of the originating country. But had he decided on any kind of arrangement with a German firm in the early 1920s, Hornby would have had to contend with a prejudice against German goods which, although understandable, was by no means insurmountable.

The finish of Hornby trains underwent alteration in 1925. All the locomotives were now painted and lettered in the goods or passenger styles of the LMS or LNER, and more expensive locomotives had twin headlamps fixed on their buffer beams. Except for the bogie Pullmans, most of the rolling stock including the re-designed four-wheeled coaches, could be purchased with the lettering of the same two railway companies as the locomotives.

At the end of 1925, the first Hornby electric train, based on the well known Metropolitan underground trains was announced (Fig. 55). It had a high-voltage motor operating from a DC mains supply, thus creating a situation where up to 230-volts could be present in the track. A firm would never be allowed to put such a device into the hands of children today, but in mitigation it must be remembered that the fortunate few who enjoyed electricity at this time were, if anything, more aware of its dangers than their contemporaries today.

Electric track was already available in the Hornby series (probably because the tooling for the track was ready before the finalisation of electric motor production. It is unlikely that the track was marketed to encourage customers to use other makes) and an interesting sidelight was the note in the Hornby catalogues to the effect that standard track was suitable for 'clockwork and steam trains'. It is believed that Frank Hornby did consider adding steam-driven locomotives to his range, but he must have abandoned the idea later. However, the note about the suitability of Hornby track for steam trains still appeared in catalogues until 1935.

Christmas 1925 saw the beginning of another feature that older readers will recall: *Hornby Train Week*. Dealers throughout the country put on special displays of Hornby Trains during that week and in their advertisements, Meccano Ltd urged boys to go to the dealers: and to take Dad with them!

Fig. 57

"Royal Scot"

Always on Time!

HORNBY TRAINS

BRITISH AND GUARANTEED

Manufactured by

Meccano Ltd., Old Swan, Liverpool

This is No. 3C L.M.S. "Royal Scot" Pullman Train, one of the famous trains in the Hornby System. It is seen passing under a Hornby Signal Gantry.

102

Fig. 58

FOR THE 1926 SEASON, THE Hornby Control System was introduced. This was an ambitious idea for clockwork layouts, as most of them were not permanent, and had to be dismantled when their owners had finished playing with them. The Control System (Figs. 63 & 64) enabled signals and points to be operated from a lever-frame housed in the signal cabin, and in addition, specially fitted locomotives could be stopped, reversed or restarted by means of a special control rail, also operated from the central-lever-frame. The system comprised control wires, which were threaded through brackets attached to the rails, and lever frames and accessories fitted with special attachments to take the wire. The whole system was not really suitable for temporary railway layouts, but was probably quite effective when applied to permanent installations. The rail for controlling locomotives must have had its limitations, especially when youthful enthusiasts operated it with trains

moving at high speeds! This particular aspect of the control system was abandoned in 1929 and the whole control system survived for only another nine years.

The year 1926 also saw two innovations at opposite ends of the price range. At the upper end, another electric set joined the Metropolitan Train. This newcomer was the 'Riviera Blue' train (Fig. 59) consisting of a 4–4–2 loco in Nord colours with two coaches to match. The electric version was 4-volt, designed to work from an accumulator, and a clockwork version was also available. The other new item was the first of the Hornby 'M' Series. This series ran until the end of Hornby's Gauge '0' era as their cheap line, although what 'M' stood for is still a mystery. The M1/2 loco was a simple but sturdy toy engine which sold, together with a tender, two Pullman coaches and a set of rails for 7/6d. This was obviously brought out to compete with cheap foreign sets. The M3 loco was the old 'German' type

The *Riviera "Blue" Train*

Fig. 60

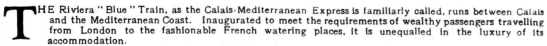

Fig. 59

Fig. 61

Fig. 62

THE Riviera "Blue" Train, as the Calais-Mediterranean Express is familiarly called, runs between Calais and the Mediterranean Coast. Inaugurated to meet the requirements of wealthy passengers travelling from London to the fashionable French watering places, it is unequalled in the luxury of its accommodation.

The Coaches, the property of the International Sleeping-Car Company, are built of steel, wood being used for internal decorations only. The exteriors are elaborately finished with royal blue panelling with gold-leaf lining, hence the title of the train.

The "Blue" Train, introduced last year to the Hornby Series, is a model of this famous train. Distinguished in appearance, strongly built and beautifully finished in correct colours, it is supplied with either electric (4-volt) or clockwork loco.

104

with new lithography, coupled to a typical Hornby tender. It sold complete with two wagons and rails for 15/-.

Up to 1926, Hornby Trains were only available in the styles of the LMS and LNER. Then Great Western colours were introduced, and finally at the end of 1928, the Southern Railway was recognized. It has been suggested that, as the factory was in Liverpool, the designers considered the Southern Railway too remote to bother with at least for the first eight years of Hornby Trains, coupled with the cost factor of permutating many items in four liveries. However, with a few exceptions, all Hornby locomotives and rolling stock items were available, from 1929, in the colours of the four famous lines. Then, as now, railway enthusiasts had strong loyalties to one particular railway, not always for the most logical reasons!

A landmark in Hornby history was the introduction of the No. 3 locomotives for the 1927/28 season. These were of French design, based on the 'Riviera Blue' engines, and may even have initially been made in Hornby's French factory at Bobigny. To begin with, the No. 3 locomotives, carrying such famous names as 'Royal Scot' and 'Flying Scotsman' were painted in British liveries, though still retaining French-type chimneys and safety valves. Later, they were modified to make them more English in appearance, and they became very popular as Hornby's largest engines, capable of running at good speeds on two-foot radius track, due to their flexible 4–4–2 wheel arrangement. Clockwork or 4-volt electric versions were available, indicating that Hornby had decided not to proceed further with high-voltage motors, although the original Metropolitan locomotive remained in the catalogue until 1928.

The Hornby system was now developing rapidly, and another announcement in November 1929 brought several new locomotives to the series. Predominant amongst these were the No. 2 Specials, true-to-type engines for each railway company, representing respectively the LMS Compound, LNER Shire (Fig. 61), GWR County and Southern L1 classes. Unlike the previous policy of merely painting an identical locomotive in different styles, four completely different models were produced which closely resembled the actual locomotives.

The other models introduced for the 1929/30 season were the No. 1 Special – a powerful four-wheeled engine of generous proportions (Fig. 60) – and the No. 2 Special Tank (Fig. 62), a modernised version of the No. 2 Tank (Fig. 54) but with a 4–4–2 instead of a 4–4–4 wheel arrangement.

Fig. 63

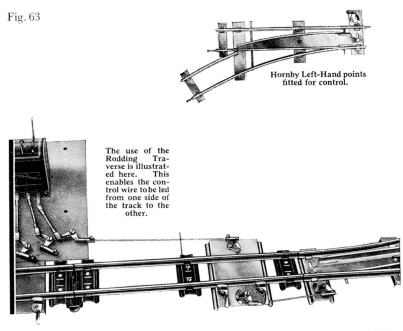

Hornby Left-Hand points fitted for control.

The use of the Rodding Traverse is illustrated here. This enables the control wire to be led from one side of the track to the other.

The late 1920s also brought additions to the range of Hornby rolling stock and accessories. The original green-and-cream Pullman coaches were replaced by new models in correct Pullman colours, fitted with corridor connections which could actually be joined together. Popular goods vehicles included three biscuit vans and five petrol tankers, all beautifully enamelled in the colourful styles of the appropriate private owner. Platforms for extending stations enabled boys to have as long a platform as their space allowed; and two imposing engine sheds, probably the largest and most elaborate single models Hornby ever made, were available.

At the lower-price end, the 'M' series trains were brought up to date. Two modern-looking locomotives, the larger of which had a reversing mechanism, were supplied in sets, the smaller one selling for only 5/-.

By 1930, the No. 2 Tender and Tank locomotives had been withdrawn from the series. Compared with the No. 2 Special versions, they had an old-fashioned look, attractive to present day collectors, but not to boys at the time.

The original 1920 locomotive was still in the series, though much modified. Enamelled and fully lined-out in the passenger or goods style of the four railway companies, it now carried appropriate numbers as well in place of the '2710'. The dome, previously brass, was now painted to match the body, and twin headlamps were fixed in position. Short couplings replaced the earlier somewhat oversized ones, and engine and tender were now closely coupled together. In all, it had become a very handsome locomotive demonstrating Hornby's policy of constant up-dating.

In 1930, it was possible to build a complete model railway with main line, branch line, stations and sidings, using only Hornby components. Perhaps the only things missing were human and animal figures, but these were readily obtainable in lead from most toy shops, although they were somewhat overscale. It must have been a source of great satisfaction to Frank Hornby to see his trains in use all over the world and to hear in Britain the term 'Hornby Train' become a household word used to describe any tinplate trains, whether of Hornby manufacture or not.

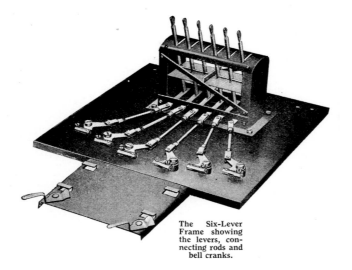

The Six-Lever Frame showing the levers, connecting rods and bell cranks.

Fig. 64

A Hornby "Distant" Signal fitted for Control Working. The bell crank and coupling at the base of the post enable connection to be effected with the Lever Frame.

Fig. 65

SEPTEMBER 1931 WAS A WATERSHED in the Hornby Train story. The *Meccano Magazine* for that month announced the modernization of the Hornby Series together with the introduction of many new items. Changes throughout the system included the lowering of the buffer height on all locomotives and rolling stock; the incorporation of a new type of base for goods vehicles; and the announcement that automatic couplings which engaged on impact were to be fitted to all stock in future. The old-style No. 1 locomotives were replaced by new, modern looking types with high boilers and squat chimneys and domes. Six new goods vehicles together with several new items of rolling stock were introduced, and most significantly, the prices of some items were reduced.

As with changes in Meccano, these Hornby modifications did not, of course, happen overnight. Not only were large stocks of the old-style items held, but for a time the factory produced hybrid vehicles having some pre- and some post-1931 features. However, the style of Hornby Trains was set for the next decade, and to some extent, for the post-war period also. Hornby reached its zenith in both quality and quantity in the years between 1931 and 1939. A feature of this period was the extension of electrical items in the Hornby Series. Most houses were now electrified in this country, and model trains operated from the house mains, through a suitable transformer, became a viable proposition. Although some low-voltage models for use with accumulators were always available, the 20-volt system was gradually standardised for all Hornby locomotives, the larger of which was also equipped for automatic reversing from the lineside as indeed were several 6-volt versions. Many accessories such as signals and stations were optionally available fitted with electric lighting, using an output socket on the transformer, and a common earth return via the track.

During 1937, two new locomotives joined the Hornby series, both high quality models in the higher price range. One of these, a true-to-type model of the Southern Railway 'Schools' class (Figs. 67 & 68) was designated No. 4, although it really fitted into the No. 2 Special Series, giving previously neglected Southern enthusiasts two different true-to-type models from which to choose.

The other locomotive was the finest ever made by Hornby in '0' gauge: the famous 'Princess Elizabeth' (Figs. 65 & 66). Meccano Ltd pulled out all the stops to give this locomotive publicity, and to launch it at the time when the LMS railway company was publicising the real engine.

Hornby's locomotive was a realistic model in every sense. The tapered boiler, six-coupled wheels, valve motion and external details of the original were all accurately reproduced. Priced at five guineas (£5.25) it was expensive by Hornby standards, but cheaper than other versions of similar locomotives by British and Continental manufacturers to whom Hornby had now thrown down the gauntlet. It is interesting to speculate on what other scale models Hornby would have produced had it not been for the outbreak of World War 2.

At the same time, Hornby introduced solid steel, scale model track, so that their new engine could show its paces. With wide-radius curves this track was ideal for those fortunate enough to have the space available, and the fact that so much survived in good order after over thirty-five years is indicative of its durability.

To appeal to younger enthusiasts, Hornby made a series of complete model railways. Each had one of the cheaper train sets plus a station, a tunnel, a footbridge and other accessories. The collections were packed in attractive boxes, complete with trays in the larger sets, and were eye-catching items when displayed in shop windows.

From the middle 1930s, tinprinting was extensively used for coaches and vans in the Hornby Series. Previously most of these items had been stove enamelled, unlike the products of their competitors, who in the main used the tinprinting process. Certainly much more detail was possible with tinprinting, although it is arguable that a richer finish could be achieved through stove enamelling.

Modern coaches, both corridor (Fig. 69) and surburban, in the styles of the four railway companies were now tinprinted, as were open wagons and an extensive range of vans for special traffic like meat, fish and bananas.

Hornby had also given some attention to the scenic side of model railways by producing tunnels, cuttings and fields made of wood and cardboard suitably finished to represent grass. These items were made to fit the geometry of the Hornby rail formations and were suitable for temporary as well as permanent layouts.

Lineside effects such as human and animal figures as well as cars and lorries were now available in the Dinky Toy series to which reference will be made later.

Fig. 66

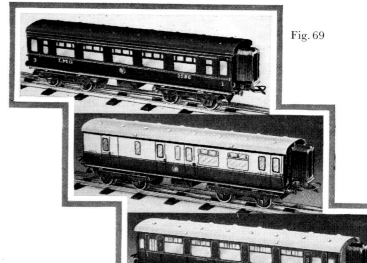

Fig. 69

Fig. 67

Fig. 68

No doubt Hornby had many new things planned for the 1940s, in fact, an artist's impression of scale model coaches appeared in an advertisement for the 'Princess Elizabeth' locomotive, but these were not produced. Although the manufacture and sale of Hornby Gauge '0' continued in the early years of World War 2, like all Meccano products it ceased with the Government order banning metal toys.

Unlike Meccano however, most of the Hornby Series did not re-appear at the end of hostilities.

In 1938, Hornby introduced their 'Dublo Trains' in Gauge '00'. From a small beginning, this range expanded in post-war years to become what was probably the finest model railway system ever offered to the public.

This is the
No. 2 Special Pullman
Train L.M.S.

Fig. 70

WHEN THE WAR ENDED IN 1945, the *Meccano Magazine* promised that Hornby Trains would soon be back, and it showed a picture of their 'Eton' locomotive, one of the near-scale models of the late pre-war period. Indeed, some Hornby Trains were to be seen in dealers' shops at Christmas 1945 and again in 1946, but these were almost certainly old stock, released with Government permission. When new Hornby Trains *did* appear once more in 1947, only the smaller four-wheeled variety was made. There were probably several reasons for this: the Company naturally concentrated on their main product – Meccano – which with Dinky Toys, sold well to the toy-starved children of the immediate post-war years. When material and machine capacity could be used again for trains, the decision

had to be made whether to concentrate on '0' or '00' gauge. Research would have revealed that tastes had changed since 1939. Limited room space did not allow the large layouts of previous years and, at the same time, boys had become more sophisticated, wanting trains that closely resembled the real thing. Clearly '00' had come to stay in the model railway world, so Hornby concentrated on developing their Dublo range, and '0' gauge Hornby trains became toys for younger children. It seems likely that this trend towards the smaller gauge would have happened even if there had been no war, and this fact, was discernible even in 1938 when Dublo trains were first made.

For a year or so no catalogues were published, some of the smaller train sets being the only items available. Then in 1948,

Fig. 71

Fig. 73

Fig. 72

HORNBY GAUGE O TRAINS

THE COMPLETENESS OF THE HORNBY GAUGE O RAILWAY SYSTEM

From the day of their introduction Hornby Trains have always represented the latest model railway practice. Designs are continually being improved and new items added so that the system is complete in practically every detail. There are Locomotives for all duties, driven by electric motors or by clockwork. There is Rolling Stock of all kinds, including Corridor Coaches, Pullman Cars, ordinary Coaches and Guard's Vans for passenger services; and there are numerous and varied Wagons and Vans for freight working.

The Accessories are now better than ever before. Stations, Signals and Signal Cabins, Engine Sheds, Level Crossings and other items can be obtained wired for electric lighting. Miniature Trees and Hedging provide a splendid scenic setting for any layout; Tunnels add realism to the track; miniature Railway Staff and Passengers give "life" to station platforms; and there are Animals for lineside fields.

The splendid fun of running a Hornby Railway is real and lasting, because of the exceptional strength and reliability of Hornby Locomotives, the realistic appearance and easy running of the Rolling Stock, and the wide range of effective Accessories—all designed and built in proportion and all splendidly finished.

HORNBY ELECTRIC AND CLOCKWORK LOCOMOTIVES

Hornby Electric Locomotives, of which there is a wide selection, are fitted with powerful and efficient motors capable of hauling heavy loads at high speeds, but always under perfect control. All Hornby Electric Locomotives can be controlled for speed, and for starting and stopping, from the lineside.

Hornby Clockwork Locomotives are the longest-running locomotives of their respective types in the world. The motors are perfect mechanisms with accurately cut gears. All the locomotives can be braked either from the cab or from the track by means of a suitable brake rail.

THE FAMOUS HORNBY REMOTE CONTROL

The largest Hornby 20-volt Electric Locomotives are fitted with the famous Hornby Remote Control. This makes possible starting and stopping; controlling for speed, easy round the curves, faster along the straight; and reversing trains at the end of the run or when shunting, without any need to touch the Locomotive at all. Everything is done from outside the track! In conjunction with the automatic couplings fitted to the Rolling Stock, Remote Control makes possible the most realistic operation.

THE FINISH OF HORNBY LOCOMOTIVES

Hornby Locomotives are finished in the passenger traffic colours of the four British Railway groups, red for L.M.S., light green for L.N.E.R., and dark green for G.W.R. and S.R. Locomotives can be obtained to special order finished in goods traffic colours—black for L.M.S., L.N.E.R. and S.R., and dark green for G.W.R.

Be Chief Engineer of your own Railway, like this boy!

Ready to give the "Right Away!"

HORNBY

CLOCKWORK TRAINS 'O' GAUGE

One of the attractions of a Hornby Clockwork railway is being able to start in a small way with a train and track, and then add to the equipment from time to time. The choice of Hornby trains ensures reliable performance, all components being tested and guaranteed before despatch from the Meccano Works.

No. 20 GOODS TRAIN SET
Contains No. 20 Locomotive (non-reversing), No. 20 Tender, two No. 20 Wagons and Rails.

No. 21 PASSENGER TRAIN SET
Contains No. 20 Locomotive (non-reversing), No. 20 Tender, two No. 21 Coaches and Rails.

No. 30 GOODS TRAIN SET
Contains No. 30 Locomotive (reversing), No. 30 Tender, No. 30 Wagon, No. 30 Goods Van and Rails.

No. 31 PASSENGER TRAIN SET
Contains No. 30 Locomotive (reversing), No. 30 Tender No. 31 Coach 1st/2nd, No. 31 Coach Brake/2nd and Rails.

No. 45 TANK GOODS TRAIN SET
Contains No. 40 Tank Locomotive (reversing), No. 50 Wagon, No. 50 Lumber Wagon, No. 50 "SHELL" Tank Wagon and Rails.

No. 41 TANK PASSENGER TRAIN SET
Contains No. 40 Tank Locomotive (reversing), two No. 41 Coaches, No. 41 Passenger Brake Van and Rails.

Train Sets No. 20, 21, 30 and 31 are supplied with 1 ft. radius rails requiring a space of 3 ft. 3 in. by 2 ft. 6 in. Train Sets No. 41 and 45 are supplied with 2 ft. radius rails requiring a space of 5 ft. 4 in. by 4 ft. 6 in.

Load up the Goods!

What opportunities there are for lasting fun with a goods depot made up of Hornby equipment. Hornby Clockwork locomotives—now in British Railways colours—are long-running and strong-pulling, and there is a variety of rolling stock and accessories to build up an exciting model railway. In the Hornby railway scene below, effective use is being made of Dinky Toys No. 973 Goods Yard Crane, price 11/6. (incl. Tax)

HORNBY TRAINS

Fig. 74

an illustrated folder was issued showing a small range of post-war trains which was never extended. It included the 'M' sets, virtually the same as the pre-war series, plus the equivalent of the No. 1 goods and passenger sets (See page 114). The tank locomotive (Fig. 73) was actually the pre-war M3 with minor modifications and now called No. 101. The tender engines were very similar to the pre-war No. 1 type except that they were now sprayed in matt finish instead of the pre-war shiny enamel. No doubt Hornby used the same enamel for these as for Dublo locomotives. The finish on some coaches and wagons was also modified usually being lettered in the post-war style. Some bogie coaches and goods vehicles were listed for a time, and if the vans were not of post-war manufacture they were certainly finished in post-war style. However, all bogie items were soon deleted leaving a rather small selection of four-wheeled stock to make up the series. Some accessories re-appeared too, although cost cutting simplifications could be detected: for example the station had no fencing, and plain rather than latticed signal posts were used once stocks of the latter were exhausted.

To begin with, post-war trains were advertised as being available in the colours of the four main railways. In fact very few, if any, GW or SR locomotives or coaches were made after 1948, although up to then pre-war items in post-war boxes could be found, as well as 'hybrid' items. The range remained fairly static for some years, and then Meccano Ltd changed locos and rolling stock to BR colours (see page 116). These items were first illustrated in the *Meccano Magazine* April 1954. The tank engine was now lithographed in black, while the tender engines were enamelled in either black or green, and all three were lined-out and carried the BR emblem. Rolling stock items were gradually changed over to BR finish too, and at about the same time (c1951) plastic wheels replaced the old tinplate ones. Even seasoned enthusiasts discovered that the new wheels gave very smooth running, superior even to the pre-war die-cast wheels which Hornby had fitted to selected vehicles.

In 1957, goods vehicles were re-designed (Figs. 71 & 72) with a new type of base and fitted with separate brake levers. The bodies of some items were also modified, and a completely new vehicle – the Saxa Salt Wagon (Fig. 70) – became the only really new standard post-war vehicle. This new series, called No. 50, was tin-printed, following the trend that had begun twenty years before.

To the 'M' series was added an up-dated version of the larger engine, called the No. 30. Completely new wagons and coaches were produced to go with it, all equipped with a new efficient type of simple coupling.

The year 1958 evidenced the final phase for Hornby gauge '0', and soon after that time, deletions began to reduce the range. First to go were the large tender engines designated No. 50 or 51 depending on the colour, and this left the No. 40 tank engines as sole survivors of a once-proud range. The old 'M' series, now numbered 20 and 30, continued to the end of the era. The last year in which '0' gauge was supplied in quantity was 1964, and by this time the buildings and further rolling stock had been deleted. Stocks in dealers' shops must have been quite high because Hornby Gauge '0' items, including locomotives, could be found in small out-of-the-way shops as late as 1970. By this time, the cult of Hornby collecting had become established, and for several years, small bicycle and sweet shops became the happy hunting ground for the collecting fraternity. Maybe there are still stocks of '0' gauge to be found, but I would be surprised if much more comes to light. Naturally enough the demand, so small during the final years of Hornby tinplate trains, has now grown with the collecting craze, but it is most unlikely that Meccano Ltd (or indeed Rovex Ltd) will ever make tinplate trains again. Their demise was brought about by a war, and a change in public taste. The surviving 'Princess Elizabeths', Compounds, coaches etc, remain the legacy of this era, at peace now on collectors' shelves. Such is the market acceptance of the name *Hornby* when linked with model trains, that an entirely new generation of plastic trains (a continuation of the Triang system still manufactured by Rovex Ltd.) now bear this proud name.

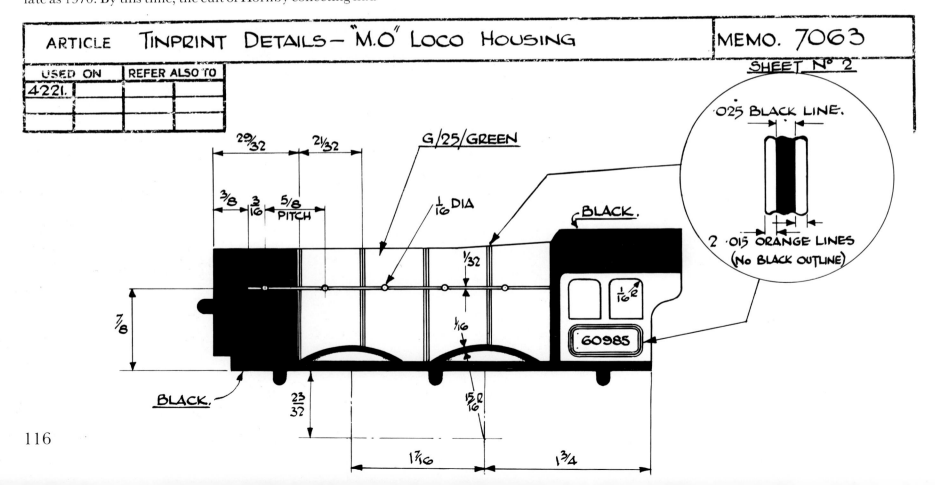

THE PERFECT TABLE RAILWAY

The remarkable success of the Hornby-Dublo Railway introduced last year has proved our claim that this is the finest system in the world for the development of a complete miniature railway where space is limited. The trains are actually one seventy-sixth of the size of real trains, and are marvellous scale models of their prototypes.

Hornby-Dublo electric locomotives are fitted for remote control; starting, stopping, reversing and speed regulation are all carried out from the lineside by the movement of a single lever. All Hornby-Dublo coaches, vans and wagons have automatic couplings.

The great new feature of the Hornby-Dublo System this year is the introduction of Isolating Rails for dividing a layout into separate sections that can be made "alive" or "dead" as desired. By means of these Rails, and special Switches (D2), endless fun can be had by controlling two or more trains independently at the same time. All kinds of interesting shunting operations can be carried out, every movement being made as on real railways.

Other new features include Electrically-Operated Points, and large radius Curved Rails, which, used in conjunction with the standard Dublo Rails, form a perfect double track.

Hornby-Dublo electric trains operate on Direct Current at 12 volts. This current may be obtained in three different ways—first, from Alternating Current mains supply through a Dublo Transformer and a Dublo Controller No. 1; second, from Direct Current mains supply through a D.C. Converter and a Dublo Controller No. 1; third, from Accumulators giving 12 volts, with a Dublo Controller No. 1A.

This attractive layout shows the splendid possibilities of the Hornby-Dublo System. There is a double track main line serving two stations, and an interesting goods yard, and yet the whole is accommodated on a board measuring only 8 ft. x 4 ft.

By means of Isolating Rails and Switches the trains can be operated independently of one another. An engine can shunt wagons in the goods yard in the centre of the layout while the streamlined express dashes round the inner road, or the goods train runs round the outer track. Points and Signals are electrically operated from special Switches.

HORNBY DUBLO
Gauge OO

L.M.S. EXPRESS PASSENGER TRAIN
HAULED BY THE
"DUCHESS OF ATHOLL" LOCOMOTIVE

EDP2 HORNBY-DUBLO

ELECTRIC PASSENGER TRAIN SET, L.M.S.

This wonderful Train Set represents the highest degree of realism ever attained in Gauge OO, both in general design and extent and perfection of detail. The components comprise the locomotive and coaches of a typical L.M.S. express in its characteristic red livery. The Locomotive, "Duchess of Atholl", is a splendid reproduction of one of the non-streamlined "Duchess" class. These powerful and attractive-looking locomotives are employed mainly in the working of the principal fast and heavy trains between London and Scotland and London and Liverpool.

The Coaches are modelled on the very latest L.M.S. standard corridor stock used for main line working. One of them is a first-third, and the other a brake-third with guard's and luggage accommodation at the rear end. These Coaches are particularly attractive; they have real cut-out windows glazed with celluloid inside. Another feature that adds to the realism is a corridor partition inside each Coach. Automatic couplings are fitted. The Locomotive is not supplied with Clockwork mechanism.

EDP2 Electric Passenger Train Set, L.M.S., contains Locomotive "Duchess of Atholl" (automatic reversing), Tender, first-third Corridor Coach, brake-third Corridor Coach, seven Curved Rails, one Curved Terminal Rail and two Straight Rails. The Set includes Dublo Controller No. 1 for use with Dublo Transformer (for A.C. mains) or D.C. Converter (for D.C. mains). Transformer or Converter not included. Price **92/6**

For districts where no electric supply is available.

EDPA2 Electric Passenger Train Set, L.M.S. (with Dublo Controller No. 1A for use with 12-volt accumulators). Price **84/-**

The components of the above Train Set are obtainable separately at the following prices:—

EDLT2 Electric Locomotive (Automatic Reversing) and Tender L.M.S. ... ... Price 45/-
EDL2 Electric Locomotive L.M.S. (Automatic Reversing) without Tender ... ... Price 39/-
Tender D2 L.M.S. ... ... Price 6/-
First-Third Corridor Coach, D3 L.M.S. ... ... Price 6/9
Brake-Third Corridor Coach, D3 L.M.S. ... ... Price 6/9
Dublo Controller No. 1 (for use with Dublo Transformers or D.C. Converter) ... ... Price 21/-
Dublo Controller No 1a (for use with 12-volt accumulators) ... ... Price 12/6

EDLT2 Hornby-Dublo Electric Locomotive "Duchess of Atholl" (Automatic Reversing) and Tender. Price 45/-

HORNBY DUBLO

EDP1 ELECTRIC & DP1 CLOCKWORK PASSENGER TRAIN SETS, L.N.E.R.

EDP1 Electric Passenger Train Set, L.N.E.R.

EDG7 Electric Tank Goods Train Set, G.W.R.

This L.N.E.R. Express Train Set consists of a streamlined "Pacific" with an 8-wheeled corridor Tender, and a Two-Coach Articulated Unit. The engine modelled is "Sir Nigel Gresley", named after its famous designer. The Articulated Coaches make up a two-coach unit or "twin", with a corridor connection. Automatic couplings are fitted.

ELECTRIC

EDP1 Electric Passenger Train Set, L.N.E.R., contains Streamlined Locomotive "Sir Nigel Gresley" (Automatic Reversing), Tender, Two-Coach Articulated Unit, seven Curved Rails, one Curved Terminal Rail and two Straight Rails. The Set includes Dublo Controller No. 1 for use with Dublo Transformer (for A.C. mains) or D.C. Converter (for D.C. mains). Transformer or Converter not included. **Price 70/-**

For districts where no electric supply is available.

EDPA1 Electric Passenger Train Set L.N.E.R. (with Dublo Controller No. 1a for use with 12-volt accumulators). **Price 61/6**

CLOCKWORK

DP1 Clockwork Passenger Train Set, L.N.E.R., contains Streamlined Locomotive "Sir Nigel Gresley" (Reversing), Tender, Two-Coach Articulated Unit, eight Curved Rails and two Straight Rails. **Price 39/6**

The components of the above Train Sets are obtainable separately at the following prices:—

EDLT1 Electric Streamlined Locomotive (Automatic Reversing) and Tender L.N.E.R. ...	Price 29/6
DLT1 Clockwork Streamlined Locomotive (Reversing) and Tender L.N.E.R.	Price 23/-
EDL1 Electric Streamlined Locomotive L.N.E.R. (Automatic Reversing) without Tender	Price 25/-
DL1 Clockwork Streamlined Locomotive L.N.E.R. (Reversing) without Tender	Price 18/6
Tender D1 L.N.E.R.	Price 4/6
Two-Coach Articulated Unit D2 L.N.E.R.	Price 6/6
Dublo Controller No. 1 (for use with Dublo Transformers or D.C. Converter)	Price 21/-
Dublo Controller No. 1a (for use with 12-volt accumulators) ...	Price 12/6

EDG7 ELECTRIC AND DG7 CLOCKWORK TANK GOODS TRAIN SETS

The powerful Tank Locomotive in these Train Sets is a particularly attractive model representing a type that is extensively used by the four main line companies. It is available in the style and finish of each company.
The Open Wagon represents the 12-ton vehicle adopted as a standard for the conveyance of general goods by each of the companies. The 12-ton Van is a true-to-type model of the actual vans used for general traffic requiring protection from the weather. Each Brake Van follows the latest practice of its company. Automatic couplings are fitted.

ELECTRIC

EDG7 Electric Tank Goods Train Set, L.M.S., L.N.E.R., G.W.R. or S.R., contains Tank Locomotive (Automatic Reversing), Open Goods Wagon, Goods Van, Goods Brake Van, seven Curved Rails, one Curved Terminal Rail and two Straight Rails. The Set includes Dublo Controller No. 1 for use with Dublo Transformer (for A.C. mains) or D.C. Converter (for D.C. mains). Transformer or Converter not included. **Price 55/-**

For districts where no electric supply is available.

EDGA7 Electric Tank Goods Train Set. (With Dublo Controller No. 1a for use with 12-volt accumulators). **Price 46/6**

CLOCKWORK

DG7 Clockwork Tank Goods Train Set, L.M.S., L.N.E.R., G.W.R. or S.R., contains Tank Locomotive (Reversing), Open Goods Wagon, Goods Van, Goods Brake Van, eight Curved Rails, and two Straight Rails. **Price 27/6**

The components of the above Train Sets are obtainable separately at the following prices:—

EDL7 Electric Tank Locomotive (Automatic Reversing) ...	Price 17/6
DL7 Clockwork Tank Locomotive (Reversing)	Price 12/6
Goods Brake Van D1	Price 2/6
Open Goods Wagon D1	Price 1/4
Goods Van D1	Price 1/6
Dublo Controller No. 1 (for use with Dublo Transformers or D.C. Converter)	Price 21/-
Dublo Controller No. 1a (for use with 12-volt accumulators)	Price 12/6

EDLT1 Electric Streamlined Locomotive "Sir Nigel Gresley" (Automatic Reversing) and Tender, L.N.E.R.

Price 29/6

EDL7 Electric Tank Locomotive (Automatic Reversing), G.W.R. Available also in L.M.S., L.N.E.R. and S.R. finish.

Price 17/6

GOODS BRAKE VAN D1
L.M.S.
This Van is coloured in the latest L.M.S. Bauxite brown.   Price 2/6

12-TON OPEN GOODS WAGON D1
L.N.E.R.
L.N.E.R. Open Goods Wagon, finished in grey with white lettering.
Price 1/4

MEAT VAN D1
L.M.S.
Scale model of the latest ventilated meat vans. Finished in L.M.S. Bauxite brown.   Price 1/6

12-TON GOODS VAN D1
L.N.E.R.
The vertical boarding of standard N.E. vans is a feature of this vehicle; red-brown finish. Price 1/6

CATTLE TRUCK D1
G.W.R.
This model, and also the L.M.S. model below, have pierced openings. Finished in grey. Price 1/6

GOODS BRAKE VAN D1
G.W.
A fine model of the characteristic 20-ton long-bodied G.W.R. Goods Brake Van.   Price 2/6

12-TON OPEN GOODS WAGON D1
L.M.S.
The standard L.M.S. Open Goods Wagon, finished in the company's characteristic Bauxite brown.
Price 1/4

MEAT VAN D1
S.R.
A realistic model of the steel-ended type of van. The vehicle is finished in buff.   Price 1/6

12-TON GOODS VAN D1
L.M.S.
Typical of the latest vans for goods traffic; finished in L.M.S. Bauxite brown.   Price 1/6

CATTLE TRUCK D1
L.M.S.
An attractive model fully detailed, finished in Bauxite brown.
Price 1/6

GOODS BRAKE VAN D1
L.N.E.R.
An accurate model of the standard L.N.E.R. 20-ton Goods Brake Van.   Price 2/6

12-TON OPEN GOODS WAGON D1
G.W.R.
G.W.R. standard Open Goods Wagon, finished in grey with white lettering.   Price 1/4

HIGH-SIDED WAGON D2
L.M.S.
Represents the standard type of mineral wagon with high sides. Finished L.M.S. Bauxite brown with diagonal white stripe.   Price 1/6

12-TON GOODS VAN D1
G.W.R.
Conforms to the latest G.W. standards in design and finish; grey with white lettering and white roof.   Price 1/3

FISH VAN D1
N.E.
A characteristic N.E. van used for perishable traffic. Finished in red-brown with white roof and lettering.   Price 1/6

GOODS BRAKE VAN D1
S.R.
The latest type of 25-ton Goods Brake Van operated by the Southern Railway.   Price 2/6

12-TON OPEN GOODS WAGON D1
S.R.
Model of standard 12-ton Open Goods Wagon, finished in S.R. chocolate brown with white lettering.   Price 1/4

HIGH-SIDED WAGON D2
L.N.E.R.
Finished in grey with diagonal white stripe.   Price 1/6

12-TON GOODS VAN D1
S.R.
A modern 12-ton van for general goods; S.R. chocolate brown finish with white lettering.   Price 1/6

HORSE BOX D1
N.E.
Model of the latest type, with full details. Finished in teak brown with white lettering.   Price 1/6

**PETROL TANK WAGON
"POWER ETHYL" D1**

Finished in green with gold and
red lettering.   Price 2/6

PETROL TANK WAGON "ESSO" D1

Finished in buff with bright blue
lettering.   Price 2/6

**OIL TANK WAGON
"ROYAL DAYLIGHT" D1**

Finished in bright red with gold
lettering.   Price 2/6

**HIGH-SIDED COAL WAGON D2
L.M.S AND N.E.**

A model of the standard type high-
sided mineral wagon, with a
realistic load of coal.   Price 1/9

**COAL WAGON D1
L.M.S., N.E., G.W., S.R.**

A standard open wagon with
realistic load of coal.   Price 1/7

**HIGH-CAPACITY WAGON D1
N.E.**

Scale model of the L.N.E.R. bogie wagons used
for brick traffic.   Price 3/6

**TWO-COACH ARTICULATED UNIT D2
L.N.E.R.**

A perfect representation of the teak-finished Corridor
Articulated Units used on the principal L.N.E.R.
expresses.   Price 6/6

**FIRST-THIRD CORRIDOR COACH D3
L.M.S.**

A splendid reproduction of the latest type of L.M.S. corridor coach
with real cut-out windows glazed with celluloid inside. Its style and
finish follow closely the details of the real thing.   Price 6/9

**BRAKE-THIRD CORRIDOR COACH D3
L.M.S.**

Designed to run with the first-third coach, with which it
is identical in style and finish.   Price 6/9

**CORRIDOR COACH D1
L.N.E.R.**

An accurately detailed model of a standard L.N.E.R.
teak-finished Corridor Coach.   Price 3/6

DUBLO TRANSFORMERS

Dublo Transformer No. 1 (Output 10 VA at 12 volts).
For running one Hornby-Dublo Train.
Price 9/6

Dublo Transformer No. 2 (two outputs
of 10 VA at 12 volts). For running
two Hornby-Dublo Trains on separate
tracks by means of two No. 1 Dublo
Controllers.   Price 12/6

Available for the following Alternating Current supplies: 100/110 volts,
50 cycles, and 210/240 volts, 50
cycles. They can be specially wound for other supplies,
if required.

DUBLO CONTROLLER No. 1
(for use with Dublo Transformers and D.C. Converter).

This Controller is fitted with
a single handle by which a
train can be started, stopped,
reversed and regulated for
speed. A circuit breaker is
incorporated.   Price 21/-

DUBLO CONTROLLER No. 1a
(for use with 12-volt
accumulators).

This Controller, similar to No. 1 described above, is for
use with 12-volt accumulators.   Price 12/6

D.C. CONVERTER

(Two outputs of 10VA at 12 volts)
For running Hornby-Dublo Trains
from Direct Current (D.C.) mains.
For use with one Dublo Controller
No. 1 to run one train, or with
two No. 1 Controllers to run two
trains, each on a separate track.
Wound for 210-240 volts; wound
for other voltages to special
order.   Price 39/-

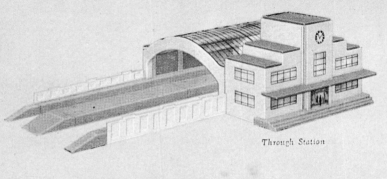

Through Station

CITY STATION OUTFIT D2

This Outfit has been specially designed for building either of two splendid city stations.

The Terminal Station illustrated on the left is an imposing model in the modern style, with three platforms covered by an arched roof span in celluloid. The front of the station, with its steps, awning and clock tower is particularly realistic.

The Through Station shown on the right is an equally effective model, built up from the same components and ideal for through running on a large layout. **Price 25/-**

The components of the above Outfit can be purchased separately at the following prices:

				Price
Station Building, D2	...	...	each	**8/6**
Arched Roof, D2	...	...	"	**10/-**
Centre Platform, D2	...	...	"	**11d.**
Side Platform, D2	...	...	pair	**3/3**
Centre Platform Ramps, D2	...	each	**4d.**
Side Platform Ramps, D2	...	"	**3d.**
Platform Buffers—Single, D1	...	"	**6d.**
Platform Buffers—Double, D2	...	"	**1/-**

Terminal Station

MAIN LINE STATION D1

A particularly fine model in wood of a modern-style station. It is long enough to accommodate a three-coach train, and is supplied with printed gummed slips giving a choice of four names— "Berwick" (L.N.E.R.), "Penrith" (L.M.S.), "Truro" (G.W.R.) and "Ashford" (S.R.). Size: Length 24in., width 4⅛in., height 3⅞in. **Price 6/9**

ISLAND PLATFORM D1

This platform can be used separately between two tracks, or in conjunction with the Main Line Station, which it resembles in design and construction. Size: Length 24in., width 2⅝in., height 2⅞in. **Price 4/-**

GOODS DEPOT D1

A realistic depot for goods traffic in the same style as the Main Line Station and Island Platform. Size: Length 12in., width 4in., height 2½in. **Price 4/-**

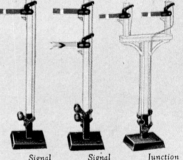

SIGNAL CABIN D1

A typical example in wood of a medium-sized signal cabin. Supplied with four gummed slips printed with the names "Berwick", "Penrith", "Truro" and "Ashford." **Price 11d.**

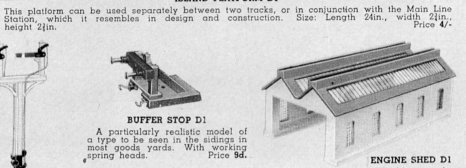

Signal D1   *Signal D2*   *Junction Signal D3*

All Hornby-Dublo signals carry semaphores of the latest upper-quadrant type.

SINGLE ARM SIGNAL D1
"Home" (as illustrated) or "Distant" **Price 1/-**

*SINGLE ARM SIGNAL ED1
Electrically Operated. **Price 3/6**

DOUBLE ARM SIGNAL D2
"Home" and "Distant" **Price 1/3**

*DOUBLE ARM SIGNAL ED2
Electrically Operated. **Price 6/-**

JUNCTION SIGNAL D3
"Home" (as illustrated) or "Distant" **Price 1/6 each**

*JUNCTION SIGNAL ED3
Electrically Operated. **Price 6/3**

* Designed to work off a Dublo Transformer or D.C. Converter. The same Transformer or Converter that supplies current to the Trains can be used. The Signals are controlled by means of the Switch D1.

BUFFER STOP D1

A particularly realistic model of a type to be seen in the sidings in most goods yards. With working spring heads. **Price 9d.**

MINIATURE PASSENGERS D2

The Set includes three men and three women passengers. **Price 1/-**

MINIATURE RAILWAY STAFF D1

This Set consists of six figures, Driver, Porter, Ticket Collector, Stationmaster, Guard and Shunter. **Price 1/-**

ENGINE SHED D1

An attractive two-road Building, modern in style, with windows along each side, and a roof glazed with celluloid, in two bays each with smoke vent. The Shed will accommodate two Hornby-Dublo Express Locomotives and their Tenders. **Price 10/6**

FOOTBRIDGE D1

Attractive model of an up-to-date reinforced concrete footbridge. It spans a double track, and is complete with stairways and intermediate landings. **Price 3/6**

TUNNEL D1 (Short)

This Tunnel is 5½in. long and is suitable for either curved or straight track. **Price 1/3**

TUNNEL D2 (Long)

This Tunnel is 11½in. long. It can only be used on straight track. **Price 1/8**

Hornby-Dublo Trains are one seventy-sixth of the size of real trains. They enable you to lay out a complete railway on your dining table!

MANUFACTURED BY MECCANO LTD., BINNS ROAD, LIVERPOOL 13

Fig. 75

123

UNTIL THE MID-1930s Hornby Gauge '0' Trains were an obvious choice for anyone wanting a train set, or a more ambitious layout in the home. In order to develop a really comprehensive system however, a large room was needed, preferably set aside as a permanent railway room. Many boys had to be content with temporary layouts which took an hour or more to set up on the dining room floor, only to be dismantled when father came home for his tea! The need for a temporary system dictated many of the features of Hornby Trains such as sharp curves and out-of-scale accessories.

Shortly before World War 2, Meccano Ltd developed a model railway system to a smaller scale with the aim of enabling an interesting layout to be set out on a normal-size dining table. The result was Hornby Dublo, announced in the September 1938 issue of *Meccano Magazine*. Dublo was Hornby's trade name for gauge '00', a system whose gauge, ie, the distance between the rails – 16.5mm was approximately half that of Gauge '0'. This meant that a layout needing a space of, say, 4metres by 2metres in gauge '0' could be reproduced in Dublo on the average extended dining room table, and this feature was emphasised in Meccano Ltd's advertising.

There was more to Dublo however, than merely saving space; from the start, the system was designed to incorporate many advanced model railway features. The electric motors fitted to Dublo engines were DC, allowing a much better degree of control than with the AC type used in some rival systems. Pre-war Dublo track had solid brass rails although later this was changed to steel. The relationship of Dublo wheels to track was obviously carefully worked out at Binns Road because Dublo trains negotiated points more smoothly than most. A rather surprising thing was the provision of both clockwork and electric locomotives with the appropriate track. One would have supposed that by 1938 most houses had electricity, and in any case, Dublo trains could easily be operated from batteries.

The initial releases enabled an interesting railway system to be assembled (see pages 117–122). The two die-cast locomotives were both LNER types; the streamlined pacific 'Sir Nigel Gresley' – then the pride of that line – and an 0–6–2 tank locomotive closely resembling the N2 class which was also available in the colours of the other three railway companies. Passenger stock took the form of a tinprinted LNER corridor coach and a two-coach articulated unit. Goods vans, open wagons and a brake van for each railway company completed

124

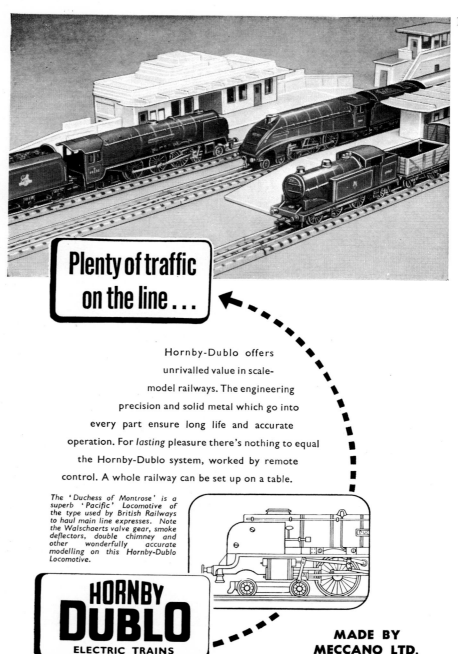

Fig. 76

Plenty of traffic on the line . . .

Hornby-Dublo offers unrivalled value in scale-model railways. The engineering precision and solid metal which go into every part ensure long life and accurate operation. For *lasting* pleasure there's nothing to equal the Hornby-Dublo system, worked by remote control. A whole railway can be set up on a table.

The 'Duchess of Montrose' is a superb 'Pacific' Locomotive of the type used by British Railways to haul main line expresses. Note the Walschaerts valve gear, smoke deflectors, double chimney and other wonderfully accurate modelling on this Hornby-Dublo Locomotive.

HORNBY DUBLO ELECTRIC TRAINS

MADE BY MECCANO LTD.

Fig. 77

A *wide variety of*
HORNBY DUBLO
Gauge '00' Rolling Stock
makes railway working more fun

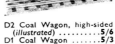

D2 Coal Wagon, high-sided
(*illustrated*) **5/6**
D1 Coal Wagon **5/3**

Fig. 78

SOUTHERN 2594

D1 Bogie Bolster Wagon **7/6**

D1 High Capacity Wagon **7/6**

Fig. 79

D1 Meat Van **4/11**

D1 Goods Brake Van B.R. (L.M.R.) **6/9**

D1 Fish Van...........**4/11**

D1 Open Wagon (*illustrated*) **4/4**
D2 High-sided Wagon......**4/8**

D1 Goods Van.......**4/11**

D1 Oil Tank Wagon ...**5/3**

D1 Horse Box **4/11**

D2 Mineral Wagon....**4/11**

D1 Cattle Truck **4/11**

D11 Coach Brake/3rd B.R. (E.R.).....**9/-**

D12 Coach 1st/3rd B.R. (L.M.R.)....**12/9**

Fig. 80

ROYAL MAIL

the range of rolling stock for 1938. Station buildings were of wood, a new departure for Hornby; and tunnels, signals and miniature figures were also available.

During 1939, there were various additions to the Dublo range, including items actually introduced after the outbreak of war. Three attractive tank wagons, a variety of different vans,

and a high-capacity bogie wagon augmented the original rolling stock. A large station complete with covered section appeared, together with an engine shed, in the fateful month of September 1939. By February 1940, Dublo was being advertised as the 'ideal blackout hobby for boys and their fathers', and in that month electrically operated points and signals were introduced. Meccano Ltd had scheduled their LMS Duchess locomotive for late 1940, and some present day collectors claim that it actually appeared. However, the

Company's official position is that it did *not* appear on the market until after the war.

Hornby Dublo re-appeared in December 1947. Only three sets were available initially; two pre-war plus the long awaited 'Duchess of Atholl' with two LMS coaches. An improved type of coupling was fitted to the new trains, the LNER pacific was modified to bring it into line with the real engine, and two separate coaches replaced the articulated unit previously included in the set.

Times were hard, materials were in short supply, and it was some while before additions were made to the Dublo range. In the early 1950s demand was very much greater than supply, and queues formed in some shops when the quota of Dublo arrived.

By 1949, the catalogue listed most of the vans and wagons of the immediate pre-war period together with a new range of die-cast station buildings. The price of the 'Duchess of Atholl' set was nearly £8 in 1952, a sizable sum for an ordinary family. During the next three years, only a few minor items appeared, such as a water crane, a loading gauge and an uncoupling rail, although supplies did gradually become more plentiful. During the following year, all Hornby Dublo locomotives, coaches and wagons were altered to British Railways livery, the two express engines becoming the 'Duchess of Montrose' and the 'Silver King' both finished in glossy paint, (though the Company soon reverted to matt finish). Several new die-cast wagons appeared, including mineral and bogie bolster wagons. Electrically operated points and signals were re-introduced, and with the supply position improving, it was possible to build an attractive layout using Dublo material.

During the next few years, the system expanded rapidly. Two new engines appeared, a BR 2–6–4 tank and a Western Region 'Castle' class, bringing the total Dublo loco stud to five. Coaches now included BR maroon-and-cream, and Western Region liveried varieties, corridor and surburban, while new wagons in both tinplate and die-cast styles had appeared. A working novelty was the TPO (Travelling Post Office) Mail Van (Fig. 80) which picked up and dropped miniature mail bags whilst on the move.

The year 1958 was a significant one in Dublo history as it saw the introduction of the first diesel and the first of a series of plastic rolling stock. A new steam-outline engine also appeared in that year, the LMR 8F freight loco. The first of the super-detail series of plastic vehicles was a 20-ton bulk grain wagon to be followed by other wagons, vans and goods brakes. These magnificent items of rolling stock had only one fault; they made the standard tinplate wagons look inferior by comparison!

In 1959, a major event in the Dublo world was the introduction of 'two-rail' track and locomotives. This system, by which current is picked up and returned through the wheels from the two running rails, was already being used by other manufacturers in Britain and abroad. For a time Hornby produced both the three- and two-rail systems side by side, but the former was eventually dropped. Many enthusiasts, consider that Meccano Ltd were ill-advised to make this change, and that they should have continued to develop the original system. Although this view is based more on nostalgia than on commercial considerations, it is interesting to note that Hornby's oldest rival, Märklin, was able to continue with its somewhat out-dated centre stud pick-up system.

The last Hornby Dublo catalogue to be printed appeared in 1964, and illustrated the final two-rail range. Eight steam outline engines were included, the later ones being Southern Region types, a 'West Country', and an 0–6–0 tank. Four diesel locomotives were available, and the last Dublo loco of all – an electric overhead pantograph type. A large range of coaches included Pullman and sleeping cars, all with tinplate sides and detailed plastic ends and roofs. No less than thirty-five goods vehicles were listed, all plastic or die-cast, while the buildings were now plastic, sold in kit form for simple assembly with nuts and bolts.

In 1965, Tri-ang, who had taken over the Meccano factory, issued a folder in which they announced that six Dublo engines and several accessories would be incorporated into their own Tri-ang Railways System, but in the event, these items were soon deleted from that system.

So ended what was probably the finest model railway system ever to be produced in Britain, inaugurated in 1938 and discontinued in 1965. At the time of writing, collectors are busily buying-up the considerable quantities of Hornby Dublo still to be found on the second-hand market. Fortunately it was very robust and usually owned by older boys, so much has survived in excellent condition. Interest in the system is growing on the part of collectors, and a later volume in this series will be devoted entirely to this subject.

Fig. 81

Fig. 85

New Modelled Miniatures Sets
Trains, Motor Vehicles, and Farm Animals

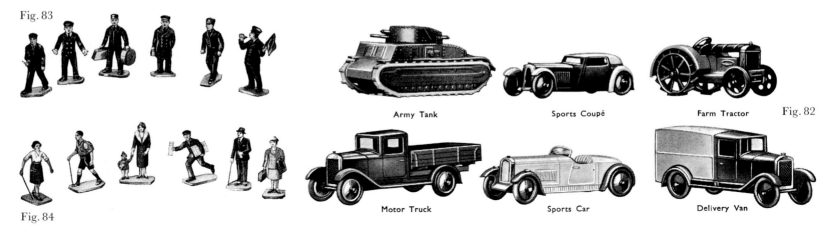

Fig. 83

Fig. 84

Army Tank	Sports Coupé	Farm Tractor
Motor Truck	Sports Car	Delivery Van

Fig. 82

Fig. 86

Fig. 87

Fig. 88

Modelled Miniatures No. 13, "Hall's
Distemper." This is a novel accessory
for lineside use.

TO THE NAMES 'Meccano' and 'Hornby Trains', which became
household words, must be added the third: Dinky Toys.
Probably better known after the Second World War in the form
of model cars and lorries, they actually first appeared at the end
of 1931 when they were called 'Modelled Miniatures'.

The first set, designated Modelled Miniatures No. 1 (Fig. 83)
consisted of six cast figures representing a station master, ticket
collector, guard, engine driver and two porters. These models
were beautifully painted, presumably by hand, and the fine
details of their faces and uniforms withstood examination even
under a magnifying glass. A set of farm animals (Fig. 85) and a
set of passengers (Fig. 84) were the next two in the series, the
latter including a male and female hiker, so typical of the 1930s.
Further sets of railwaymen were produced by painting some of
the original station staff figures in different styles, thus the
station porter became, in turn, both a hotel porter and a fitter!

Then in December 1933, as a direct response to America's
'Tootsie Toys', the first vehicles (Fig. 82) were introduced in a
set of six: an army tank, a tractor, two cars, a lorry and a van.
These were intended as line-side effects for model railways, and
the presence of the tank is hard to explain, unless Meccano Ltd
had cast an eye on the cheap lead models made by competitors.

REALISTIC DESIGNS

Fig. 89

The road vehicles did not represent any particular cars or commercial vehicles, and were fitted with solid metal wheels. The complete set of six sold for 4/- in 1933. A totally different set was a small model train of the 'push-along' variety comprising a tank engine and four wagons.

The name 'Dinky Toys', or rather 'Meccano Dinky Toys', was used for the first time in April 1934. The word 'Meccano' was later dropped, and these toys have been known by the shorter name ever since. The April 1934 *Meccano Magazine* announced new vehicles, some of which were now fitted with rubber tyres. The open racing car, which became a firm favourite for playground races, appeared then, as did the cars in the No. 24 series which are now collectors' pieces along with most other pre-war Dinky Toys. The seven cars making up set No. 24 (the eighth was an ambulance) were freelance models called simply 'sports tourer', etc, but they were closely based on real cars, and the later versions had different radiators and were stamped with real car names. A set of commercial vehicles was also produced, together with new versions of the original van, each finished in the style of a well-known company. A disadvantage of these vehicles from the model railwayman's point of view, was that they were not built to any particular scale. The commerical vehicles were about right for '00' gauge,

Fig. 90

Dinky Toys No. 60r
EMPIRE FLYING BOAT "CALEDONIA"
This is a splendid model of the famous Empire Flying Boat that made the experimental flights across the Atlantic recently, in preparation for a regular air service between this country and America. The "*Caledonia*" has a wing span of 114 ft., and is fitted with four Bristol "Pegasus X" engines that give it a top speed of nearly 200 m.p.h.
Models of five other Empire Flying Boats—"*Canopus*," "*Corsair*," "*Challenger*," "*Centurion*" and "*Cambria*" will be available shortly. Price 1/- each

Fig. 91

but the cars were too big for this and too small for gauge '0', the size of contemporary Hornby Trains. However, as contemporary model railway photographs illustrate, modellers were not so fussy about scale in the 1930s, and items built to suit gauges '00', '0' and '1' could often be seen mixed indiscriminately on model railway layouts.

Like all Meccano products, the early Dinky Toys were beautifully painted and looked very smart with their white tyres. At this time the idea of treating Dinky Toys as collectables took root and has continued ever since. Lucky indeed was the boy in 1934 who had the foresight to keep his Dinky cars in mint condition rather than give them away or push them around the playground.

During the next five years, Meccano Ltd produced a large number of Dinky Toys which could be divided conveniently into several themes. The human figures were re-moulded to a slightly smaller scale, and eventually consisted of station staff, passengers, engineering staff and hotel employees. In addition there were postmen, policemen, AA and RAC men, and the original farm animals plus a shepherd, dressed in a smock and carrying a crook in the style of the previous century!

Other themes were represented by aeroplanes and ships, being based on real prototypes and modelled to a very small scale. Civilian and military aircraft were also represented, and the series included such prestige items as the Empire Flying Boat (Fig. 90). Pride of place in the ship series was held by a model of the *Queen Mary* (Fig. 92), with a de luxe version

available in a presentation box. Fitted with rollers, it could be propelled across the 'sea' by youthful owners.

The small-scale Dinky Toy railway trains now included models of the GWR Rail Car and a streamlined train representing the LNER *Silver Jubilee* (Fig. 91). However, the largest group in the Dinky Toy series has always been road vehicles, and the cars in the No. 24 set were joined by a group of British saloons, and later a most attractive American car set. Models of buses and trains, fire engines and a 'mechanical horse' and trailer augmented the original set of commercial vehicles.

As 1939 approached, military models began to appear. The army series had tanks, lorries and scout cars together with appropriate personnel, and some of the aeroplanes appeared later with a camouflage finish.

All these and more Dinky Toys were available up to the early war years, and some new models were still introduced after the hostilities had begun. As with other Meccano products, present-day collectors still argue as to what was actually produced during the time immediately before toy production ceased and in the early years of its resumption. Mention should also be made of the most famous Dinky Toy of all, the Triumph Dolomite Sports Car of 1940. Most collectors agree that this model, although advertised, never actually appeared, nonetheless a few test samples may have been produced. It has now entered the folklore of Dinky Toys where conjecture is almost as exciting as the real object.

Fig. 92

Fig. 93

Have you seen the NEW **DINKY SUPERTOYS?**

These wonderful models are similar in style to the famous Dinky Toys, but much larger. The Foden Wagon, for instance, is 7½" long, and the Guy Lorry 5¼" long. The great amount of accurate detail included gives the models a strikingly realistic appearance.

●

	Price incl. Tax
No. 501 Foden Diesel 8-wheel Wagon	10/-
No. 502 Foden Flat Truck	10/-
No. 503 Foden Flat Truck with tailboard	10/-
No. 511 Guy 4-ton Lorry	7/-
No. 512 Guy Flat Truck	7/-
No. 513 Guy Flat Truck with tailboard	7/-
No. 701 Shetland Flying Boat	7/6

Made in England by **MECCANO LIMITED**

Dinky Supertoys No. 501 Foden Diesel 8-wheel Wagon

Dinky Supertoys No. 502 Foden Flat Truck

Dinky Supertoys No. 511 Guy 4-ton Lorry

Dinky Supertoys No. 701 "Shetland" Flying Boat

ALTHOUGH THE EARLIEST post-war Dinky Toys were almost certainly 'unfrozen' war-time stocks, Meccano Ltd concentrated on new models as soon as conditions allowed. In April 1946, the first new Dinky Toy was announced: a Jeep in military style. This was quickly followed by three new cars and two new aeroplanes. Some pre-war, re-issues, appeared next, although with slight changes, such as dished wheels on which all tyres were now black instead of the pre-war white.

In October 1947, the inside cover of the *Meccano Magazine* carried an announcement of Dinky Supertoys (Fig. 93) which, as the text said, were 'similar to Dinky Toys but much larger'. The first two were Foden eight-wheeled vehicles, a wagon, and a flat truck. They were beautiful models about 190mm long, packed in individual blue boxes with a picture of the vehicle on the lid. The price was 10/- each, which was rather expensive, by 1947 standards, when the average price of similar toys was around 2/6d.

Supertoy commercial vehicles had such an attractive appearance that they appealed to adults as well as children, and thus prompted 'impulse buying'. Other road vehicles and a model flying-boat were added to the Supertoy range during the following months, while at the same time, new additions to the standard Dinky Toy series included cars, buses, a modern tractor and a diesel roller.

A new departure in June 1948 was the introduction of a garden roller to be followed by two models of lawn mowers, a sack truck, and a wheelbarrow. These models – larger in scale than existing Dinky or Supertoys – were presumably introduced for their play value rather than to augment any particular theme. To the Supertoy range meanwhile had been added a crawler tractor, a dumper truck, and a petrol tanker.

In December 1948, the *Meccano Magazine* began to feature articles on Dinky Toys, which thereafter became a regular feature. The first article described that month's new issues: the

.Fig. 94

Supertoy Tanker and the Standard Vanguard saloon. A good marketing move by Meccano Ltd was to run a feature on, say, bulldozers in the magazine, followed in the next month by an announcement of a Dinky Supertoy bulldozer, to which most of that month's Dinky Toy article was devoted.

Throughout 1949, new Dinky and Supertoys were announced and in December three new models were introduced: a Supertoy van, (available in several finishes) a working mobile crane, and a three-wheel farm truck. The early 1950s were years of shortages, especially of metal, and although new Dinky Toys did not appear every month, many new lines were introduced including smaller cars and lorries. During 1950, Meccano Ltd temporarily dropped the 'Supertoy' label, possibly due to difficulty in differentiating between a Dinky Toy and a Supertoy.

In June 1952, the pre-war station figures and farm animals were re-introduced alongside two new sets of figures to a smaller size more-suited to '00' gauge. Also re-introduced were five aeroplanes and three racing cars, one of which, the small open racer, dated back to 1934. The following year, a set of contemporary racing cars was introduced which proved very popular. These were to a larger scale than previous racing cars, each with a driver, and wheels 'borrowed' from the Supertoy lorries.

In the *Meccano Magazine* for October 1953, an announcement was made of a reduction in the price of Dinky Toys due to 'a new Works with a most up-to-date plant, resulting in improved methods of production'. This new works was at Speke, near Liverpool Airport. At the end of 1953, a series of army models began with the introduction of the Scout Car, finished in army green. Notable models in 1954 were the Jaguar XK120 and seven additional army vehicles.

In 1955, the 'Supertoy' label was re-introduced, but this time being applied only to the larger vehicles, the medium sized vans and lorries continuing as Dinky toys. From March of that year, the *Meccano Magazine* began to illustrate new Dinky Toy issues in full colour on the back cover. In January 1956, under the banner 'Gayer than ever', Dinky cars went into vivid two-tone finishes. This followed the American lead fashion in real cars of the time, when it was a case of obtaining your Ford in any colour, so long as it was caramel and pastel pink!

A range that was of interest to the model railway man was that introduced in December 1957 and known as Dublo Dinky

Toys. These were cars, lorries and vans made to '00' scale and intended as lineside effects for Hornby Dublo Trains.

From April 1958, Dinky cars were fitted with plastic windows, in response to Mettoy's Corgi series, and in February 1959, the Dinky Rolls Royce Silver Wraith appeared with a host of special features. These included independent suspension, a feature that not even the real car possessed. The Corporal Missile Rocket Launcher (which actually fired nylon rockets) was introduced at the end of 1959.

The 1960s were years of more and more Dinky 'features'. Car doors, windows and boots that opened, and on some models even head and tail lights, and on fire engines there were lights which flashed as the model was pushed along.

In 1964, Meccano Ltd was taken over by Lines Bros. No great changes were detected in Dinky Toys around that period, but deletions of the older models were accelerated. To see how the original Company's Dinky Toy policy had developed it is worth reviewing the models introduced during the year prior to the takeover.

Fig. 95

133

Fig. 96

As usual, cars were the favourite models, and the year began with a 'scoop' when the Dinky version of the Triumph 2000 coincided with the release of the real car. Other cars followed, some with Dinky 'firsts' like the Corsair with 'jewelled headlights', and the Mercedes 600 with boot, bonnet, and all four doors opening.

Dinky entered the vintage stakes in 1964 with a Model 'T' Ford complete with driver and passenger in period dress (Fig. 94). At Christmas, a special version of this model appeared with a Santa Claus in the driving seat. One of the last models to be called a 'Supertoy' before Meccano Ltd dropped the name for the second and final time, was the Vega Luxury Touring Coach. This model had flashing indicators, which operated when it was steered in the appropriate direction. A Routemaster bus, with internal detail, driver and 'clippie' appeared in June 1964, and is still available at the time of writing. A very unusual model was an eight-wheeled chassis with moving prop shaft, representing real vehicles seen on the roads before completion. Another rather surprising model was a loudspeaker van, on the side of which was the legend 'Vote for Somebody' (Fig. 95).

The Lines Bros take-over of Meccano Ltd changed many products and while this sounded the death knell for Hornby Trains, Dinky Toys survived, and new models, many of which are still available, are described in the next chapter.

Fig. 97

FROM 1965, NEW DINKY TOYS appeared fairly regularly every month, with cars still the main interest, closely followed by the machines of the fighting services and a sprinkling of models inspired by space fiction.

The Model 'T' Ford was followed by another vintage car, the bull-nose Morris, which was soon to be available, also as a comic version. Meccano Ltd did not make any further vintage cars, possibly due to competition from other die-cast car makers, who specialised in such models. However, many models of modern cars appeared over the next three years, the majority of them equipped with special features such as steering, removable luggage, opening doors, bonnets and boots. The Aston Martin model had simulated 'wire' wheels, and the Mini – in addition to opening doors – had front seats which tilted.

To lend truth to the statement that 'there is always something new from Dinky Toys', a model of an Army Para-Moke appeared in November 1966 complete with a parachute that really worked.

In 1967, the popular television marionette programmes of Gerry and Sylvia Anderson began to influence Dinky Toy production, and the first two models introduced were Lady Penelope's rocket-firing Rolls Royce 'FAB 1', and the Thunderbird 2 craft from the *Thunderbirds* series. These were soon followed by *Captain Scarlet's* Spectrum Pursuit Vehicle, and other futuristic craft.

The Dinky Cars of the late 1960s were mainly based on exotic sports models. Then, in June 1969, came 'Speedwheels'. An article in the next month's *Meccano Magazine* described them as follows: 'Speedwheels are free-rolling wheels incorporating a special low-friction bearing which when mounted on new style axles, runs more smoothly, more quietly and very much longer than anything previously fitted to a Dinky Toy'. The first model to carry the distinction of these wheels was the Pontiac Parisienne which also had retracting radio aerials.

In October 1969, to coincide with the film *Battle of Britain*, a Dinky Toy 'Spitfire' appeared with a propeller that could be driven by a battery-operated electric motor. In December of that year, another innovation was the 'Dragster', supplied with a starter unit, which was a spring device for projecting the dragster on its journey. Other action features introduced at about this time were retractable undercarriages for planes and a single-decker bus with an operating bell.

In 1972, Dinky Kits were introduced, each consisting of a set of parts to build a Dinky Toy similar to those already included in the range. The die-cast finished parts simply screwed together leaving the painting to the constructor, with a phial of paint included in the kit. Although of interest to more adult enthusiasts who could paint models – such as buses – in their own styles, youthful modellers must have found it very hard to obtain a finish approaching that of Meccano Ltd.

A review of Dinky Toys of the 1970s brings the story to a peak for thereafter model car production was to assume less significance. Cars, mainly of the sporting or luxury variety, still predominate all with special features including opening doors. The only car without opening doors was the NSU RO 80 but it had operating head and tail lights with a solid body to house the batteries.

The 'way-out' models, mainly based on Childrens' television programmes, include two self-propelling vehicles; Sam's Car with a clockwork mechanism (the only Dinky Toy to be so fitted), and the Pink Panther car with inertia drive. At the time of writing, six buses of various types and sizes, are available together with numerous breakdown, police and fire vehicles. There are many other commercial and construction vehicles from which to choose, and some, like the Coles Hydra Truck, are large elaborate productions with many working features. Lastly, representing the services, there are army vehicles, guns and tanks, to a larger scale than before, a Missile Firing ship and numerous aircraft.

The *Meccano Magazine* still carries a feature in each issue describing the latest models in 'Dinky Toy News'. A recent introduction has been a Ford Capri car built to a scale of one twenty-fifth, making it 180mm long – a far cry from the original cars – and a model which, it is assumed, will be the forerunner of others to this scale once again to meet specific competition, this time Italian. Two boats have also appeared recently; one, an Air Sea Rescue Launch, which has a separate life raft and 'ditched' pilot while another actually fires plastic shells. These boats, mounted on Speedwheels are obviously intended for 'serious' play.

Dinky Toys satisfy two distinct markets: children and adult collectors. Quite rightly Meccano Ltd built 'play value' into some Dinky Toys, hence the missile firing devices and Speedwheels. At the same time, car and commercial vehicle models are now so accurate that collectors buy them as soon as they appear. The pre-war model cars are crude by comparison, but they have a 'period' charm, and as with all things rarity enhances their desirability with collectors.

Fig. 98

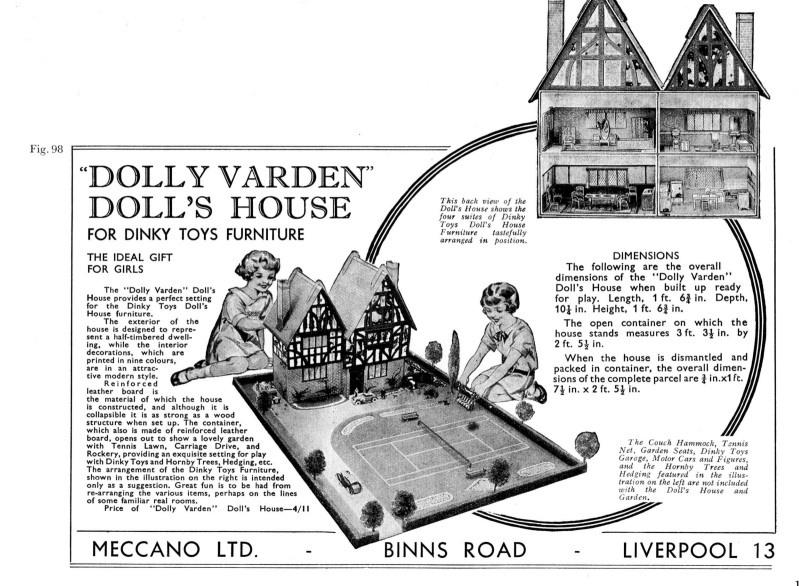

"DOLLY VARDEN" DOLL'S HOUSE

FOR DINKY TOYS FURNITURE

THE IDEAL GIFT FOR GIRLS

The "Dolly Varden" Doll's House provides a perfect setting for the Dinky Toys Doll's House furniture.

The exterior of the house is designed to represent a half-timbered dwelling, while the interior decorations, which are printed in nine colours, are in an attractive modern style.

Reinforced leather board is the material of which the house is constructed, and although it is collapsible it is as strong as a wood structure when set up. The container, which also is made of reinforced leather board, opens out to show a lovely garden with Tennis Lawn, Carriage Drive, and Rockery, providing an exquisite setting for play with Dinky Toys and Hornby Trees, Hedging, etc. The arrangement of the Dinky Toys Furniture, shown in the illustration on the right is intended only as a suggestion. Great fun is to be had from re-arranging the various items, perhaps on the lines of some familiar real rooms.

Price of "Dolly Varden" Doll's House—4/11

This back view of the Doll's House shows the four suites of Dinky Toys Doll's House Furniture tastefully arranged in position.

DIMENSIONS

The following are the overall dimensions of the "Dolly Varden" Doll's House when built up ready for play. Length, 1 ft. 6¾ in. Depth, 10¼ in. Height, 1 ft. 6¾ in.

The open container on which the house stands measures 3 ft. 3½ in. by 2 ft. 5½ in.

When the house is dismantled and packed in container, the overall dimensions of the complete parcel are ¾ in. x 1 ft. 7½ in. x 2 ft. 5½ in.

The Couch Hammock, Tennis Net, Garden Seats, Dinky Toys Garage, Motor Cars and Figures, and the Hornby Trees and Hedging featured in the illustration on the left are not included with the Doll's House and Garden.

MECCANO LTD. - BINNS ROAD - LIVERPOOL 13

Fig. 99

THIS BRIEF REVIEW of other Meccano products includes those which were short-lived, and those which were perhaps different in character from the main products described in this survey. The list is meant to be indicative rather than exhaustive.

Most Meccano products were intended primarily for boys, although a few girls have been Meccano enthusiasts and some have figured in the lists of prize-winners in Meccano contests. However, in July 1936, a product appeared which was designed especially for girls: the 'Dolly Varden' Doll's House (Fig. 98). Made of leather board, the house was collapsible, and the container opened up to form a base, arranged as a garden. The house itself represented a half-timbered dwelling, and four Dinky Toy furniture sets were available, separately, for bathroom, bedroom, dining room and kitchen. The original illustration showed a tennis net and a couch hammock, but these were never actually produced. The house was priced at 9/6d in 1936 but by 1939 – the last time it was advertised – it had been reduced to 4/11d. This doll's house is possibly the rarest of all Meccano's products and one of the few items I have not personally seen.

In June 1963, a circular jig-saw puzzle was produced, using illustrations from the coloured covers of *Meccano Magazines*. The centre showed a 'West Country' class locomotive, and the segments were pictures of traction engines, ships, trains and yachts. The jig-saw was made of cardboard, measuring 508mm in diameter, and contained five hundred pieces. Five years later, Meccano Ltd marketed a jig-saw puzzle-making machine. A small hand-driven machine, resembling a miniature vice, this tool cut card into shapes which could be varied by changing the angle of the card between cutting operations and by moving the card through varying distances.

Also appearing in 1963 were the 'Circuit 24' Racing Sets which were among the less successful of Meccano's imports. Sectional track pieces with the usual slot pick-up, were assembled into circuits on which the cars raced, controlled by hand-held units. This type of layout was very popular in the 1960s and several manufacturers were already established in this field. However the major difference with Circuit 24 cars was that instead of an electric motor, they had an electric oscillator, which propelled the vehicle via a ratchet wheel. Three types of car and a Go-Kart were available, with accessories such as fences, walls and a variety of track sections.

In March 1964, a very different product appeared called

Fig. 100

Fig. 101

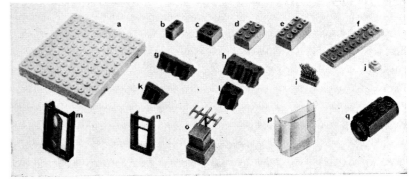

'Super-Skates'. These were roller skates without straps, available in one size only and suitable for children from four to fourteen. Special features were rubber wheels and a thumb screw adjustment, which, in conjunction with a spring-loaded front, ensured a good and rapid fit.

In July 1964, the Hornby Speedboats, referred to earlier, were joined by an exciting newcomer, the Hornby Hoverer (Fig. 99). This was a 15″ model of a hovercraft powered by a 'Glo-Plug' motor, retailing at £5. 12. 6d. It worked in a similar manner to the real craft and could either be free flown or tethered to a pole and flown in a circle.

New products were appearing thick and fast in 1964, and yet another new line for that year was Play-Doh. This was a modelling compound available in various bright colours, which, if returned to its container immediately after use, remained pliable, but which set hard if left in the air for several days. A press with a set of dies was supplied enabling various shapes to be produced. Play-Doh is still manufactured, although it is no longer associated with Meccano Ltd. Towards the end of 1964, 'Cliki' (Fig. 100) – a plastic building set – appeared, based on a series of interlocking blocks. There were two sets (both imported), Cliki and Cliki-Plus, the former building small houses and push-along toys, the latter enabling more engineering-type models, such as cranes, to be constructed. Features of Cliki were roof tiles and glazed windows, while Cliki-Plus outfits contained pulleys, cranks and hooks. The basic interlocking blocks bore a remarkable resemblance to Lego, a building toy which continues to enjoy great popularity.

Of Meccano's recent products, by far the most important – Plastic Meccano – was introduced in August 1965. This product retains the basic principles of its famous parent: Strips, Girders and Brackets, held together by Nuts and Bolts. In the case of Plastic Meccano however, all the parts are brightly coloured in yellow, red and blue and are extra large to enable them to be used by small children. Originally there were three sets, but the range of Plastic Meccano has been extended having proved popular for use in Childrens' Homes and Junior Schools. There are currently four basic sets in the series plus a 'Workbox' set. There are also two study sets for schools (not strictly Binns Road products, although packaged there), designed to teach elementary geometry and mechanics. Another development has been the use of Plastic Meccano with standard Meccano Parts. Meccano Ltd produce a flexible tank-type Track Set for use with either Plastic or Metal Meccano, and a plastic Sprocket provides the escapement wheel in the Meccano Clock Kit. Advanced modellers have also made use of other plastic parts, in particular the Gears.

In 1968 the company made miniature sewing machines for girls. Known as the Jones/Meccano Sewing Machine, it was based on full sized Jones machines and produced a lockstitch. Two models were available, one hand- and one electrically-operated selling at £6 and £9 respectively. The current models, with a modern streamlined metal casing, are called 'Starlet'. The electric version is battery operated incorporating a foot switch.

A very brief mention must be made here of three more post-war Meccano products. A delightful train set intended for the very young appeared in December 1965. Based on 'Percy the Small Engine' in the books by Rev W Awdry, it contained a plastic tank engine with a cheerful face on the smoke box door and two goods trucks. In 1968, a series of children's records was issued featuring well-known artists such as Johnny Morris and Muriel Young bearing the 'Pied Piper' label. A novelty produced recently is the Apollo Astrolite, a spinning-disc operated by cord stretched between the hands, which whistles and lights up as it spins.

The most recent Meccano product, at the time of writing, is Prima, aimed at the pre-school market and allied to Plastic Meccano. This product consists mainly of slotted plastic strips and discs from which very young children can make shapes by pushing them together. The No. 1 outfit simply consists of shaped pieces, while the No. 2 outfit has in additon, Axle Rods, Wheels and Connecting pieces. It is pleasing to record that the very latest Meccano product, like the first one seventy-five years ago, still helps children to exercise their inventiveness.

Fig. 102

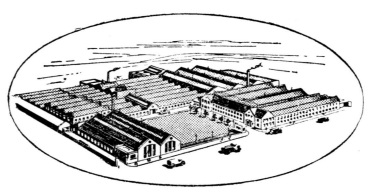

London Warehouse :
Meccano Ltd.,
5/6, Marshall Street,
London, W.1.

London Office & Warehouse :
Meccano Ltd.,
Walnut Tree Walk,
Kennington Road, London, S.E.11.

Meccano Agencies :

Algiers,	Bogota,
Amsterdam,	Bombay,
Auckland,	Brussels,
Barcelona,	Buenos Aires,
Basle,	Cape Town.

Head Office and Factory :
OLD SWAN, LIVERPOOL.

Meccano Company Inc.,
Elizabeth, New Jersey, U.S.A.

Meccano (France) Ltd.,
78-80 Rue Rébeval,
Paris XIXeme.

Meccano G.m.b.H.,
Alte Jacobstrasse 20-22 (Bergmannshof),
Berlin SW.68.

Canadian Office and Warehouse :
Meccano Ltd.,
45, Colborne Street, Toronto.

Meccano Agencies :

Constantinople,	Malta,
Durban,	Monte Video,
Genoa,	Oslo,
Iquitos,	Stockholm,
Johannesburg,	Sydney.

DURING ITS HISTORY, Meccano Ltd had several overseas factories (Fig. 102), in addition to Meccano being made under licence in other countries. In retrospect, the main interest in the products of these factories is the extent to which they differed from those of Liverpool.

Meccano had an American Company with a factory located in New Jersey. From 1920 until 1928, Meccano and Hornby Trains were made there, after which, following lengthy patent litigation, the business was sold to the A C Gilbert Company who made products bearing the Meccano name – but differing from those of the parent company – for sale only in the United States.

The American catalogue shows American Meccano as similar to the Liverpool product, except for minor variations such as electric motors. However an American-style Hornby Train, different from any produced in Liverpool, was on sale for a few years in the United States. The clockwork locomotive was something like the standard Hornby M1 in general construction, but had typical American features such as bell, headlamp and cowcatcher. Finished in red or green, the loco and tender bore the number 2527, and the couplings were simply the combined hook-and-loop type. The passenger car was a four wheeled Pullman-type, coloured green or yellow, with the names 'Washington', 'Madison' or 'Jefferson'. There were three freight vehicles, a yellow box car, a red tank wagon and a caboose, finished in green or brown. American rolling stock became familiar in this country when, following the

141

closing of business in New Jersey, American-style goods and passenger vehicles were sold in the UK refitted with British couplings.

After 1928, the Meccano factory in New Jersey turned out several products which included Meccano standard parts together with some of new design. Snap Rivets sets contained standard, X series, and new design parts, assembled by snap rivets instead of Nuts and Bolts. Shipbuilding outfits combined Meccano parts with a special hull, which enabled ships to be built which actually floated. Before the Meccano name was dropped by the American company, other unrelated products, including microscopes and model greenhouses, were made.

The French Meccano factory at Bobigny has a long history. Production now centred at Calais, still continues although Meccano France is no longer a subsidiary of Meccano Limited. In pre-war days, French Meccano resembled its British counterpart except for minor variations, but there were interesting differences in French Hornby Trains. Locomotives were similar to Binns Road products although naturally they were painted and lettered in French styles. Vans and wagons were also similar, although most could be obtained fitted with the characteristic 'vigie' or brakeman's hut. Signals were of French design, and an interesting set – never duplicated in this country – consisted of four different whistles, one for each of the main French railways.

After World War 2, French products diverged from those of Liverpool. Meccano continued, painted until very recently in blue and gold, with a few parts in red. Post-war French Hornby was quite different from the British product. Electric as well as clockwork trains were available in Gauge '0', and up to 1956 these included a streamlined 4–4–2 locomotive with matching coaches, in additon to four-wheeled steam- and electric-outline locomotives which continued to be made for some years after that date. Rolling stock was typically French in style and included four-wheeled and bogie coaches, vans and wagons. Solid cast-metal wheels and an automatic coupling of similar, but shorter style to the British Standard type, were fitted. Several wooden buildings were included in the range of accessories, and the larger two-storey station was particularly attractive.

The smaller French Hornby system, corresponding to Dublo, was called 'AcHo'. The name was derived from 'H0' (Half 0), a Continental scale slightly smaller than '00' but using

the same gauge of track. In 1961, several items from the French range were made available in Britain for use on Dublo two-rail layouts. The steam outline locomotive was a 2–6–2 Tank of continental design sporting a multiplicity of domes and outside pipes on the boiler. Another attractive loco was the SNCF B16000 overhead electric type, complete with two pantographs. Finished in grey, it was a massive and powerful locomotive and long bow-ended, green SNCF coaches were available for haulage by this loco. A fine main line Co Co Diesel was also offered and goods rolling stock resembled the Dublo SD series, moulded in plastic to mainly SNCF designs. Station buildings, also of plastic, were most attractive, and the main line station had an imposing entrance and even included a sunken garden.

A different range of Dinky Toys is made by the French Factory, and as might be expected, cars by Simca and Peugeot predominate, although a sprinkling of American saloons can also be found. Many French Dinky vehicles have white tyres like the pre-war British types. Among some interesting commercial vehicles perhaps the most attractive was a fire engine with a delightfully old-fashioned open cab. Several French Dinky toys including Berliet lorries and the 2CV Citroën car were on sale in Britain for a time.

Meccano parts have also been made in other countries under licence. In Spain, until 1960, they were manufactured by a company called Poch, whose series included parts long obsolete from the standard Liverpool range, such as Sand Rollers and Train Couplings, the latter being sought by enthusiasts as replacement fittings for Hornby Trains of the 1928–30 period.

In Argentina, Exacto SRL still manufactures Meccano parts under licence. Their products cover seventy-five percent of the Liverpool range plus some special parts. Included among the latter are Strips, Angle Girders and Plates of non-Liverpool-standard sizes, and parts now obsolete in the UK. Argentine Meccano is made in grey, yellow and blue.

This has been, of necessity, a brief survey of overseas Meccano products. Many, because they were indistinguishable from the UK types, have already been covered in earlier chapters. Obsolete items of foreign manufacture are of course extremely rare, and of great interest to the collector. The American Hornby Locomotive for example, is hard to find even in the United States, where the hobby of collecting old toys has achieved even greater popularity than in Britain.

Fig. 103

IN THE 1930s the *Meccano Magazine* was far more than an advertising medium for Meccano products and a manual of hints on how to use them. It was both these but also a lot more. Running to over one hundred pages at its peak, it was, with its coloured cover, a monthly source of delight to its many thousands of readers. Articles and pictures dealt with all those things which interested boys: models, toys, sport, engineering wonders, stamps, photography and even a page of jokes called 'Fireside Fun'.

The first issue of *Meccano Magazine* came out in September 1916. In a message to Meccano boys, Frank Hornby told of the rapid growth of the Meccano hobby in the fifteen years since its invention. The rest of the four-page issue was devoted to descriptions of models, recently introduced parts, and a model-building contest with a £50 first prize. Several articles were merely advertisements for Meccano, including one that

said 'Meccano Beats Germans Hollow'; dubious advertising, but one must remember it was 1916!

The first Meccano Magazines were free, postage only being charged. Issues were produced bi-monthly until July-August 1922, by which time the Magazine had grown to eight pages and the cost was 1d. From September 1922, it was decided to publish the magazine monthly, and at that time the publication had a line-drawn cover in black and white. In 1924, the price rose to 2d, and the first coloured cover was introduced. With an ever increasing number of pages, the price went up to 3d in 1925 and 6d in 1927. By this time the contents had changed from matters of a purely model-building interest to the well-remembered format of the 20s and 30s. Inside the front cover and on both sides of the back cover were full-page advertisements, usually for Meccano or Hornby Trains, but sometimes the products of other manufacturers were carried.

"Meccano Magazine"

RAILWAYS
COMPETITIONS
AERONAUTICS
LATEST PATENTS

WONDERFUL
MACHINERY
LIVES OF FAMOUS
INVENTORS
ELECTRICITY
FAMOUS BRIDGES

The " Meccano Magazine " is the Meccano boy's newspaper. He reads it regularly and corresponds with his friend the Editor when he feels inclined.

The Magazine tells him of the latest Meccano models ; what Meccano Clubs are doing ; how to correspond with other Meccano boys ; the Competitions that are running. It contains splendid articles on such subjects as Railways, Famous Engineers and Inventors, Electricity, Bridges, Cranes, Wonderful Machinery, Aeroplanes, Latest Patents, Radio, Stamps, Photography, Books and other topics of interest to boys, including suggestions for new Meccano

parts and correspondence columns in which the Editor replies to his readers' enquiries. The publishing date is the 1st of each month.

Write to the Editor, " Meccano Magazine," Binns Road, Liverpool, enclosing 6d. in stamps. He will then forward a specimen copy of the " M.M.", post free. If you wish to become a regular subscriber the rates are 4/– for six issues or 8/– for twelve issues, post free.

If you prefer to do so, you may order the Magazine from your Meccano dealer or from any newsagent or bookstall, price 6d. Order early to avoid disappointment.

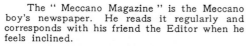

A Fine Engineering Monthly for Boys

Fig. 104

Some twelve more pages of advertisements appeared in each magazine, and the names of the regular ones – Bowman Steam Engines, Seccotine, Lott's Bricks, Harbutt's Plasticine – must have been known to every schoolboy of that period. Their appearance could be relied upon, month after month.

Regular articles in 1927 included (in serial form) Frank Hornby's tour around the world, 'Lives of Famous Inventors', 'Air News', 'Railway News', 'Engineering News', and 'Stamp Gossip'. Meccano pages included well established features like 'New Models', 'In Reply' and 'Suggestion Section', but as yet there were no pages devoted to Hornby Trains.

The Magazine's format remained basically the same up to World War 2. The quality of the coloured covers improved during the 1930s and some very striking ones were produced. Regular articles on Hornby Gauge '0' – and later Dublo Trains – were joined from time to time by features on other Meccano products like Kemex Sets, Elektron Sets and Hornby Speed Boats. Advertisements were now placed at both front and back of the magazine so that they could be omitted, if desired, when binding into yearly volumes. A large percentage of advertisements were now for the increased range of Meccano products, but Hamleys, Lotts and Tri-ang usually took full-page spaces.

144

Fig. 105

145

The Editor of the *Meccano Magazine* was not named in pre-war issues but we now know that up to 1924 it was Frank Hornby, Ellison Hawkes took over until 1932 and W H McCormick from that date and right through the wartime period.

For a time after September 1939, the magazine continued as before. The format remained unchanged, although the number of pages fell to fifty by the end of 1939, and then to thirty-five by the end of 1940. Prices of Meccano products were advertised with purchase tax shown separately, and of course articles took on a war-time flavour with descriptions of life in the services, and a feature on 'Leaders in the War'. By December 1941, the number of pages had been reduced to thirty, and the Editor announced that the following month's issue would be in 'pocket' size instead of the usual 280 × 203mm. In the event, this size – 203 × 140mm – continued up to the end of 1960. As the war dragged on, the magazine shrunk to twenty pages or on occasion, less. Meccano products together with all metal toys ceased, but articles on Meccano and Hornby Trains continued, along with many of the old features and the coloured cover. The issue for June 1945, announcing VE Day, still carried two train articles and two on Meccano. The back cover announced that the famous products would soon be back. This was repeated every month until December 1945 when the return of some Meccano Sets and Dinky Toys was promised for Christmas, though the Gauge '0' trains did not re-appear for yet another year. The issue for December 1946 contained forty-two pages, with many of the old advertisements alongside those of Meccano Ltd.

Paper, as well as metal, was in short supply in the years that followed, and it was not until 1953 that the magazine began to resemble its old-self, with sixty pages, improved paper and photographs, and advertisements front and back as in earlier days. The Editor, at this time, although still anonymous, was Frank Riley, and the magazine was to undergo little change up to December 1960. From the next month's issue however, there were major changes. The size was enlarged to 240 × 190mm, Geoffrey Byrom became Editor and, although not apparent to the reader, the publishers changed from Meccano Ltd to the International Publishing Corporation. However, advertisements for Meccano products (now in colour) appeared on the inside and on the back cover, and articles on Meccano and Hornby Trains could still be found alongside an increasing number of general interest articles.

In January 1964, publication was taken over by Thomas Skinner and Co, and readers were promised a 'new look' magazine. This came with the March issue, the Editor remained the same but the magazine reverted to the pre-war format, albeit with revised, up-dated, layouts. Articles appeared on racing drivers, television programmes and even pop groups. Meccano products were restricted to an eight-page section, but wide coverage was still given to their advertising.

Following the take-over of Meccano by the Lines Brothers Group, there was an interim period after which time Doug McHard assumed the Editorial chair. Once again the number of the magazine's pages was increased, and became devoted more to hobbies such as model aircraft, plastic modelling and model car racing, whilst continuing its coverage of Meccano. By that time of course, Hornby trains were obsolete, and not surprisingly Tri-ang Trains were featured instead.

A crisis occurred in July 1967, the magazine was to cease production! After more than half a century, economic circumstances had forced a shut-down. Yet by January 1968, the old magazine was back though under new management, and reduced in size to 240 × 178mm. It was published by the Model Aeronautical Press Ltd (later Model and Allied Publications), with John Franklin as Editor.

The format did not greatly change, and Meccano was still featured much as before, but new sections were devoted to reviews of toys and models of various other makes. Dave Rothwell took over as Editor in April 1969 and he was succeeded by V E Smeed two years later, but the magazine had changed little during this period.

The monthly magazine ceased in December 1972, although Meccano Limited continued to publish the magazine as a quarterly until October 1976. During 1976 the magazine was offered to a completely independent magazine, *Meccano Engineer*. In January 1977 the new *Meccano Magazine*, incorporating *Meccano Engineer*, was published. Initially published as a quarterly, it is hoped at some time in the future it will revert to a monthly issue. Thus it has fallen to Mike Nicholls, the new Editor, to continue, in close association with the original Meccano Company, the long and honourable tradition of *Meccano Magazine*.

With many changes in size, shape, colour and format, the *Meccano Magazine* has spanned three generations with sections on Meccano model building as the only constant factor; another tribute to Frank Hornby's first and best invention.

Fig. 106

IT IS NATURAL FOR PEOPLE with similar interests to seek one another out, and as early as 1919, Frank Hornby realised that there was a desire for some kind of organization catering for Meccano Boys. In that year, the Meccano Guild was formed by Meccano Ltd, and in a little over ten years it grew to include 100,000 boys in a world-wide fellowship. Of course, it was all good advertising for Meccano, but Frank Hornby was genuinely interested in making boys' lives happier and brighter, and was rightly convinced that his invention could help achieve this.

The Meccano Guild encouraged local clubs which grew to a total of more than five hundred. Each had an adult leader, but the other officials and members were mainly boys whose chief interest lay in building Meccano models as individual or group projects.

In 1928, the Company founded a similar organization for train enthusiasts and called it the Hornby Railway Company. The *Meccano Magazine* reported that boys were rushing to join this organization, and by the outbreak of World War 2, 10,000 boys had become members. Nearly four hundred branches were formed at home and overseas, with the chief pursuit of combining Hornby equipment to form large layouts.

The *Meccano Magazine* reported news for Meccano Clubs and Hornby Railway Company local branches each month, and many photographs appeared over the years. Both groups diversified into other activities such as sports, camping and rambling and it would be true to say that model railway equipment of other than Hornby manufacture found its way on

to some Branch layouts.

As might be expected, the war curtailed club and branch activities and cut off supplies. However, after the war both began to flourish once more as new groups were formed. Until 1964, Meccano Ltd continued to sponsor these along with a rather less-well-supported Dinky Collectors' Club. With the take-over of the Meccano factory however, company sponsorship officially ceased.

Fortunately, in more recent years there has been a re-birth of rather similar national and local organizations. Some Meccano clubs never died but continued much as before, though independently. In the last three years, several new clubs have sprung up, consisting for the most part, of adult model builders. At the time of writing, clubs of this kind exist in Alcester, Henley-on-Thames, Birmingham, and Huddersfield as well as in Australia, New Zealand and South Africa; and a club for younger enthusiasts is well established in Stevenage, and no doubt others will be formed, as interest in Meccano is still growing rapidly.

The Hornby Railway Collectors' Association was formed in 1969 by a group of Bedfordshire enthusiasts, the author being a founder member. It has grown into an international body with about five hundred members, and frequent local meetings are held. The aims are to foster the hobby of collecting and operating Hornby Gauge '0' and Hornby Dublo Trains. Some members already own fine collections, while others are busy compiling a detailed history of these much-loved trains which are unhappily no longer manufactured. A monthly magazine is circulated to all members, and Annual General Meetings are held at various locations throughout the country.

What causes a middle-aged man to cherish toys which were originally intended for children? As far as Meccano is concerned the word 'toy' is incorrect. Meccano is a medium whose full potential has not yet been fully realised; even by those who have the time and skill, together with very large collections of parts, which enables them to build 8ft long locomotives or complex electronically-controlled mechanisms.

With Hornby Trains, it is probably pure nostalgia, and the desire to own now something possibly missed in childhood. Indeed the cult of collecting any or all the products of the famous factory in Binns Road, Liverpool is growing; praise indeed for the genius who brought them all into being during the first thirty or so years of this century.

Fig. 107

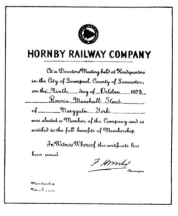

1901 JANUARY 9 — Patent No. 587 granted for what becomes *Mechanics Made Easy*, marketed in England by Frank Hornby, 18 James Street, Liverpool. Original wholesalers: George Philip & Son of London; Philip, Son & Nephew of Liverpool.

1901 — From this year until 1909, many parts of the *MME* system (Although a considerable quantity are bought-in) are manufactured at Hornby's one-room factory at 12 Duke Street, Liverpool.

1906 — Hornby forms a partnership with David Hugh Elliot of Liverpool. *Mechanics Made Easy* continues to operate from James Street, where the outfits are assembled and packed after being transported from Duke Street, London. Wholesalers now Philip & Tacey Limited.

1906 JANUARY 16 — General patent granted in USA.

1907 SEPTEMBER 14 — Trade name '*Meccano*' registered at Designs Registry of the UK Patent Office. Proprietor of Trade Mark named as Frank Hornby of 12 Duke Street, Liverpool.

1908 JUNE 4 — Meccano Ltd is incorporated as a joint stock company with a nominal capital of £5000. Directors: Hornby and Elliot. Manager: George Jones (from Kodak Ltd). Subscribers for share capital were: Frank Hornby, Arthur Hooton (Bank Manager), Edward M D Warry (Bank Cashier), George Jones, Montague Henry Hill (Banker), Leonard George Hill (Banker), Owen William Owen (Solicitor). Registered Office: 12 Duke Street, Liverpool.

1909 MARCH 29 — Registered Office now at the new factory at 274 West Derby Road, Liverpool.

1911 TO 1913 — Hornby is granted several German Trade Marks, but no patents to safeguard his products.

1912 AUGUST 7 — Meccano (France) Ltd is incorporated, and the Registered Office (as of August 8 1912) is 274 West Derby Road.

1913 — During this year, Meccano GmbH is registered in Germany; the Registered Office is at Bürohaus Börse, Burgstrasse 28, Berlin. (The West Berlin Chamber of Commerce and Industry has no record of the Company's registration, as the relevant papers appear to have been destroyed during the First World War.)

1913 SEPTEMBER 8 — Meccano Inc registered in the USA.

1914 — At the outbreak of war, the German Government confiscates Meccano GmbH, which is subsequently sold to Märklin et Cie, who continue to manufacture Meccano-style construction outfits under their own name.

1914 AUGUST 28 — Meccano Ltd moves to the new purpose-built factory in Binns Road, Liverpool. The new factory is funded from an issue of £50,000-worth of Debenture Stock which was subscribed during 1913 and 1914. The Registered Offices of Meccano Ltd and Meccano (France) Ltd are moved to Binns Road.

1915 — The first £500 Meccano Competition. Meccano Inc (of USA) publish '*Frank Hornby – The Boy Who Made $1,000,000 With A Toy*' by M P Gould; copies of this are available as prizes in a competition.

1916 SEPTEMBER/OCTOBER — First edition of *Meccano Magazine* is published.

1917 — Legal proceedings in America over Meccano patents are instigated by Hornby. Litigation won by Hornby, resulting in injunctions on American Model Builder, Structo, and Erector. A C Gilbert (Erector) buys-up valid patents of the other defendants and re-designs Erector to overcome the results of Hornby's suit.

1919 — The Meccano Guild is formed as a 'world-wide alliance of Meccano Boys'.

1920 — Constructional Hornby Trains are introduced as an extension of the Meccano system. The Metal Box Company becomes the main source of lithographic tin-printing for the Company's products.

1921 — A factory is opened outside Paris at Boissy for the manufacture of French Hornby, Meccano, and –

in the 1930s – of French Dinky Toys.

1925 Production of constructional Hornby Trains ceases. Meccano now tooled-up for model train production from specially-made components.

1928 Hornby Railway Company formed as a guild for Hornby Train enthusiasts. The depression results in the closure of Meccano's New York Office, and A C Gilbert takes over Meccano Inc.

1929 Introduction of the celebrated No. 2 Special Hornby Series semi-scale locomotives.

1931 TO 1933 The field is widened: Aeroplane Constructor Outfits, Motor Car Constructor Outfits, Elektron, Kemex, and 'X'-Series. Meanwhile, large and complex models demonstrate the adequacy and versatility of the standard parts range.

1933/1934 *Modelled Miniatures* – the fore-runners of Dinky Toys – are introduced to compete with the American Tootsie Toys. In fact, Meccano purchased American Kippa machines to make the first Modelled Miniatures.

1936 SEPTEMBER 21 Frank Hornby dies, leaving as directors his sons Roland and Douglas, George Jones, Ernest Bearsley and Walter Hewitt. Roland Hornby succeeded his father as chairman.

1938 Among the diverse range of products made at Binns Road at this time are Hornby Speed Boats, Kemex Chemistry Sets and Elektron Electrical Sets and Dolly Varden Doll's Houses. The Hornby Dublo Model Train System is introduced, stimulated by the growing success of the Trix-Twin Model Railways inspired by Bassett-Lowke.

1939 TO 1945 At the outbreak of war, Meccano Ltd begins to turn to government work. Meccano production is gradually phased-out, but large stocks exist from the pre-war years; however, stocks of some parts are exhausted by December 1940. *Meccano Magazine* continues to be published, but following a government order of September 30, 1943, the sale of Meccano has to cease.

1945 DECEMBER The first 'unfrozen' pre-war Meccano sets appear in the shops.

1946 NOVEMBER The first post-war Meccano sets appear in the shops.

1947 TO 1948 Full production and availability is gradually resumed.

1950 MAY 2 Douglas Hornby dies.

1951 MARCH 9 Following a shortage of steel and other metals due to a government re-armament programme, the Meccano factory at Speke has to shut down (It was to reopen in October 1953 as a Dinky Toy factory). The metal shortage is so acute that the Company considers returning to war-time-style instrument production for the defence programme.

1954 Meccano Ltd is making pre-tax profits in excess of £500,000 and part of the equity is offered to the public. New Meccano parts are introduced to extend the post-war range.

1955 Pre-tax profits approach £1,000,000.

1956 OCTOBER 31 Meccano Ltd acquire new works at Aintree for £75,000 as a 33,600 sq ft extension to the Company's production facilities.

1958 APRIL Dinky Toys fitted with Plastic Windows, are introduced.

1959 In response to overwhelming competition from Tri-ang and other two-rail '00' systems, Hornby Dublo introduces a two-rail system as a replacement for its old three-rail system. The capital cost of this late change of policy is to cause a great strain on the Company's liquidity from hereon.

1960 Meccano take over Bayko from Plimpton Engineering. In the same year, competition in the form of the Danish Lego system appears; this latter concept is to dominate the plastic toy construction market and is one of the principal causes of Bayko's failure to earn profits for Meccano Ltd.

1962 British Electric Traction purchase 12½ % of the Company's equity. By 1964 BET hold some 30% of the equity.

1963 For the eighth year in succession, Meccano Ltd achieves export turnover in excess of £1,000,000, but nonetheless Meccano announce an interim trading loss of £28,858. The reasons given are a world-wide recession in the market for train sets, increasing costs coupled with an inability to increase retail prices in view of strong competition, and unexpected disruption of product distribution in the USA.

1963 AUGUST 21 At a shareholders' meeting, Roland Hornby reveals a trading loss of £164,534 for the year. He announces 'a complete change in production, management and selling'. Plant at the two ancillary factories at Speke and Fazakerley is moved to the new 20,000 sq. ft extension to the Binns Road factory. In order to centralise and economise production, Roland Hornby is 'hopeful that the trading of the Company will be fully balanced . . . and profitable' during 1964.

1964 FEBRUARY 14 Following an estimated loss of ' . . . not more than £250,000 . . . ' during the whole of the previous year, Meccano's directors advise shareholders to

| 1964 | accept the Lines Group £781,000 offer for all Meccano Ltd's share capital. | the decision by the USA Gallaher Group not to invest £5 million, the Lines Group is forced into liquidation. Meccano-Tri-ang goes into voluntary liquidation as part of the break-up of the Lines Group. All assets are transferred to a new company called Maoford Ltd, which is subsequently re-named Meccano (1971) Ltd, and trade continues. An expected profit of £150,000 is announced for the year, and with Secretary-of-State approval, Meccano (1971) Ltd is re-named Meccano Ltd. Meccano Ltd is | | sold to Airfix Industries Ltd. The name Hornby is acquired by Dunbee-Combex which had previously acquired Rovex which included Tri-ang Trains but not the trade name Tri-ang. French Meccano and Hornby are sold to General Mills of America. |

1964 — The Hornby name is gradually phased out; the tools for the Hornby Dublo range are sold to G & R Wrenn Ltd, a subsidiary company within the Lines Group.

1970 MAY 28 — The original company name is changed to Meccano-Tri-ang Ltd.

1971 — Following poor trading, the calling-in of millions of pounds-worth of bank loans, and

1972 TO 1976 — The Meccano product range is extended again.

1976 — The 75th anniversary of the first *Mechanics Made Easy* patent is reached, with the demand and production of the Meccano system higher than ever before.

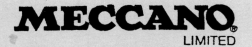

LIMITED

P.O.BOX No.4   BINNS ROAD   LIVERPOOL L13 1DA   Telephone 051-228 2701
Telegrams MECCANO, LIVERPOOL   Telex 629246

30th November 1979

Dear Customer,

The Board of Meccano Ltd., regrets to announce that the continuing and heavy losses of its factory at Binns Road, have resulted in a decision to cease to manufacture at the close of business on Friday, 30th November 1979.

Meccano Ltd., will however continue into the 1980's as a sales and marketing organisation providing your business with full support in your efforts to sell the Dinky and Meccano ranges. Our TV advertising will continue as planned this Christmas. We look forward to showing you our new toys at the Trade Fairs in January and to your continued support for our products in the future.

Yours faithfully,

RAY McNEICE
Managing Director

Index of Illustrations & Source Material

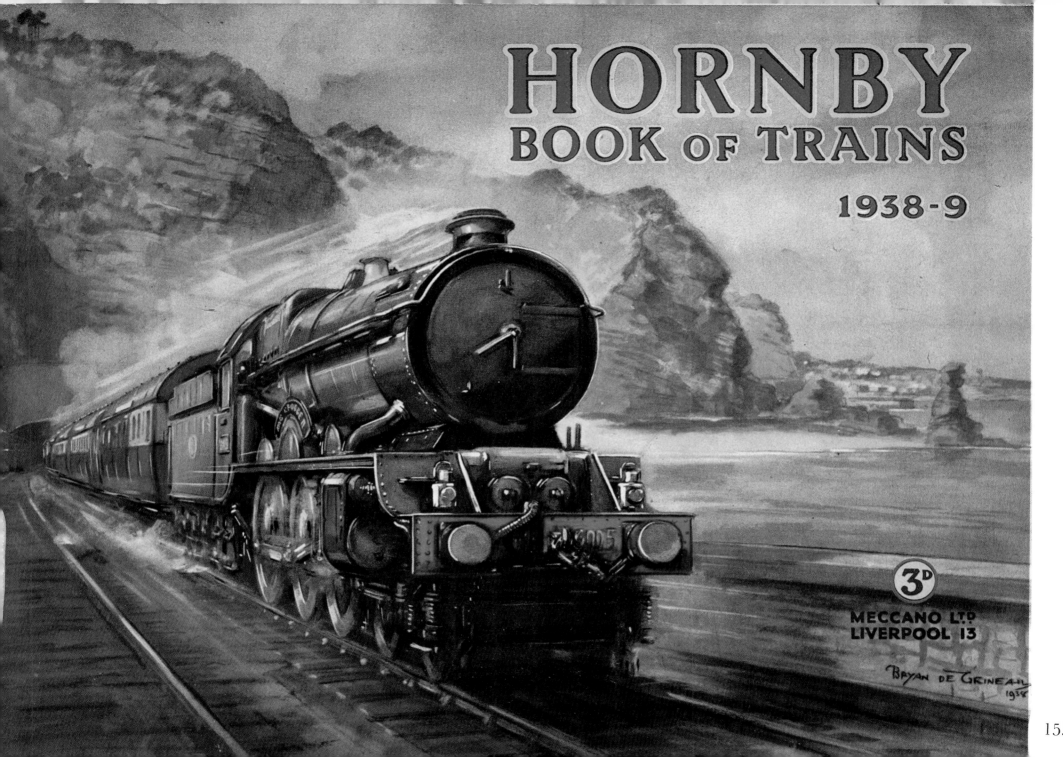

HORNBY
BOOK OF TRAINS

1938-9

3D

MECCANO LTD
LIVERPOOL 13

Bryan de Grineau
1938

Foreword

Almost everybody is familiar with at least the main features of the operation of passenger trains, but to most of us the working of goods trains is a mystery. A train of 50 or 60 wagons passing slowly through a station irritates us with its insistent clatter. We are thankful when it has gone, and probably we never give it another thought. Yet that clattering train may be of far greater value than the express passenger train for which we are waiting. In the first article in this book we describe some of the interesting and ingeniously-constructed vehicles that have been designed to handle the wide variety of goods dealt with by the railways as "Common Carriers," and the trains in which they run.

The splendid cover design to this book and the illustration above show that aristocrat of G.W.R. expresses, the "Cornish Riviera Limited," which links London with the romantic shores of Cornwall. Its running, like that of all other G.W.R. expresses, is safeguarded by a wonderful system of automatic train control, the operation of which is described in our second article.

The third article deals with the remarkable progress in luxury travel that has been made during recent years by both the East Coast and the West Coast Routes from London to Scotland.

The fourth article tells the story of the Travelling Post Office, which has been a regular feature of railway operation for exactly 100 years. It describes how the exchange of mails is carried out at wayside stations while the mail trains are travelling at full speed.

Many years of development have resulted in a splendid series of train and steamer services linking Britain with France. The principal Continental Boat expresses of the S.R. and the remarkable Train Ferry service form the subject of the final article.

For assistance in the preparation of this book we wish to express our indebtedness to the Postmaster-General, The British Railways' Press Office, the London, Midland and Scottish Railway, the London and North Eastern Railway, the Great Western Railway and the Southern Railway. The photograph of the G.W.R. train on page 6 is by Mr. J. G. Muir; that of Norton Fitzwarren on page 8 is by Mr. D. Fear; the "Irish Mail" illustration on page 52 is by Mr. S. Garbutt; the Shakespeare Cliff Tunnel photograph on page 54 is by Mr. J. M. Tomlinson, and the "Newhaven Boat Express" on page 55 is by Real Photographs Company.

"Common Carriers"; How the Railways deliver the Goods

Our railways are "Common Carriers", which means that they must be ready to accept for transport any load that is offered to them. As they cannot pick and choose their freights, they must have equipment that is capable of handling efficiently anything from a packet of pins to a ship's rudder, not to mention livestock, minerals, foodstuffs and a host of other things.

In recent years great progress has been made in the handling of freight by rail in order to keep pace with modern demands for service. New locomotives, equipment and methods of handling have been introduced, and to-day railway freights move much faster than they did ten years ago. More than one million freight wagons are moved from point to point as required. Last year 286,617,000 tons of freight and 9,103,000 head of livestock were transported by the four main line railways. Freight trains varying from 100 tons to 1,000 tons capacity journeyed 140,109,000 miles.

In providing the type of service required by modern conditions the railways make the best possible use of one of their greatest advantages—the facility to transport material in bulk at high speed. "Next day" delivery has become the rule rather than the exception, and this has meant the institution of a large number of express freight trains consisting of vehicles specially designed for fast running and headed by engines capable of maintaining high rates of speed with heavy loads. Actually there are now nearly 700 express freight trains running in this country over the 24 hours, where five years ago there were 338; and the fastest of them make their journeys at average speeds of 45 m.p.h. or so, while others are timed at speeds of about 40 m.p.h. The longest non-stop run of all freight services in the country is shared by two trains of the L.M.S. between London and Liverpool. The faster of these is the 7-45 p.m. from Camden, covering the 191 miles to Edge Hill, Liverpool, at an average speed of 38.97 m.p.h.

An essential feature of the vehicles composing such trains is the provision of automatic brakes that can be controlled from the engine in the same manner as those on passenger trains. These would be of little use, however, with the ordinary loose-chain couplings employed on slow goods and mineral trains; so screw couplings are provided, springs are secured by bolts, and axle-boxes are oil-lubricated, making the wagons or vans similar to passenger stock as far as the brakes, draw-gear and running equipment are concerned.

There is an atmosphere of romance about these night freight flyers. Watching one of them dash through a wayside station, one catches something of this as the bulky shape of an engine is followed by a long line of vans and sheeted wagons, dark and mysterious looking, brought up in the rear by a swaying goods brake van with its tail and side lamps forming the red-studded points of an inverted triangle. It is thrilling, too, to watch the departure of an express goods train from a big freight yard; let us do so in imagination. We find the train already made up, and the guard in possession of his van. He walks down one side of the train to the engine, taking note of any vehicles to be detached en route. He sees that all hand-brake levers are in the "off" position and that all loads are secure, and looks over the fastening of all couplings, doors and wagon sheets. We follow him to the engine, where he compares notes with the driver as to the load and to the running times of the train. He now returns to his van along the other side of the train in order to examine the doors, sheets and brakes on that side. We will stay at the front, however, near to the locomotive.

Half a minute to go! The enginemen are ready, the driver looking at his watch and then back along the length of the train for the guard's signal, while the fireman busies himself with the last-minute details of his preparations for a strenuous trip. The train has been inspected throughout and the engine is plainly eager to be off, a plume of steam hissing from the safety valves. The yard starting signal is already clear, and then at last comes the guard's "right-away" signal, a green lamp shining from the tail-end of the train 35 wagon-lengths away. A hoot from the whistle, and the din of the safety valves lessens and then stops as the engine makes its first few mighty puffs as it slowly gets hold of the load. The fireman is already plying his shovel, and

(Above). Brick wagons being shunted at Ferme Park Yards, L.N.E.R. Each wagon holds 19,800 bricks.

(Right). A main line coal train on the L.N.E.R. The engine is one of the powerful three-cylinder 2-8-0s built specially for coal and mineral traffic.

the glare from the open fire door flickering under the effect of each staccato blast casts weird shadows on the footplate and on the billowing steam that rolls overhead. The wagons pass, loaded with the myriad things that make up a city's trade, the wheels of each beating in turn more rapidly on the rail joints; and at last comes the brake van with its little stove chimney smoking cheerily, the guard leaning out and watching, the progress of the train through the yard. So the train passes out of sight and becomes a low rumble that rapidly dies away in the distance.

Among the fastest and most important express freighters are those carrying perishables and foodstuffs generally. Fish from Aberdeen and Grimsby, fresh meat from Scotland, frozen meat from Liverpool, milk from the Midlands and the West, fruit, vegetables and general produce are all conveyed by fast freight trains. Some idea of their importance is shown by the frequent use of express passenger locomotives on these trains. For instance, on the fish trains from Aberdeen that are run by both L.M.S. and L.N.E.R. routes, even 4-6-2 locomotives can sometimes be seen. By either route the long journey from the Granite City up to London is covered in something over 13 hours. Average speeds are thus relatively high, and the restriction of loads to a definite maximum according to the class of train makes the passenger engine suitable for express freight work.

For the most part fish is packed in ice in crates and is carried in fish vans which, however much they differ in detail, are all arranged so that there is ample ventilation. Special ventilated vans also are used for fresh meat traffic, but a great deal of meat nowadays is carried in special containers, which in effect are separate wagon or van bodies that can be carried on railway trucks or road vehicles. They

(Right). A transformer loaded on a special well wagon.

(Circle). Transferring a container from road to rail vehicle.

(Bottom). A train of milk tank wagons. The wagon next to the tender is carrying a road-rail tank.

are transferred from one to the other at terminal points by crane power, and avoid the loss of time caused by the transhipment of individual loads from road to rail and vice versa. The L.M.S. 9.45 a.m. Scottish Meat Special from Aberdeen to Broad Street, quite an institution on the system, conveys its traffic by containers alone, and the meat is actually on sale in butchers' shops within 24 hours of its leaving Aberdeen. A considerable amount of L.M.S. traffic in chilled or frozen meat originates in Liverpool and a notable train for its conveyance is the 4-55 p.m. from Alexandra Dock, which is timed over certain sections of its journey up to London at speeds of over 45 m.p.h. At one part of its journey from the Dock to Edge Hill, the great marshalling centre of the Liverpool area, it passes within a stone's throw of the Meccano Factory. It may be hauled by a 4-6-0 express engine of the "Jubilee" or "Patriot" series of class 5XP, or by one of the very capable Stanier engines of class 5P5F. At Edge Hill additional vehicles that have been worked in separately from Canada Dock are attached, and the train is soon on its way to London. Stops are made at Rugby and Willesden, but the whole journey including stops is covered in just over 7 hours.

An express freight train on the G.W.R. headed by a "Hall" class locomotive.

Milk traffic always used to be associated with the rumbling of milk churns on station platforms and the juggling performances carried out by porters trundling two churns at once. Churns are still used for local milk traffic or where small quantities are involved, but a great deal of milk now travels in bulk in special tank wagons. The tanks are glass-lined, and insulated with layers of cork to ensure their contents being kept at an even temperature, and the wagons are fitted with automatic brakes for fast running

The organisation necessary to place fresh milk on the breakfast table every morning is very interesting, and as an example let us take the working of the G.W.R. Cornish milk traffic. Under modern arrangements milk depots, such as that of Nestlé's Milk Products Ltd., at Lostwithiel, in Cornwall, are situated in the producing areas. The milk is collected in churns from the different farms by railway lorries, and a familiar feature at the roadside in many districts is the raised loading platforms provided where it would be difficult for a heavy lorry to reach the farm itself. On these platforms or stands milk brought from the farm is placed ready for collection, and on them the lorry driver places as many empty churns as he takes up full ones. At the depot the milk is tipped into a tank attached to a weighbridge, weighed, and then pumped into storage tanks. Later it flows through a cooling apparatus and is fed into the railway tank wagons. After its railway journey the milk undergoes the various processes connected with bottling, and is sent on its way for delivery.

In addition to the ordinary railway tank wagons there are in use special road-rail milk tank trailers. On the road these run on pneumatic tyres, haulage being by motor tractors. The tractors also are used in the loading operations, which are carried out from the platform endways on to railway wagons specially designed for the purpose. These wagons have two raised rails running longitudinally, so arranged that they serve as a track for steel drums fitted on the

inside of the road wheels of the trailers. The rails relieve the pneumatic tyres of the weight of the trailer, about 14 tons or so when the tank is full. When in position the road vehicle is prevented from moving by wheel-bars and chains.

In addition to the carriage of milk in this way the railways have considerably developed their facilities for the transport in bulk of acids, edible and other oils, and tar. The number of wheeled road-rail tank trailers in service is growing, but for service over both road and rail, separate tanks without wheels are specially favoured, owing to the fact that they are cheaper to construct and maintain, no special cartage equipment is required for their collection and delivery, and they can be easily loaded and unloaded by crane.

Interesting differences exist in the methods employed in handling fruit traffic according to the kind of fruit and the season. Plums, for instance, are picked

(Above). A busy scene at Paddington Goods Station, showing the great variety of barrels, crates and boxes.

(Right). An army tank on an S.R. well wagon.

when ripe, and the better kinds are packed in the familiar "chips" or baskets. They are carried on shelves in specially constructed and ventilated fruit vans. As with·milk traffic, railway lorry service plays a large part in the work. The companies' motor vehicles collect their freight from plantations within a radius of five to ten miles from the stations. With this traffic "next morning" deliveries are essential, and special trains are arranged to convey the fruit to all parts of the country.

Strawberries form a highly perishable traffic; the season is often confined to the hottest part of the year, so that the very heat that ripens the fruit hastens its deterioration afterwards. This has led to the introduction of insulated containers and the use of refrigeration for this traffic. Refrigeration is effected by what is known as "dry ice", actually solid carbon dioxide, carried in specially fitted bunkers under the roof of the containers.

In contrast to ripe fruit and other perishables which need to be well ventilated, and in some cases to be kept cool by refrigeration, bananas are kept unripe by refrigerating apparatus on ship-board during their journey from overseas but are ripened during their railway journey in this country. Garston and Avonmouth are noted ports for this traffic, and during the season many trains of special banana vans, steam heated in the winter time, are run from these points.

Among recent types of vehicles evolved for the transport of fruit and vegetables are some covered vans on the G.W.R. which have the usual ventilated slots in the sides and ends of their bodies covered with gauze. This permits of the free circulation of air even to the lowest layers of a load, but at the same time protects the load from possible dust and dirt.

In addition to trains such as those we have dealt with so far, the loads of which are confined to traffic of a particular kind, there are many express freight trains that carry miscellaneous loads. Among them is one of the fastest, if not actually the fastest freight train in the world, the 3-35 p.m. of the L.N.E.R. from King's Cross to Glasgow. This is a train with a tradition of service behind it, for it commenced to operate in 1897, although then leaving at 3-25 p.m. It is variously referred to as the "3-35 Glasgow Goods" or "3-35 Scotsman", the latter name suggesting something of its importance by the association of its name with the various passenger "Scotsmen". It reaches

Glasgow at 5-15 a.m. after a journey of 441.4 miles, and vigorous running is necessary to observe the sharply-timed schedules between intermediate stops.

The well-known "K3" class 2-6-0s of the L.N.E.R. have made a special reputation on this train, although it is possible to see other engines on this duty, such as the unique Gresley 2-6-2s of the "Green Arrow" series.

The S.R. operate various services between the South and West and London, and the imported traffic from Southampton Dock, consisting of meat, fruit and so on, is considerable. A notable S.R. express freight train is the 9-38 p.m. that runs up from Exeter to Nine Elms, the great S.R. London Goods Depot. This train speeds up to city markets a variety of West country produce, and it is sometimes referred to by S.R. men as "The Market", or "The Flyer".

In the naming of freight trains the G.W.R. seem to have made the greatest progress. Some of the titles have long been in use among the men who work the trains. The significance of "The Meat" is obvious, the train being one that is run from Birkenhead to Smithfield. Some names indicate points of origin or destination or the district served, such as "The Cornishman"; while others have fanciful names, such as the "Flying Pig".

We are all familiar with coal trains, and it is fascinating to stand at some lineside point on one of the great coal-carrying routes and to watch the procession of long coal trains passing. Much of this traffic is carried in private owners' wagons, most of them boldly lettered with the names of the colliery merchants or colliery company owning them; and many display bright and sometimes even startling colour schemes. The extent of the coal traffic and the running conditions of the Midland route of the L.M.S. have caused the use of the most unusual locomotives of regular main line service in this country. These are the articulated 2-6-0+0-6-2 "Beyer-Garratts", the most powerful locomotives on the L.M.S. They regularly haul trains of 90 loaded wagons, or an average gross tonnage of 1,400, in the up direction between Toton Sidings near Nottingham, where the traffic is concentrated,

(Circle). L.M.S. tank locomotive for local goods traffic.

(Above). A consignment of buoys loaded on G.W.R. "crocodile" wagons.

(Right). The "3-35 Glasgow Goods" of the L.N.E.R. hauled by a "Green Arrow" locomotive.

and Cricklewood, where the trains are broken up and the traffic distributed. The load in the down direction is 100 empty wagons.

The L.M.S. have also powerful 2-8-0 tender engines for heavy coal and mineral traffic, and good use is made of the type on the L.N.E.R. and the G.W.R. The L.N.E.R. seem to delight in producing exceptional engines; in addition to a 2-8-0+0-8-2 "Beyer-Garratt" engaged in banking duties on coal trains in South Yorkshire, they have on main line duty a couple of powerful 2-8-2s or "Mikado" freight engines, the only ones of their kind in the country.

A traffic of importance on the L.N.E.R. is the carriage of bricks from the Fletton brickfields near Peterborough. Bricks have become of such consequence in recent years that express services are operated for their conveyance, special brick wagons being used with a capacity of 50 tons each or nearly 20,000 bricks. Their sides can be dropped for convenience in loading and unloading, and the vehicles have automatic brakes and are equipped in every way for fast running.

Although not one of the "heavy" lines, the S.R. have some awkward consignments to deal with from time to time. There were, for instance, 70 lions in 15 cages that required to be taken from Newhaven to Olympia. Lifting the cages by crane was a delicate proceeding, as may well be imagined! The handling of unusual loads has in recent years been reduced to something of a fine art by the provision of special rolling stock and other equipment. Boilers, army tanks, ship's propellors and electrical machinery are among the many varied loads that may require special handling.

Items of unusual bulk or weight may need special provision making for them. Suitable wagons must be requisitioned, clearance of fixed structures must be studied and the route to be taken has to be selected with extreme care. Tracks may require slewing at certain places, signals may require to be partially dismantled and Wrong Line Working intermittently may be necessary in order to provide clearance. To avoid interference with traffic, loads of this kind are usually moved at week-ends, but in spite of all the difficulties entailed the capacity of the railways for handling the traffic is such that on one section alone of the L.M.S. last year over 3,400 exceptional loads were carried, this being 700 more than in the previous year. The items included machinery of all description, a complete automatic telephone exchange, the world's largest hollow steel forging, ships' lifeboats,

(Above). Girders loaded on special trolleys. The girders themselves connect the trolleys in pairs.

(Below). Filling the ice bunkers of a container with "dry ice".

locomotives for export, coaches and electrical transformers. For nearly 700 of these consignments it was necessary for special notices to be prepared advising the staff of the running of these loads and of the routes over which they were to travel.

In addition to the special methods developed for the handling of perishable traffic and the transport of heavy loads attention has been devoted in recent years to schemes for preventing possible damage in transit to general goods. The shocks of shunting tend to cause some displacement of wagon loads and some classes of goods, of course, are more liable to damage than others, no matter how well they are packed and how carefully they are stowed in the vehicles. Some years ago the G.W.R. commenced experiments with a system of movable partitions that could be fitted across the interior of some of their goods vans. The scheme has proved very successful and additional vans equipped with these partitions have been put into service. More recently the L.M.S. and the G.W.R. have introduced special shock-absorbing wagons. On these the wagon body literally "floats" on the wagon chassis, for it is allowed independent longitudinal movement, this being cushioned by means of horizontal india-rubber springs. Additional protection is afforded by special shock-absorbing buffers. For loads consisting of glassware, earthenware, china and so on, such vehicles are particularly valuable. Glass requires very careful handling, and much traffic of

An out-of-gauge load. Ship's rudder loaded for rail transport.

this kind is conveyed packed in crates and cases. Containers also are used for the carriage of glass articles of many kinds.

Sheet and plate glass are conveyed in specially constructed well wagons having capacities varying from 8 to 30 tons. Some of these vehicles are fitted with special stanchions between which large sheets of glass can be loaded. As a general rule glass traffic is carried by ordinary freight services, but if the consignment is of unusual shape and size a special service is arranged. A short time ago special Sunday working was arranged for the conveyance of the largest plate ever made at a glass works at Barnby Dun. Sixty men were required to handle the consignment, which travelled to London in a special wagon. The load was then transferred to a road vehicle and carried to its destination.

Train Running on the G.W.R.: Protection by Automatic Train Control

In almost all its phases G.W.R. practice is strongly individual, and has been so since Brunel laid out his London and Bristol main line on a grand scale a hundred years ago, and adopted the unique broad gauge of 7ft. 0¼in. During the present century the

The system is a well-tried one. Preliminary experiments were begun in the early years of this century, and the first installation in actual service was brought into use in 1906 on the Henley branch. Later in the same year a further application was completed on the Fairford branch, and in 1908 the four main line tracks between Reading and Slough were equipped. In 1912, the four-track section between Slough and Paddington came under automatic train control.

The next extension took place in 1929, and with this 372 miles of track had been equipped. A great step forward was made in 1931 when the system was brought into use on the main line routes to Plymouth, Swansea, Newport and Gloucester, among others. The section from Swansea to Fishguard was completed in 1937 and soon after it was decided to complete the installation over the remaining sections of main line between Plymouth and Penzance, and between Wolverhampton and Chester.

The apparatus fitted on the permanent way consists of an immovable ramp, about 40ft. long, fixed between the running rails. The ramp is a steel inverted T-bar mounted on a baulk of timber. At its highest point it is 3½in. above rail level, and it is connected electrically with a switch in the signal box. This switch is operated by means of the lever controlling the distant signal. When the latter is "clear" and a train can proceed, current flows to the ramp, but this remains "dead" electrically when the distant signal is in the "caution" position. Where colour-light signals are used matters are so arranged that the ramp cannot be electrified until the distant signal is showing a green light indicating "clear".

On the engine there are a contact shoe, an electrically-controlled brake valve and siren combined, and an electric bell. The contact shoe is fixed on the centre line of the engine, and projects downward to within 2½in. of rail level. It is free to rise vertically, and as it is in line with the

G.W.R. set the standard in high speed train running, and pioneered in principles of locomotive design and operation that have since been followed elsewhere. Alone of British railways the G.W.R. have consistently applied a system of automatic train control, familiarly known as A.T.C., for the safe working of its traffic. By the time schemes in hand are completed this system will have been installed over the whole of 2,852 miles of main line track, thus affording automatic safety on all the chief routes operated by the company. There is little doubt that the long immunity of G.W.R. trains from serious accident during the past 30 years or so has largely been due to the efficiency of the apparatus.

Other companies have tried various systems from time to time and experiments are still in progress. At the time of writing the interesting L.N.E.R. decision to equip their main line between Edinburgh and Glasgow with automatic train control has just been made known, the Hudd inductive system with which experiments have been made by the L.M.S. and the S.R. having been adopted.

The G.W.R. system of automatic train control has as its primary object the giving of an audible warning in the locomotive cab to a driver when his train is approaching a distant signal in the "caution" position, and the automatic application of the brakes if this warning is disregarded. This makes it certain that the train will be held up before it reaches the next stop signal. Another distinctive audible indication is given when the distant signal shows "line clear". The two signals given to the driver are the sounding of a siren in the cab indicating "caution", and the ringing of a bell to show that the line is clear. Each therefore is a sound message from the signalman to the driver that cannot fail to attract his attention.

(Top). A G.W.R. express leaving Chester.

(Centre). Cab view of a G.W.R. locomotive fitted with automatic train control apparatus.

(Right). G.W.R. enginemen at work

ramp it is lifted 1in. whenever this is passed over. A switch attached to the shoe is closed when the engine is not over a ramp, and the brake valve is kept shut by the electro-magnet controlling it being energised by current from a battery carried on the engine.

When the engine passes over a "dead" ramp, the signal being at "caution", the switch is opened by the raising of the shoe, the circuit is broken, and the de-energised electro-magnet allows the brake valve to admit air to the brake pipe, causing the siren to operate and the brakes to be applied. This effect continues until the driver acknowledges the signal by raising a small handle on the apparatus in the cab. When a "live" ramp is passed over the circuit on the engine is again broken, but current from the ramp now energises the electro-magnet, thus keeping the brake valve shut and at the same time causing relays to operate and so ring the bell. In order to prevent waste of engine battery power an automatic cut-out is provided, which comes into operation when an engine is stationary.

The locomotives that work over various sections of London Transport electrified lines require a slight modification of the engine apparatus. Contact of the engine shoe with the centre rail is avoided by the fitting of a device that lifts the collector shoe clear while the engine is over such electrified sections.

A further modification has been applied experimentally to a few engines in order to do away with the engine battery and to simplify the electrical apparatus. In this the "clear" indication in the cab is produced by a mechanically-operated gong when current is picked up from the ramp.

A special demonstration of the working of the G.W.R. system to illustrate the degree of safety attained was made early this year. For this purpose it was arranged that a main line distant signal should be kept in the "caution" position, and the enginemen were instructed to ignore the signal entirely. Steam therefore remained on, and the speed of the train on passing over the ramp was 59 m.p.h., but the train was stopped by the automatic application of the brakes in a distance of 900 yards. From the stopping point to the home signal was a further 450 yards, so that the train was brought to a stand in an easy manner with this distance to spare. The train on this occasion weighed 304 tons and the locomotive and tender approximately 126½ tons.

A further move to aid enginemen and to promote safety in operation has been the installation of speedometers on the whole series of G.W.R. locomotives engaged on express passenger traffic. Provision of such instruments assists the correct observance of speed restrictions and thus ensures safety, while at the same time it prevents the hindrance to traffic caused by reductions of speed well below the limits laid down. The "Kings" and the "Castles", as the premier express classes, were the first to be dealt with, and towards the end of 1937 it was decided to equip the older "Star" and "Saint" classes as well. All the main line express locomotives

engaged on high-speed services on the L.M.S. and the L.N.E.R. also are fitted with speedometers.

The apparatus adopted as standard for G.W.R. engines consists of an alternating current generator mounted on a suspending bracket below the footplate. The generator is driven by means of bevel gears and a balanced slotted link connection from a small return crank incorporated in the crank pin washer of one of the trailing coupled wheels. The current generated is conveyed through an armoured cable to a voltmeter placed in the cab in front of the driver. Its voltage is proportional to the speed, and the dial of the instrument is graduated not in volts, but in miles per hour. A rectifier is incorporated to ensure that the speedometer needle shows the correct indication whether the engine is running in either the forward or backward direction. The use of the slotted link, the outer end of which is closed by means of a removable

(Right). Speedometer driving arrangements on a G.W.R. locomotive.
(Centre). The A.T.C. apparatus and speedometer dial.
(Bottom). The "Cheltenham Flyer" leaving Swindon.

distance piece, permits of the coupling rods being taken down without it being necessary to dismantle the speedometer gear.

The most famous G.W.R. express is the "Cornish Riviera Limited", which is shown in the cover illustration to this book. The operation and equipment of this train represent all that is best in G.W.R. practice, and the journey from the busy City to the picturesque Cornish Coast is completed in 6 hours. The present-day service has developed from the original "Riviera Express" of 1904, and for over 20 years the train made the longest regular non-stop run in the world, between Paddington and Plymouth, a distance of 225¾ miles. Almost from the first the train has been distinguished by the employment of special stock, and the spacious vehicles shown in our illustrations are reserved for this service alone. Actually they are the widest coaches in the country running in main line express service, measuring 9ft. 7in. overall; they are easily distinguished by the pronounced curve of their sides and their set-in doorways.

Locomotive performance of the highest standard has always been demanded on this service. The train of 1904 consisted of seven vehicles and weighed under 200 tons behind the tender, but the "Limited" of to-day is made up to a maximum of 14 coaches with an empty weight of 465 tons. In addition progressive accelerations have resulted in a schedule requiring practically the mile-a-minute rate throughout the run from Paddington to Plymouth.

Another point of development concerns the route followed. For the first two years of its existence the "Riviera Express" had to cover slightly over 246 miles in order to reach Plymouth from Paddington. It then followed the original route of Brunel via Swindon and Bristol. It has been part of G.W.R. policy during this century to reduce the distance on many of the chief routes by the building of short cuts. This principle was applied to the road to the West and in 1906 the "Riviera" first made use of the shortened route afforded by the opening of the Westbury and Castle Cary cut-offs, which reduced the distance beween London and Plymouth by some 20 miles.

The "Cornish Riviera Limited" now leaves Brunel's old main line at Reading and proceeds up the valley of the Kennet past Newbury and Savernake to Westbury. Until a year or two ago it was here that slip coaches destined for Weymouth used to be detached from the tail of the train, in the days when three separate slip portions were conveyed. These were detached one after the other at Westbury for Weymouth, at Taunton for Minehead and Ilfracombe, and at Exeter for Torquay respectively. Revised working arrangements during the past few years, doing away with slip coaches on the "Riviera", have resulted in its becoming a truly Cornish express.

Westbury station is not now passed through by the "Cornish Riviera Limited"; avoiding lines that were brought into use some years ago, in order to ease the passage of fast trains, are taken instead by this and other West of England expresses. A similar state of affairs exists at Frome. Then comes Castle Cary, where the Weymouth line diverges, and soon Cogload Junction is reached, where the old route via Bristol now joins the Westbury line by means of a fly-over junction. Taunton, the scene of the slipping of the Minehead and Ilfracombe coaches, is next passed, and there follows the climb up Wellington bank, scene of so many speed exploits of up trains, to Whiteball summit. Near the summit is Whiteball tunnel, the longest on the journey; and on emerging from the tunnel the "Cornish Riviera Limited" is in Devon.

Exeter is passed, and then from Exminster to Newton Abbot there is practically a level run, much of the line being carried on a ledge cut out in the base of the cliffs; but the route becomes literally mountainous over the latter stages of the run on the South Devon line. After it has swept through the tunnels under the red cliffs along the seashore between Dawlish and Teignmouth, where the train is shown in the cover illustration, stiff gradients confront the engine, with slopes of 1 in 57, 1 in 41 and even one length of 1 in 36! This is on the climb to Dainton, and on passing through Dainton Tunnel there is a similarly sharp decline at 1 in 37. This only precedes a severe

climb to Rattery; from Rattery to Wrangaton matters are eased somewhat. There is still another sharp drop at 1 in 42 from Hemerdon before Plymouth is reached.

First choice for this Paddington to Plymouth stretch are the locomotives of the "King" class. These are four-cylinder 4-6-0s, and they are the most powerful of their type in the country, for power is certainly needed to haul the "Cornish Riviera Limited". "King" class locomotives are not allowed to run over Saltash Bridge by reason of their weight. For the Cornish section of the journey, therefore, lighter but still very powerful engines are required. The efficient "Castles" and the useful "Halls" are chiefly employed for the energetic running required by the "Limited" on this last stretch of the journey.

The character of the route now changes; numerous valleys have to be crossed by lofty viaducts, masonry or steel girders having replaced the timbered structures of Brunel. The longest is Truro Viaduct and the highest is St. Pinnock Viaduct. It is an "up and down" sort of run through Cornwall, past Liskeard and Lostwithiel to Truro, the county town and junction for Falmouth; then comes the mining district full of associations with Richard Trevithick, the Cornishman who constructed the first railway locomotive. Redruth, Camborne, Helston, St. Erth follow, and then finally Penzance, the end of a run of 305¼ miles.

Other trains that have brought fame to the G.W.R. are the "Torbay Express", another heavy long-distance train run at an average speed approaching 60 m.p.h.; the faster but lighter "Cheltenham Spa Express", popularly known as the "Cheltenham Flyer", and "The Bristolian". The "Cheltenham Flyer", with its 71.4 m.p.h. sprint over the 77¼ miles from Swindon to Paddington, was for a time the fastest train in the world. The "Bristolian"—a younger service—was inaugurated in 1935 to mark the centenary of the formation of the G.W.R., and to provide an improved service between London and Bristol, the extremities of the original line. It runs down from Paddington via Bath at an average of 67.6 m.p.h. and returns via Badminton at 67.1 m.p.h. On the down journey it passes through Box Tunnel, nearly two miles long. The "Irish Mail" Expresses of the G.W.R. between Paddington and Fishguard pass through the Severn Tunnel, which is the longest under-water tunnel in the world, and is 4 miles 624 yards long.

(Above) "Line clear"! Norton Fitzwarren Junction, on the route of the "Cornish Riviera Limited".

(Left). The "Cornish Riviera Limited" leaving Paddington, hauled by a "King" class locomotive.

Rival Roads to the North: Developments of Fifty Years

ultimately "*The Flying Scotsman*" did the journey in 7 hrs. 32 mins., the run of 124¼ miles from Newcastle to Edinburgh being accomplished in 124 minutes. This great run finished the racing, officially at any rate. Realising the futility of such hectic competition, the rival authorities met in conference, and after considerable discussion agreed that the scheduled times should be fixed at 7¾ hrs. for the East Coast route and 8 hrs. for the West Coast, thus establishing the superiority to Edinburgh of the former route, which it has held ever since.

Unofficially, however, the racing was not quite at an end. The East Coast drivers were not satisfied with their time of 7 hrs. 32 mins., and they made a special effort to eclipse all previous performances. As a result they succeeded in bringing "*The Flying Scotsman*" to rest in Edinburgh 7 hrs. 26¾ mins. after leaving London, thus cutting 5¼ mins. off the record. During this run it was reported that four consecutive miles had been covered at 76.6 m.p.h. This was a remarkable speed for that time, although the train weighed only 100½ tons, or one-fifth the load of "*The Flying Scotsman*" to-day. In considering these East Coast runs it must be remembered that there were then no dining cars on the Scottish trains, and a stop for lunch had to be made at York.

Seven years later another speed struggle commenced, this time to Aberdeen. Since 1890 the Forth Bridge had provided the East Coast trains with a shorter route to Perth, Dundee and Aberdeen, and up to July, 1895, they were taking 11 hrs. 35 mins. for the journey, as compared with the West Coast timing of 11 hrs. 50 mins. The West Coast decided to make an acceleration as from 1st July; the East Coast followed suit, and the race was on. After a succession of cuts the East Coast time was reduced to 8 hrs. 40 mins.,

The main railway routes between London and Scotland, the West Coast of the L.M.S. and the East Coast of the L.N.E.R., have a history probably of greater interest than that of any other railway routes in the world. To-day the rivalry between the new companies is keen but friendly; in earlier times the competition was carried on with something almost like ferocity.

Fifty years ago the East Coast Route was, as it still is, the more important of the two for Edinburgh traffic from London. Its principal day train, the 10 a.m., now famous the world over as "*The Flying Scotsman*", had been in regular daily service for 26 years. From 1876 "*The Flying Scotsman*" ran the London - Edinburgh daily journey with the greatest regularity in nine hours at a steady 44 m.p.h., including stops. At first the accommodation was confined to first-class and second-class passengers, but in 1887 third-class passengers were admitted. On the West Coast route third-class passengers had for some years been carried in the principal day train to Edinburgh, but this was a much slower journey than that by the East Coast route, taking altogether 10 hours. The West Coast

(Top). "*The Flying Scotsman*" in 1900 hauled by two North Eastern 4-4-0s.

(Centre). A racer of 1888, Caledonian No. 123.

(Right). A double-headed up East Coast express. The engines are a 4-4-0 and a 4-4-2.

authorities naturally regarded the action of their rivals in admitting third-class passengers to "*The Flying Scotsman*" as something of a challenge, and as a reply they accelerated their train to reach Edinburgh in nine hours. Then the trouble began. The East Coast people speeded up "*The Flying Scotsman*" to 8½ hours; the West Coast authorities did the same. Further drastic reductions followed, and

L.N.E.R. No. 2005 *"Thane of Fife"*, one of the giant 2-8-2s used on the difficult route between Edinburgh and Aberdeen. They are the only eight-coupled express passenger locomotives in the country.

by *"The Flying Scotsman"*, except that at Newcastle, the distance thus covered, 268½ miles, being longer than that covered by the L.M.S. train. In September, 1927, with the introduction of the "Royal Scot" locomotives on the L.M.S., non-stop running between Euston and Carlisle commenced.

In 1928 the L.N.E.R. made railway history by the institution during the summer months of the longest non-stop run in the world, that of *"The Flying Scotsman"* over the 392.7 miles between King's Cross and Edinburgh. Even with the omission of intermediate stops the time remained at the 8¼ hours of the old agreement, and this was so well within the power of modern locomotives that drivers found it difficult to fill out their time, in spite of the greatly increased loads. Apart from the novelty of the non-stop run the most interesting feature was the practice of changing the enginemen at about the mid-way point on the run. This is made possible by the use of special corridor tenders. These unusual vehicles incorporate a passageway from end to end, opening out on to the footplate at the front, and connected at the rear to the train by means of a normal corridor gangway.

With further improvements to rolling stock year by year, it seemed that the rivalry between the two routes had become one of luxury rather than of speed. In 1932, however, came

and the West Coast time to 8 hrs. 32 mins. At this stage the rival companies decided that the struggle had gone far enough, and reached an agreement that the time should be 10 hrs. 25 mins. for the East Coast and 10 hrs. 30 mins. for the West Coast.

The extensive slowing up that occurred during the War period had a deadening effect on the timings of the services between London and Scotland. Another important factor was that the trains of both routes were becoming heavier and heavier owing to the use of more luxurious stock and the introduction of dining cars. Until the appearance of the giant locomotives with which we are familiar to-day, the engines had to be handled in a very vigorous fashion in order that the trains should keep time.

From the locomotive point of view it is interesting that for many years the haulage of the principal Scottish expresses on the East Coast Route was performed almost exclusively by 4-4-2 or "Atlantic" locomotives over each stage of the journey between London and Aberdeen. This type of engine was not used at all by the West Coast companies, who relied upon 4-4-0 and 4-6-0 types. The first break from this tradition took place in 1922, when the Gresley "Pacific" type of locomotive was introduced on the G.N.R., and the North Eastern soon after introduced engines of the same wheel arrangement. It was not until 1933, however, that the 4-6-2 was adopted on the West Coast, the first engines being No. 6200, "The Princess Royal", and No. 6201, "Princess Elizabeth".

In 1923, the previously independent companies making up the East Coast Route were united as part of the L.N.E.R., and the West Coast partners lost their identity in the L.M.S. Within a few years alterations in services were made which may be considered as the first steps in the development of the present-day "Royal Scot" and "Flying Scotsman" services. In 1927 the 10 a.m. from Euston, an institution on the West Coast route dating back to 1862, became known as *The Royal Scot*, and non-stop running commenced between Euston and Carnforth, a distance of 236 miles. At the same time the L.N.E.R. decided to omit all intermediate stops made

(Above). Typical view of *"The Flying Scotsman"* as it was before the introduction of streamlined locomotives on the L.N.E.R.

(Left). *"Hardwicke"*, a famous L.N.W.R. 2-4-0 that ran from Crewe to Carlisle at 67.2 m.p.h. in 1895.

the first of a series of accelerations by which the "agreement" 8¼-hr. timing of *"The Flying Scotsman"*, to Edinburgh, and of *"The Royal Scot"*, to Glasgow, have now come down to 7 hrs. This is not the fastest schedule for the journey in operation, however. Last year a new phase began with the introduction of streamlined high-speed services between London and Scotland to mark the Coronation year. The Glasgow train of the L.M.S. is now well

A 4-4-0 express locomotive of the Caledonian "Dunalastair" series, typical of a class that did some remarkably hard work in pre-grouping days.

G.N.R. No. 1, the veteran Stirling 8ft. single-driver, that has made several special runs this year. Normally the engine is housed in York Railway Museum.

known as "The Coronation Scot", and the Edinburgh train of the L.N.E.R. bears the name "Coronation". The schedule of the former is 6½ hrs. for the 401.4 miles, and average speed of 61.8 m.p.h. Like "The Royal Scot" the train runs non-stop between Euston and Carlisle, where the enginemen are changed, the same locomotive working throughout the journey. The "Coronation" makes an average of 66.02 m.p.h., completing its journey in 6 hrs. From London to York its average speed is 71.9 m.p.h.

Special set trains were constructed for each of these services, the standard "Coronation Scot" formation consisting of nine vehicles weighing altogether 286 tons. The L.N.E.R. train includes the novelty of a streamlined tail-coach arranged as an observation car. This is always at the rear of the train, and the sight of it with its twin tail-lamps disappearing into the distance has become familiar on the L.N.E.R. The weight of the complete "Coronation" train is 312 tons behind the tender.

A special series of streamlined 4-6-2 locomotives were built at Crewe for "The Coronation Scot" service, and the first of these on a trial run from Euston to Crewe reached a speed of 114 m.p.h., the highest railway speed that had then been recorded in the British Empire. These engines are painted blue and decorated with silver bands to match the colour scheme adopted for the train. For use on other long-distance expresses such as "The Royal Scot", a further series of 4-6-2 locomotives have been built this year by the L.M.S. Five of these are streamlined in a similar manner to the "Coronation" series, but are finished in standard L.M.S. red, with gold bands running from front to rear. The other five are of normal external appearance. These "Duchesses", as they are known, form a further stage in the development

(Right). A Scottish express of the nineties on the L.N.W.R.

(Below). "The Royal Scot" leaving Euston in the earlier days of the non-stop run to Carlisle.

of the 4-6-2 locomotive on the L.M.S. The well-known "Princesses" were the first examples of the type to run on L.M.S. metals.

For high-speed trains on the L.N.E.R. a development of the Gresley "Pacific" design occurred in the shape of the streamlined "A4" series of 4-6-2s. These proved so successful that the type was adopted for general main line service. The special livery first adopted for the engines allocated to the working of the "Coronation" express has now been adopted as standard for the whole series of these locomotives. This bright shade of blue, combined with the red-finished wheels and the characteristic wedge-shape front-end, gives these remarkable engines a most distinctive appearance. It is interesting that one of them, No. 4498, has the unusual distinction of carrying the name of its designer during his term of office. This engine was actually the hundredth Gresley 4-6-2 to be built, and it was decided by the L.N.E.R. that it should be named "Sir Nigel Gresley", as a tribute to the work of their Chief Mechanical Engineer. Another of these engines, No. 4468, "Mallard", holds the world speed record for steam travel. In the course of braking trials it ran for about three miles continuously at speeds of over 120 m.p.h. and touched 126 m.p.h.

The new trains introduced this summer for "The Flying Scotsman" represent the latest in luxury for a service on which no supplementary fares are charged. To enable the public to realise actually how much progress has been made in the last half century, the L.N.E.R. assembled a "period" train representing the equipment in use in 1888, the year of the Race to Edinburgh. This old train made several special runs behind that gallant veteran of railway engines, G.N.R. No. 1, the first of the single-wheelers with 8ft. driving wheels, designed by Patrick Stirling and built at Doncaster in 1870. The train was formed of seven coaches, sturdy six-wheeled vehicles with low-crowned roofs finished in the historic varnished teak style that is as old as King's Cross itself. To board the modern "Flying Scotsman" after a run in this old train is a revelation. Externally the new train conforms to the usual teak finish. It would, in fact, seem wrong for "The Flying Scotsman" to be otherwise! Internally the coaches mark a definite advance on any other train in normal daily service that is not of the streamlined type.

(Above). "Duchess of Gloucester", the first of the most recent series of streamlined 4-6-2s on the L.M.S. These engines are painted red.

(Left). "The Coronation Scot" of the L.M.S. speeding southward in charge of a streamlined 4-6-2 locomotive of the "Princess Coronation" class.

Then come the evening long-distance sleeping car trains from Euston and King's Cross, the modern developments of the old "8 p.m." competitors of the 1895 "race". Their working varies according to the season and the demands of traffic. The "Aberdonian" of the L.N.E.R. serves Aberdeen, Inverness and Fort William. In summer this train may run in several parts, to the first of which the name "Highlandman" is given. The corresponding West Coast service is afforded by "The Royal Highlander" for Perth, Aberdeen, Inverness and Oban. Finally there are the very similarly named "Night Scotsman" and "Night Scot" trains. The former from King's Cross at 10-25 p.m. serves Glasgow, Dundee, Perth, Edinburgh and Aber-

During the summer period each of the new trains consists of twelve coaches weighing 426 tons, and during the spring service 14 vehicles are used, weighing 503 tons. In the winter 13 vehicles are used in the service.

The whole train is insulated against sound in a manner

deen; and "The Night Scot" from Euston at 11-35 p.m. normally conveys sleeping car passengers for Glasgow. These night trains are invariably heavy, for sleeping cars are weighty vehicles and the inclusion of several of them in a train adds considerably to the work required of the engine.

The "Queen of Scots" is a good example of L.N.E.R. enterprise, and in providing a late morning all-Pullman service between English and Scottish capitals it is typical of the element of novelty in operation to which the company is so partial. Unlike the other Scottish expresses it does not run via York, but diverges from the East Coast route in order to serve Leeds and Harrogate. Doncaster and Ripon are the points where the main line is left, or rejoined as the case may be, by the "Queen of Scots" trains in each direction.

In connection with their Scottish traffic both East Coast and West Coast routes maintain important hotels. There is a North British Station Hotel of the L.N.E.R. in Edinburgh and in Glasgow; and the L.M.S. have the Caledonian Hotel in Edinburgh and the Central and St. Enoch Hotels in Glasgow.

similar to that which has been so successfully used in the "Coronation" and other high-speed trains. Pressure ventilation apparatus is fitted, and this, during cold weather, automatically warms the air to a comfortable temperature. By this means fresh filtered air is delivered at floor level by way of insulated ducts. The train is electrically lighted throughout, and is coupled by means of buck-eye automatic couplers connected to indiarubber springs, with Pullman vestibules between the coaches.

In addition to "The Royal Scot", "The Flying Scotsman", and the streamlined fliers "Coronation" and "The Coronation Scot", each route to the north operates other important day and night services between London and Scotland. With the exception of the L.N.E.R. "Queen of Scots" Pullman service, which has no counterpart on the L.M.S., the trains on each route can be considered quite conveniently in pairs.

First of all there are the well-established mid-day services. There is "The Midday Scot" of the L.M.S., which is directly descended from the old favourite "2 p.m." from Euston, at one time the only train on the West Coast route composed exclusively of corridor coaches and including dining cars. For this reason it was familiarly known as "The Corridor"; the name still lingers among railwaymen although its significance has long since vanished. This train connects Euston with Edinburgh and Aberdeen, and it serves Glasgow also on days when the streamlined "Coronation Scot" does not run. The corresponding mid-day train from King's Cross is provided by the "1-20 Scotsman", a popular and therefore always a very heavy train. At the same time it is sharply booked between stops at Grantham, York, Darlington and Newcastle on its way to Edinburgh.

"The Royal Scot" in the Lune valley, hauled by a "Princess" 4-6-2.

HORNBY ELECTRIC AND CLOCKWORK TRAINS

THE COMPLETENESS OF THE HORNBY GAUGE O RAILWAY SYSTEM

From the day of their introduction Hornby Trains have always represented the latest model railway practice. Designs are continually being improved and new items added so that the system is complete in practically every detail. There are Locomotives for all duties, driven by electric motors or by clockwork. There is Rolling Stock of all kinds, including Corridor Coaches, Pullman Cars, ordinary Coaches and Guard's Vans for passenger services; and there are numerous and varied Wagons and Vans for freight working.

The Accessories are now better than ever before. Stations, Signals and Signal Cabins, Engine Sheds, Level Crossings and other items can be obtained wired for electric lighting. Miniature Trees and Hedging provide a splendid scenic setting for any layout; Cuttings and Tunnels add realism to the track; miniature Railway Staff and Passengers give "life" to station platforms; and there are Animals for lineside fields.

The splendid fun of running a Hornby Railway is real and lasting, because of the exceptional strength and reliability of Hornby Locomotives, the realistic appearance and easy running of the Rolling Stock, and the wide range of effective Accessories—all designed and built in proportion and all splendidly finished.

HORNBY ELECTRIC AND CLOCKWORK LOCOMOTIVES

Hornby Electric Locomotives, of which there is a wide selection, are fitted with powerful and efficient motors capable of hauling heavy loads at high speeds, but always under perfect control. All Hornby Electric Locomotives can be controlled for speed, and for starting and stopping, from the lineside.

Hornby Clockwork Locomotives are the longest-running locomotives of their respective types in the world. The motors are perfect mechanisms with accurately cut gears. All the locomotives can be braked either from the cab or from the track by means of a suitable brake rail.

THE FAMOUS HORNBY REMOTE CONTROL

The largest Hornby 20-volt Electric Locomotives are fitted with the famous Hornby Remote Control. This makes possible starting and stopping; controlling for speed, easy round the curves, faster along the straight; and reversing trains at the end of the run or when shunting, without any need to touch the Locomotive at all. Everything is done from outside the track! In conjunction with the automatic couplings fitted to the Rolling Stock, Remote Control makes possible the most realistic operation.

THE FINISH OF HORNBY LOCOMOTIVES

Hornby Locomotives are finished in the passenger traffic colours of the four British Railway groups, red for L.M.S., light green for L.N.E.R., and dark green for G.W.R. and S.R. Locomotives can be obtained to special order finished in goods traffic colours—black for L.M.S., L.N.E.R. and S.R., and dark green for G.W.R.

Run your own Railway! The Hornby System includes everything that is necessary to equip a complete miniature railway, either electric or clockwork, to be operated in exactly the same way as a real railway system.

"PRINCESS ELIZABETH", the most famous of L.M.S. giant locomotives, made railway history in November, 1936, when she hauled a train from Glasgow to London, 401.4 miles, at an average speed of 70 m.p.h., thus setting up a world record for long-distance non-stop steam travel. With a load of 260 tons behind the tender, maximum speeds of 95 m.p.h. were reached, and even on such trying climbs as the ascents to Beattock and Shap Summits speed did not fall below 66 m.p.h.

Yet all this was achieved in bad weather, and in spite of some 50 reductions of speed during the run that were necessary for passing round curves, through junctions, and for other reasons.

"PRINCESS ELIZABETH" was built at Crewe Works to the designs of Mr. W. A. Stanier, Chief Mechanical Engineer of the L.M.S., and was one of the first two 4-6-2 locomotives built by that Company, the other being "The Princess Royal". Massive, dignified, efficient, the "Princess" class are firm favourites on the West Coast Route. They run such famous trains as "The Royal Scot", "The Mid-day Scot" and "The Merseyside Express", whirling 500-ton loads along the steel highway with amazing ease.

Here is Driver T. J. Clarke (retired this year), who was in charge of the "Princess Elizabeth" when it made its record-breaking run. He has seen the Hornby "Princess Elizabeth" and says "It's fine!"

HORNBY ELECTRIC AND CLOCKWORK TRAINS

THE COMPLETENESS OF THE HORNBY GAUGE O RAILWAY SYSTEM

From the day of their introduction Hornby Trains have always represented the latest model railway practice. Designs are continually being improved and new items added so that the system is complete in practically every detail. There are Locomotives for all duties, driven by electric motors or by clockwork. There is Rolling Stock of all kinds, including Corridor Coaches, Pullman Cars, ordinary Coaches and Guard's Vans for passenger services; and there are numerous and varied Wagons and Vans for freight working.

The Accessories are now better than ever before. Stations, Signals and Signal Cabins, Engine Sheds, Level Crossings and other items can be obtained wired for electric lighting. Miniature Trees and Hedging provide a splendid scenic setting for any layout; Cuttings and Tunnels add realism to the track; miniature Railway Staff and Passengers give "life" to station platforms; and there are Animals for lineside fields.

The splendid fun of running a Hornby Railway is real and lasting, because of the exceptional strength and reliability of Hornby Locomotives, the realistic appearance and easy running of the Rolling Stock, and the wide range of effective Accessories—all designed and built in proportion and all splendidly finished.

HORNBY ELECTRIC AND CLOCKWORK LOCOMOTIVES

Hornby Electric Locomotives, of which there is a wide selection, are fitted with powerful and efficient motors capable of hauling heavy loads at high speeds, but always under perfect control. All Hornby Electric Locomotives can be controlled for speed, and for starting and stopping, from the lineside.

Hornby Clockwork Locomotives are the longest-running locomotives of their respective types in the world. The motors are perfect mechanisms with accurately cut gears. All the locomotives can be braked either from the cab or from the track by means of a suitable brake rail.

THE FAMOUS HORNBY REMOTE CONTROL

The largest Hornby 20-volt Electric Locomotives are fitted with the famous Hornby Remote Control. This makes possible starting and stopping; controlling for speed, easy round the curves, faster along the straight; and reversing trains at the end of the run or when shunting, without any need to touch the Locomotive at all. Everything is done from outside the track! In conjunction with the automatic couplings fitted to the Rolling Stock, Remote Control makes possible the most realistic operation.

THE FINISH OF HORNBY LOCOMOTIVES

Hornby Locomotives are finished in the passenger traffic colours of the four British Railway groups, red for L.M.S., light green for L.N.E.R., and dark green for G.W.R. and S.R. Locomotives can be obtained to special order finished in goods traffic colours—black for L.M.S., L.N.E.R. and S.R., and dark green for G.W.R.

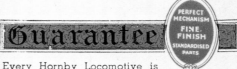

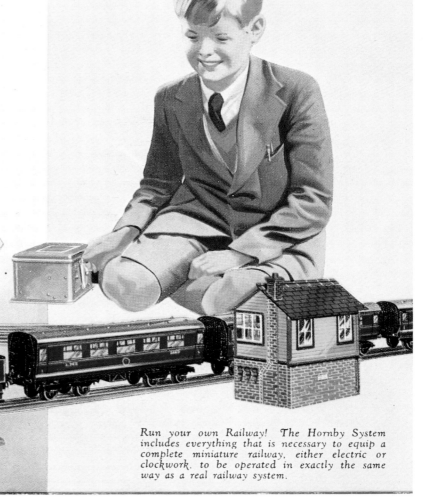

Run your own Railway! The Hornby System includes everything that is necessary to equip a complete miniature railway, either electric or clockwork, to be operated in exactly the same way as a real railway system.

400 MILES AT 70 M.P.H.

"**PRINCESS ELIZABETH**", the most famous of L.M.S. giant locomotives, made railway history in November, 1936, when she hauled a train from Glasgow to London, 401.4 miles, at an average speed of 70 m.p.h., thus setting up a world record for long-distance non-stop steam travel. With a load of 260 tons behind the tender, maximum speeds of 95 m.p.h. were reached, and even on such trying climbs as the ascents to Beattock and Shap Summits speed did not fall below 66 m.p.h.

Yet all this was achieved in bad weather, and in spite of some 50 reductions of speed during the run that were necessary for passing round curves, through junctions, and for other reasons.

"**PRINCESS ELIZABETH**" was built at Crewe Works to the designs of Mr. W. A. Stanier, Chief Mechanical Engineer of the L.M.S., and was one of the first two 4-6-2 locomotives built by that Company, the other being "The Princess Royal". Massive, dignified, efficient, the "Princess" class are firm favourites on the West Coast Route. They run such famous trains as "The Royal Scot", "The Mid-day Scot" and "The Merseyside Express", whirling 500-ton loads along the steel highway with amazing ease.

Here is Driver T. J. Clarke (retired this year), who was in charge of the "Princess Elizabeth" when it made its record-breaking run. He has seen the Hornby "Princess Elizabeth" and says "It's fine!"

HORNBY SCALE MODEL OF

"Princess Elizabeth"

20-VOLT ELECTRIC LOCOMOTIVE WITH TENDER AUTOMATIC REVERSING

This is a magnificent Hornby scale model of the L.M.S. 4-6-2 "Princess Elizabeth" locomotive. It includes all the main features of the actual engine—massive six-coupled driving wheels, outside cylinders and motion, tapered boiler and fire-box, oval-headed buffers at the front, accurate internal details of cab and tender and Royal nameplate. The new Hornby 20-volt automatic reversing motor that is fitted ensures abundant power and makes "Princess Elizabeth" the ideal engine for the fastest and heaviest trains. The enamelling and lining follows L.M.S. practice faithfully, and the general finish is of the highest Hornby quality.

Price, complete with tender, in special presentation box, **£5. 5. 0.**

"Princess Elizabeth" will run on the standard Hornby 2 ft. radius tinplate track, but in order to allow this splendid locomotive to run at its highest speed, and to show the immense loads it will pull, the Hornby Solid Steel Track (see page 49) should be used. To make up a suitable train for the "Princess Elizabeth" Locomotive as illustrated below, the L.M.S. No. 2 Corridor Coaches, featured on page 35, should be used.

QUALITY FEATURES OF "PRINCESS ELIZABETH" MOTOR

1. FIELD—Constructed of electrical steel laminations, and scientifically designed to obtain maximum power.
2. DRIVING WHEELS.—Accurately pressure diecast to give maximum adhesion and smooth running.
3. GEARS.—All gears machine cut.
4. BEARINGS. — All bearings are of phosphor bronze.

5. ARMATURE. — Of laminated electrical steel mounted on a shaft machined from specially selected high grade steel.
6. SIDEPLATES.—Hard rolled brass, rigidly connected by turned pillars.
7. COMMUTATOR.—Constructed with hard copper segments moulded into a Bakelite body.

8. BRUSH HOLDERS.—Of brass, rigidly mounted on a Bakelite moulded bracket.
9. BRUSHES.—Of self-lubricating Morganite Carbon.
10. REVERSING SWITCH—Bakelite moulded switch barrel with bronze contact springs. Working parts of the automatic mechanism are case hardened.

Gauge O

"Eton"

20-VOLT ELECTRIC OR CLOCKWORK LOCOMOTIVE

SOUTHERN
900

ETON

The "ETON" Locomotive, with Tender. Note the beautiful lines of this model, the wealth of detail and the correct colouring. It is a triumph of scale model craftsmanship.

The 20-volt electric model (No. E420) and the clockwork model (No. 4C) are identical in appearance.

This is a fine model of the first member of the famous "Schools" class, perhaps the most popular series of locomotives ever produced by the Southern Railway Company.

All who are interested in model locomotives, and especially "Southern" enthusiasts, will welcome the "ETON" model both for its beauty and its fine performance.

The E420 electric model has a 20-volt motor and is fitted with the famous Hornby REMOTE CONTROL. This means that, by the operation of the control lever on the Transformer, a train can be started, stopped or reversed without touching the locomotive at all.

The No. 4C Clockwork model is fitted with an exceptionally powerful motor that gives a long and steady run on each winding.

E420 20-VOLT ELECTRIC AUTOMATIC REVERSING	No. 4C CLOCKWORK
Locomotive (without Tender). Price 43/6	Locomotive (without Tender). Price 36/6
Tender. Price 6/6	Tender. Price 6/6

To make up a suitable train for the "Eton" Locomotive, as illustrated above, the new S.R. No. 2 Corridor Coaches should be used. Details of these are as follows:—

Hornby No. 2 Corridor Coach, Third Class   ...   .   Price **7/6**
Hornby No. 2 Corridor Coach, Brake-composite   ...   ...   Price **7/6**

The Royal Scot

Golden Arrow

No. 3C Clockwork Passenger Train Set
"The Royal Scot". L.M.S.

No. 3C Clockwork Pullman Train Set
"The Golden Arrow". S.R.

The components of the Train Sets shown on this page are obtainable separately at the following prices:—

E320 Electric Locomotive (20-volt) automatic reversing (without Tender)	Price 32/6
No. 3C Clockwork Locomotive, reversing (without Tender)	Price 22/6
No. 2 Special Tender	Price 6/6
No. 2 Corridor Coach	Price 7/6
No. 2 Corridor Composite Coach	Price 7/6
No. 2 Special Pullman Coach	Price 13/6
No. 2 Special Pullman Composite Coach	Price 13/6

The prices of Hornby Rails are given in pages 49, 50 and 51.

For particulars and prices of Transformers, see page 34.

The Train Sets listed on this page carry the names of famous British Expresses, as follows:—

"The Royal Scot"
L.M.S.

"The Flying Scotsman"
L.N.E.R.

"Cornish Riviera Express"
G.W.R.

"The Golden Arrow"
S.R.

HORNBY E320 ELECTRIC and No. 3C CLOCKWORK PASSENGER TRAIN SETS

L.M.S., L.N.E.R. or G.W.R.

20-VOLT ELECTRIC—AUTOMATIC REVERSING

E320 (20-volt). Locomotive (automatic reversing) with electric headlamp, No. 2 Special Tender, two No. 2 Corridor Coaches, one No. 2 Corridor Composite Coach, twelve EA2 Curved Rails, four EB1 Straight Rails and a TCP20 Terminal Connecting Plate. Space required—6 ft. 3 in. by 4 ft. 6 in. Price **71/6**

CLOCKWORK

No. 3C (Clockwork). Locomotive (reversing), No. 2 Special Tender, one No. 2 Corridor Coach, one No. 2 Corridor Composite Coach, twelve A2 Curved Rails, three B1 Straight Rails and a BBR1 Straight Brake and Reverse Rail by means of which the Train can be either braked or reversed from the track. Space required—6 ft. 3 in. by 4 ft. 6 in. Price **50/-**

HORNBY E320 ELECTRIC and No. 3C CLOCKWORK PULLMAN TRAIN SETS (S.R. only)

20-VOLT ELECTRIC—AUTOMATIC REVERSING

E320 (20-volt). Locomotive (automatic reversing) with electric headlamp, No. 2 Special Tender, one No. 2 Special Pullman Coach, one No. 2 Special Pullman Composite Coach, twelve EA2 Curved Rails, four EB1 Straight Rails and a TCP20 Terminal Connecting Plate. Space required 6 ft. 3 in. by 4 ft. 6 in. Price **75/-**

CLOCKWORK

No. 3C (Clockwork). Locomotive (reversing), No. 2 Special Tender, one No. 2 Special Pullman Coach, one No. 2 Special Pullman Composite Coach, twelve A2 Curved Rails, three B1 Straight Rails and one BBR1 Straight Brake and Reverse Rail by means of which the Train can be either braked or reversed from the track. Space required—6 ft. 3 in. by 4 ft. 6 in. Price **60/-**

Gauge O

THE BRISTOLIAN

THE YORKSHIREMAN

FOLKESTONE FLYER

No. 2 Special Clockwork Passenger Train Set. G.W.R.

No. 2 Special Clockwork Passenger Train Set. L.M.S.

No. 2 Special Clockwork Passenger Train Set. S.R.

"Folkestone Flyer" (S.R.)
hauled by the "L1" Class Locomotive "No. 1759"

"The Scarborough Flyer" (L.N.E.R.)
hauled by the "Hunt" Class Locomotive "The Bramham Moor"

"The Bristolian" (G.W.R.)
hauled by the "County" Class Locomotive "County of Bedford"

"The Yorkshireman" (L.M.S.)
hauled by the "Standard Compound" Class Locomotive "No. 1185"

HORNBY
E220 SPECIAL ELECTRIC and No. 2 SPECIAL CLOCKWORK PASSENGER TRAIN SETS

20-VOLT ELECTRIC—AUTOMATIC REVERSING

E220 Special (20-volt). Locomotive (automatic reversing) with electric headlamp, one No. 2 Special Tender, two No. 2 Corridor Coaches, one No. 2 Corridor Composite Coach, twelve EA2 Curved Rails, two EB1 Straight Rails and a TCP20 Terminal Connecting Plate. Space required—5 ft. 4 in. by 4 ft. 6 in. Price **76/-**

CLOCKWORK

No. 2 Special (Clockwork). Locomotive (reversing), one No. 2 Special Tender, one No. 2 Corridor Coach, one No. 2 Corridor Composite Coach, twelve A2 Curved Rails, one B1 Straight Rail and one BBR1 Straight Brake and Reverse Rail by means of which the Train can be either braked or reversed from the track. Space required—5 ft. 4 in. by 4 ft. 6 in. Price **55/-**

*The components of the above Train Sets can be purchased separately.
For prices see foot of opposite page.*

"The Scarborough Flyer"

E220 Special Electric Passenger Train Set. L.N.E.R.

"THE SCARBOROUGH FLYER" is a famous L.N.E.R. train that runs between London (King's Cross) and Scarborough, providing a speedy service to the famous Yorkshire coast resort. It is a particularly popular train, and on the first part of the down journey to York it is timed at an average start-to-stop speed of 63 m.p.h. Leaving King's Cross at 11-10 a.m. it brings Scarborough within a four-hour journey from London.

The Hornby 20-volt electric and clockwork models of "The Scarborough Flyer" have all the fine characteristics of their prototype. They are available in complete train sets, as detailed on the opposite page, or the components can be purchased separately at the prices indicated at the foot of this page.

"The Bramham Moor" E220 Special Electric Locomotive (20-volt) automatic reversing, with Tender.

The components of the E220 Special Electric and No. 2 Special Clockwork Passenger Train Sets are obtainable separately at the following prices:—

E220 Special Electric Locomotive (20-volt) automatic reversing (without Tender) Price 38/6
No. 2 Special Clockwork Locomotive, reversing (without Tender) ... ... Price 28/6
No. 2 Special Tender ... Price 6/6   No. 2 Corridor Coach ... ... Price 7/6
No. 2 Corridor Composite Coach ... ... Price 7/6

The prices of Hornby Rails are given on pages 49, 50 and 51. For particulars and prices of Transformers see page 34.

Gauge O

HORNBY *Riviera "Blue"* TRAIN SETS

ELECTRIC OR CLOCKWORK

No. 3C Clockwork Riviera "Blue" Passenger Train Set

20-VOLT ELECTRIC—AUTOMATIC REVERSING

E320 (20-volt). Locomotive (automatic reversing) with electric headlamp, No. 3 Riviera "Blue" Tender, Riviera "Blue" Dining Car, Riviera "Blue" Sleeping Car, twelve EA2 Curved Rails, four EB1 Straight Rails and a TCP20 Terminal Connecting Plate. Space required—6 ft. 3 in. by 4 ft. 6 in. The Set is supplied in correct Riviera "Blue" Train colours. Price 69/-

The components of the Riviera "Blue" Train Sets are obtainable separately at the following prices:—

E320 Electric Riviera "Blue" Locomotive (20-volt) automatic reversing (without Tender)   Price 32/6
No 3C Clockwork Riviera "Blue" Locomotive, reversing (without Tender)   Price 22/6
No. 3 Riviera "Blue" Tender   Price 5/6
Riviera "Blue" Dining Car or Sleeping Car.   Price, each, 11/-

CLOCKWORK

No. 3C (Clockwork). Locomotive (reversing), No. 3 Riviera "Blue" Tender, Riviera "Blue" Dining Car, Riviera "Blue" Sleeping Car, twelve A2 Curved Rails, three B1 Straight Rails and a BBR1 Straight Brake and Reverse Rail by means of which the Train can be either braked or reversed from the track. Space required—6 ft. 3 in. by 4 ft. 6 in. The Set is supplied in correct Riviera "Blue" Train colours.   Price 55/-

The prices of Hornby Rails, Points and Crossings are given on pages 49, 50 and 51. For particulars and prices of Transformers see page 34.

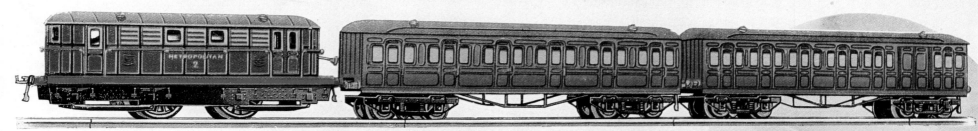

Hornby No. 3C Clockwork Metropolitan Train Set

20-VOLT AND 6-VOLT ELECTRIC

E320 (20-volt). Locomotive (automatic reversing) with electric Headlamp, First-class Compartment Coach and Brake-third Coach, both fitted for electric lighting, twelve EA2 Curved Rails and a 20-volt Terminal Connecting Plate. Space required—4 ft. 6 in. square. Supplied in standard colours of the London Metropolitan.   Price 60/-
E36 (6-volt). This set is similar to the E320 Set except that the locomotive is fitted with a 6-volt Motor (reversible by hand) and a 6-volt Terminal Connecting Plate.   Price 57/6

CLOCKWORK

No. 3C (Clockwork). Locomotive (reversing), first-class compartment coach, brake-third coach, twelve A2 Curved Rails, three B1 Straight Rails and a BBR1 Straight Brake and Reverse Rail by means of which the Train can be either braked or reversed from the track. Space required—6 ft. 3 in. by 4 ft. 6 in.   Price 40/-

The components of the Metropolitan Train Sets can be obtained separately. For prices see pages 31 and 36.

HORNBY *Metropolitan* TRAIN SETS

HORNBY E220 ELECTRIC and No. 2 CLOCKWORK TANK PASSENGER TRAIN SETS
L.M.S., L.N.E.R., G.W.R. or S.R.

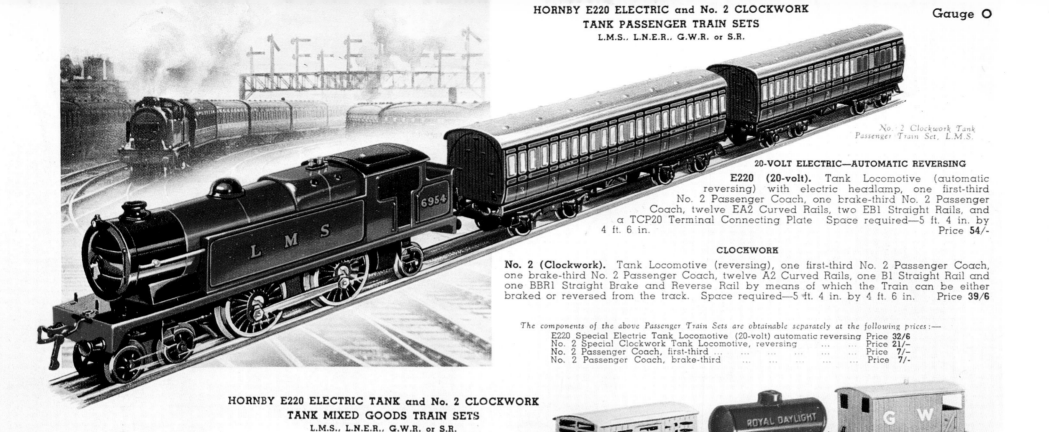

No. 2 Clockwork Tank Passenger Train Set, L.M.S.

20-VOLT ELECTRIC—AUTOMATIC REVERSING

E220 (20-volt). Tank Locomotive (automatic reversing) with electric headlamp, one first-third No. 2 Passenger Coach, one brake-third No. 2 Passenger Coach, twelve EA2 Curved Rails, two EB1 Straight Rails, and a TCP20 Terminal Connecting Plate Space required—5 ft. 4 in. by 4 ft. 6 in.   Price **54/-**

CLOCKWORK

No. 2 (Clockwork). Tank Locomotive (reversing), one first-third No. 2 Passenger Coach, one brake-third No. 2 Passenger Coach, twelve A2 Curved Rails, one B1 Straight Rail and one BBR1 Straight Brake and Reverse Rail by means of which the Train can be either braked or reversed from the track. Space required—5 ft. 4 in. by 4 ft. 6 in.   Price **39/6**

The components of the above Passenger Train Sets are obtainable separately at the following prices:—

E220 Special Electric Tank Locomotive (20-volt) automatic reversing	Price 32/6
No. 2 Special Clockwork Tank Locomotive, reversing	Price 21/-
No. 2 Passenger Coach, first-third	Price 7/-
No. 2 Passenger Coach, brake-third	Price 7/-

HORNBY E220 ELECTRIC TANK and No. 2 CLOCKWORK TANK MIXED GOODS TRAIN SETS
L.M.S., L.N.E.R., G.W.R. or S.R.

No. 2 Clockwork Tank Mixed Goods Train Set, G.W.R.

20-VOLT ELECTRIC—AUTOMATIC REVERSING

E220 (20-volt). Tank Locomotive (automatic reversing) with electric headlamp, No. 1 Wagon, No. 1 Cattle Truck, Oil Tank Wagon, Brake Van, twelve EA2 Rails, two EB1 Straight Rails and a TCP20 Terminal Connecting Plate. Space required—5 ft. 4 in. by 4 ft. 6 in.   Price **48/-**

CLOCKWORK

No. 2 (Clockwork). Tank Locomotive (reversing), No. 1 Wagon, No. 1 Cattle Truck, Oil Tank Wagon, Brake Van, twelve A2 Curved Rails, one B1 Straight Rail and a BBR1 Straight Brake and Reverse Rail by means of which the Train can be either braked or reversed from the track. Space required—5 ft. 4 in. by 4 ft. 6 in.   Price **35/-**

The components of the above Goods Train Sets are obtainable separately at the following prices:—

E220 Special Electric Tank Locomotive (20-volt) automatic reversing.			Price 32/6
No. 2 Special Clockwork Tank Locomotive, reversing			Price 21/-
No. 1 Wagon ... ... Price 1/6		No. 1 Cattle Truck ...	Price 2/3
Oil Tank Wagon ... Price 1/11		Brake Van ...	Price 2/9

The prices of Hornby Rails, Points and Crossings are given on pages 49, 50 and 51. For particulars and prices of Transformers, see page 34.

THE COMET

Gauge O

(L.M.S.)

No. 1 Special Clockwork Passenger Train Set, L.M.S.

20-VOLT ELECTRIC—AUTOMATIC REVERSING

E120 Special (20-volt). Locomotive (automatic reversing) with electric headlamp, No. 1 Special Tender, two No. 1 Passenger Coaches and a Guard's Van for L.M.S. and G.W.R., or two No. 1 Pullman Coaches and one No. 1 Pullman Composite Coach for L.N.E.R. and S.R., twelve EA2 Curved Rails, two EB1 Straight Rails and a TCP20 Terminal Connecting Plate. Space required—5 ft. 4 in. by 4 ft. 6 in. Price 48/-

CLOCKWORK

No. 1 Special (Clockwork). Locomotive (reversing) No. 1 Special Tender, two No. 1 Passenger Coaches and a Guard's Van for L.M.S. and G.W.R., or two No. 1 Pullman Coaches and one No. 1 Pullman Composite Coach for L.N.E.R. and S.R., twelve A2 Curved Rails, one B1 Straight Rail and one BBR1 Straight Brake and Reverse Rail by means of which the Train can be either braked or reversed from the track. Space required—5 ft. 4 in. by 4 ft. 6 in. Price 33/6

"The Comet" (L.M.S.)
(Illustrated above)

"Queen of Scots" (L.N.E.R.)

"Torbay Express" (G.W.R.)

"Bournemouth Belle" (S.R.)

The components of these Train Sets can be purchased separately. For prices see opposite page.

ROYAL DAYLIGHT

No. 1 Special Clockwork Tank Goods Train Set, L.N.E.R.

HORNBY
E120 SPECIAL ELECTRIC and No. 1 SPECIAL CLOCKWORK TANK GOODS TRAIN SETS
L.M.S., L.N.E.R., G.W.R. or S.R.

20-VOLT ELECTRIC—AUTOMATIC REVERSING

E120 Special Tank (20-volt). Tank Locomotive (automatic reversing) with electric headlamp, No. 1 Wagon, Oil Tank Wagon, Brake Van, twelve EA2 Curved Rails, two EB1 Straight Rails and a TCP20 Terminal Connecting Plate. Space required—5 ft. 4 in. by 4 ft. 6 in. Price 43/6

CLOCKWORK

No. 1 Special Tank (Clockwork). Tank Locomotive (reversing), No. 1 Wagon, Oil Tank Wagon, Brake Van, twelve A2 Curved Rails, one B1 Straight Rail and one BBR1 Straight Brake and Reverse Rail by means of which the Train can be either braked or reversed from the track. Space required—5 ft. 4 in. by 4 ft. 6 in. Price 28/-

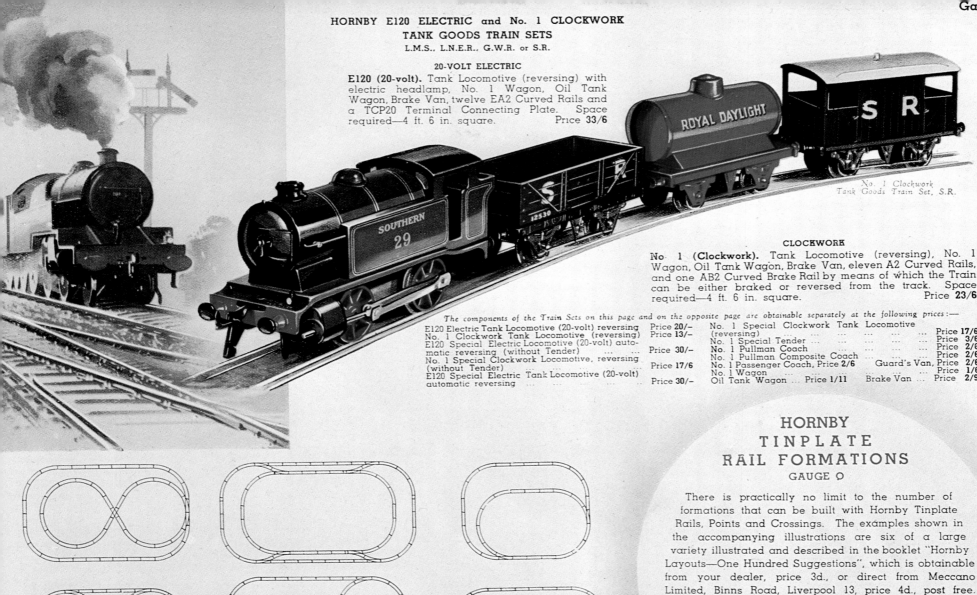

Gauge O

HORNBY E120 ELECTRIC and No. 1 CLOCKWORK TANK GOODS TRAIN SETS
L.M.S., L.N.E.R., G.W.R. or S.R.

20-VOLT ELECTRIC

E120 (20-volt). Tank Locomotive (reversing) with electric headlamp, No. 1 Wagon, Oil Tank Wagon, Brake Van, twelve EA2 Curved Rails and a TCP20 Terminal Connecting Plate. Space required—4 ft. 6 in. square. Price 33/6

No. 1 Clockwork Tank Goods Train Set, S.R.

CLOCKWORK

No. 1 (Clockwork). Tank Locomotive (reversing), No. 1 Wagon, Oil Tank Wagon, Brake Van, eleven A2 Curved Rails, and one AB2 Curved Brake Rail by means of which the Train can be either braked or reversed from the track. Space required—4 ft. 6 in. square. Price 23/6

The components of the Train Sets on this page and on the opposite page are obtainable separately at the following prices:—

E120 Electric Tank Locomotive (20-volt) reversing	Price 20/-	No. 1 Special Clockwork Tank Locomotive (reversing)	Price 17/6
No. 1 Clockwork Tank Locomotive (reversing)	Price 13/-	No. 1 Special Tender	Price 3/6
E120 Special Electric Locomotive (20-volt) automatic reversing (without Tender)	Price 30/-	No. 1 Pullman Coach	Price 2/6
No. 1 Special Clockwork Locomotive, reversing (without Tender)	Price 17/6	No. 1 Pullman Composite Coach	Price 2/6
E120 Special Electric Tank Locomotive (20-volt) automatic reversing	Price 30/-	No. 1 Passenger Coach, Price 2/6	Guard's Van, Price 2/6
		No. 1 Wagon	Price 1/6
		Oil Tank Wagon ... Price 1/11	Brake Van ... Price 2/9

HORNBY TINPLATE RAIL FORMATIONS
GAUGE O

There is practically no limit to the number of formations that can be built with Hornby Tinplate Rails, Points and Crossings. The examples shown in the accompanying illustrations are six of a large variety illustrated and described in the booklet "Hornby Layouts—One Hundred Suggestions", which is obtainable from your dealer, price 3d., or direct from Meccano Limited, Binns Road, Liverpool 13, price 4d., post free. The purpose of this book is to show how the wide range of Hornby Tinplate Rails, Points and Crossings can be employed in the assembly of clockwork and electric layouts of all kinds, from simple designs to the most elaborate formations. The Hornby Railway System is constructed to Gauge O. In this gauge the track is 1¼ in. wide, the measurement being made between the insides of the heads of the rails.

The prices of Hornby Rails, Points and Crossings, both electric and clockwork, are given on pages 49, 50 and 51.

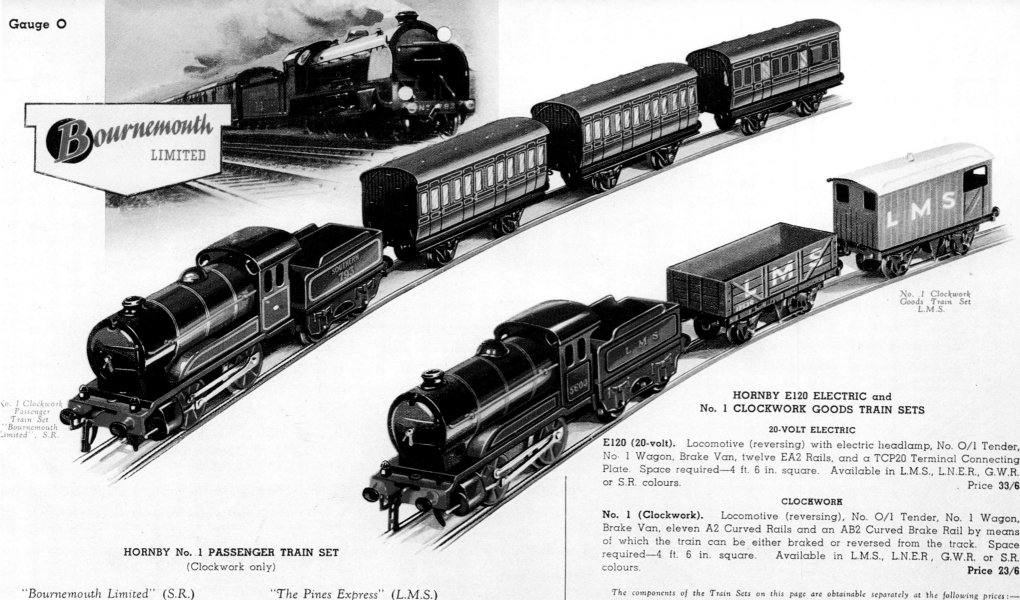

Bournemouth LIMITED

No. 1 Clockwork Passenger Train Set "Bournemouth Limited", S.R.

No. 1 Clockwork Goods Train Set L.M.S.

HORNBY No. 1 PASSENGER TRAIN SET
(Clockwork only)

"Bournemouth Limited" (S.R.)   "The Pines Express" (L.M.S.)

"Cambrian Coast Express" (G.W.R.)   "Aberdonian" (L.N.E.R.)

No. 1 (Clockwork). Locomotive (reversing), No. O/1 Tender, two No. 1 Passenger Coaches, Guard's Van, eleven A2 Curved Rails and an AB2 Curved Brake Rail by means of which the Train can be either braked or reversed from the track. Space required—4 ft. 6 in. square   Price **26/-**

HORNBY E120 ELECTRIC and No. 1 CLOCKWORK GOODS TRAIN SETS

20-VOLT ELECTRIC

E120 (20-volt). Locomotive (reversing) with electric headlamp, No. O/1 Tender, No. 1 Wagon, Brake Van, twelve EA2 Rails, and a TCP20 Terminal Connecting Plate. Space required—4 ft. 6 in. square. Available in L.M.S., L.N.E.R., G.W.R. or S.R. colours.   Price **33/6**

CLOCKWORK

No. 1 (Clockwork). Locomotive (reversing), No. O/1 Tender, No. 1 Wagon, Brake Van, eleven A2 Curved Rails and an AB2 Curved Brake Rail by means of which the train can be either braked or reversed from the track. Space required—4 ft. 6 in. square. Available in L.M.S., L.N.E.R, G.W.R. or S.R. colours.   Price **23/6**

The components of the Train Sets on this page are obtainable separately at the following prices:—

E120 Electric Locomotive (20-volt), reversing (without Tender)	Price 20/-
No. 1 Clockwork Locomotive, reversing (without Tender)	Price 13/-
No. O/1 Tender	Price 2/-
No. 1 Passenger Coach	Price 2/6
Guard's Van	Price 2/6
No. 1 Wagon	Price 1/6
Brake Van	Price 2/9

The prices of Hornby Rails, Points and Crossings are given on pages 49, 50 and 51. For particulars and prices of Transformers see page 34.

No. O Clockwork Passenger Train Set

20-VOLT ELECTRIC

EO20 (20-volt). Locomotive (reversing) with electric headlamp, No. O/1 Tender, two No. O Pullman Coaches, six EA1 Curved Rails, two EB1 Straight Rails and one TCP20 Terminal Connecting Plate. Space required—3 ft. 3 in. by 2 ft. 6 in. Available with Locomotive and Tender in L.M.S., L.N.E.R., G.W.R. or S.R. colours. Price **28/6**

CLOCKWORK

No. O (Clockwork). Locomotive (reversing), No. O/1 Tender, two No. O Pullman Coaches, six A1 Curved Rails, one B1 Straight Rail and one BB1 Straight Brake Rail by means of which the Train can be braked from the track. Space required—3 ft. 3 in. by 2 ft. 6 in. Available with Locomotive and Tender in L.M.S., L.N.E.R., G.W.R. or S.R. colours. Price **17/3**

The components of the Train Sets on this page are obtainable separately at the following prices:—

EO20 Electric Locomotive, (20-volt reversing), (without Tender) Price **19/-**   No. O Clockwork Locomotive, reversing (without Tender) Price **10/-**

No. O/1 Tender, Price **2/-**   No. O Pullman Coach, Price **1/3**   No. O Wagon, Price **1/3**   No. 1 Timber Wagon, Price **1/3**

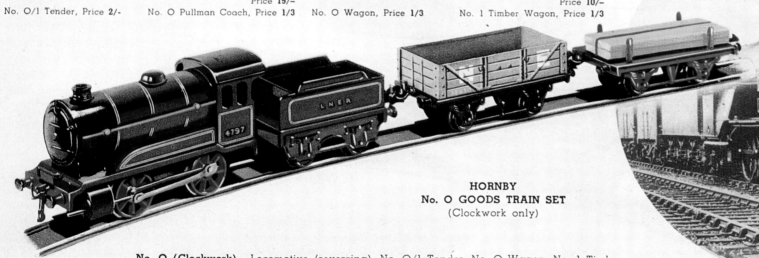

HORNBY
No. O GOODS TRAIN SET
(Clockwork only)

No. O (Clockwork). Locomotive (reversing), No. O/1 Tender, No. O Wagon, No. 1 Timber Wagon, six A1 Curved Rails, one B1 Straight Rail and one BB1 Straight Brake Rail by means of which the Train can be braked from the track. Space required—3 ft. 3 in. by 2 ft. 6 in. Available with Locomotive, Tender and Wagon in L.M.S., L.N.E.R., G.W.R. or S.R. colours. Price **17/3**

The components of No. O Goods Train Set can be purchased separately. For prices see above.

*Hornby Trains are
British and Guaranteed*

The prices of Hornby Rails, Points and Crossings are given on pages 49, 50 and 51. For particulars and prices of Transformers see page 34.

EM320 and EM36 ELECTRIC and M3 CLOCKWORK TANK GOODS TRAIN SETS

M3 Clockwork Tank Goods Train Set

CLOCKWORK

M3 (Clockwork). Tank Locomotive (reversing), available in L.M.S., L.N.E.R., G.W.R. or S.R. colours, one Goods Wagon, one Timber Wagon, one "Royal Daylight" Oil Tank Wagon, six A1 Curved Rails, three B1 Straight Rails, and one BB1 Straight Brake Rail by means of which the Train can be braked from the track. Space required—4 ft. 3 in. by 2 ft. 6 in.   **Price 16/6**

20-VOLT AND 6-VOLT ELECTRIC

EM320 (20-volt). Tank Locomotive (reversing) with electric headlamp, available in L.M.S., L.N.E.R., G.W.R. or S.R. colours, one Goods Wagon, one Timber Wagon, one "Royal Daylight" Oil Tank Wagon, six EA1 Curved Rails, two EB1 Straight Rails and one TCP20 Terminal Connecting Plate. Space required—3 ft. 3 in. by 2 ft. 6 in.   **Price 26/-**

EM36 (6-volt). This Set is similar to the EM320 Set except that the locomotive is fitted with a 6-volt motor and a 6-volt TCP6 Terminal Connecting Plate is included.   **Price 26/-**

M3 TANK PASSENGER TRAIN SET
(Clockwork only)

Tank locomotive (reversing) available in L.M.S., L.N.E.R., G.W.R. or S.R. colours, three No. O Pullman Coaches, six A1 Curved Rails, three B1 Straight Rails and one BB1 Straight Brake Rail by means of which the Train can be braked from the track. Space required—4 ft. 3 in. by 2 ft. 6 in.   **Price 15/-**

The Locomotives in the Train Sets on this page, and the No. O Pullman Coaches of the M3 Clockwork Passenger Train Set, are obtainable separately at the following prices:—

EM320 or EM36 Electric Tank Locomotive (reversible from cab)	**Price 17/-**
M3 Clockwork Tank Locomotive (reversing)	**Price 9/-**
No. O Pullman Coach	**Price 1/3**

The prices of Hornby Rails, Points and Crossings are given on pages 49, 50 and 51. For particulars and prices of Transformers see page 34.

M1 GOODS TRAIN SETS
(Clockwork only)

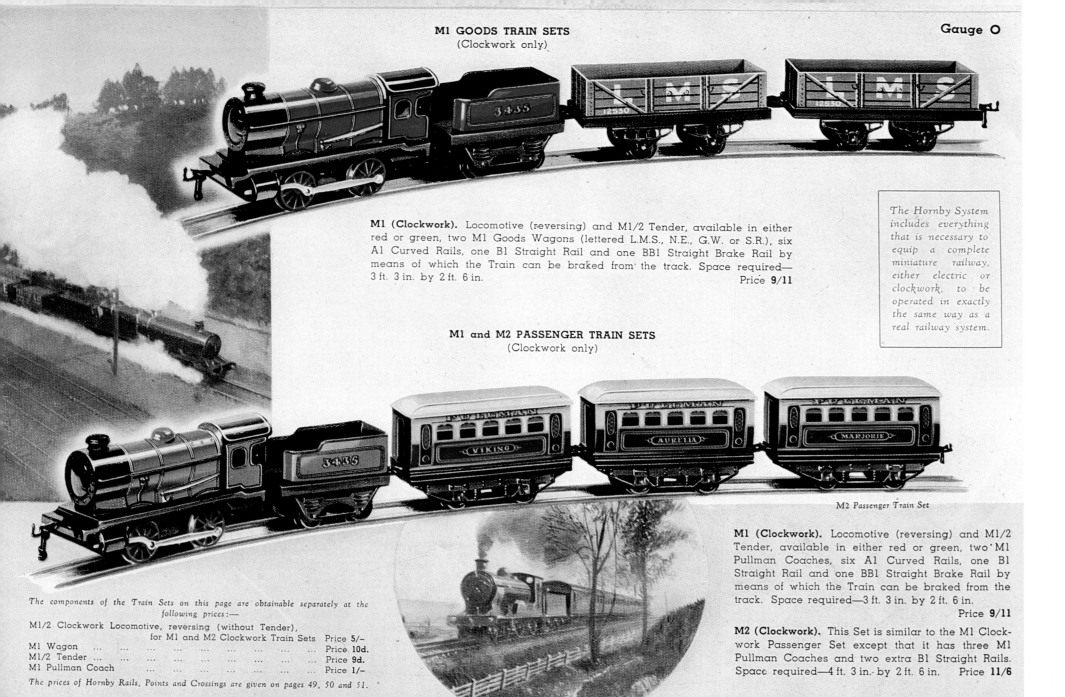

M1 (Clockwork). Locomotive (reversing) and M1/2 Tender, available in either red or green, two M1 Goods Wagons (lettered L.M.S., N.E., G.W. or S.R.), six A1 Curved Rails, one B1 Straight Rail and one BB1 Straight Brake Rail by means of which the Train can be braked from the track. Space required—3 ft. 3 in. by 2 ft. 6 in.
Price **9/11**

> The Hornby System includes everything that is necessary to equip a complete miniature railway, either electric or clockwork, to be operated in exactly the same way as a real railway system.

M1 and M2 PASSENGER TRAIN SETS
(Clockwork only)

M2 Passenger Train Set

The components of the Train Sets on this page are obtainable separately at the following prices :—

M1/2 Clockwork Locomotive, reversing (without Tender),
for M1 and M2 Clockwork Train Sets ... ... Price 5/-
M1 Wagon ... ... Price 10d.
M1/2 Tender ... ... Price 9d.
M1 Pullman Coach ... ... Price 1/-
The prices of Hornby Rails, Points and Crossings are given on pages 49, 50 and 51.

M1 (Clockwork). Locomotive (reversing) and M1/2 Tender, available in either red or green, two M1 Pullman Coaches, six A1 Curved Rails, one B1 Straight Rail and one BB1 Straight Brake Rail by means of which the Train can be braked from the track. Space required—3 ft. 3 in. by 2 ft. 6 in.
Price **9/11**

M2 (Clockwork). This Set is similar to the M1 Clockwork Passenger Set except that it has three M1 Pullman Coaches and two extra B1 Straight Rails. Space required—4 ft. 3 in. by 2 ft. 6 in.   Price **11/6**

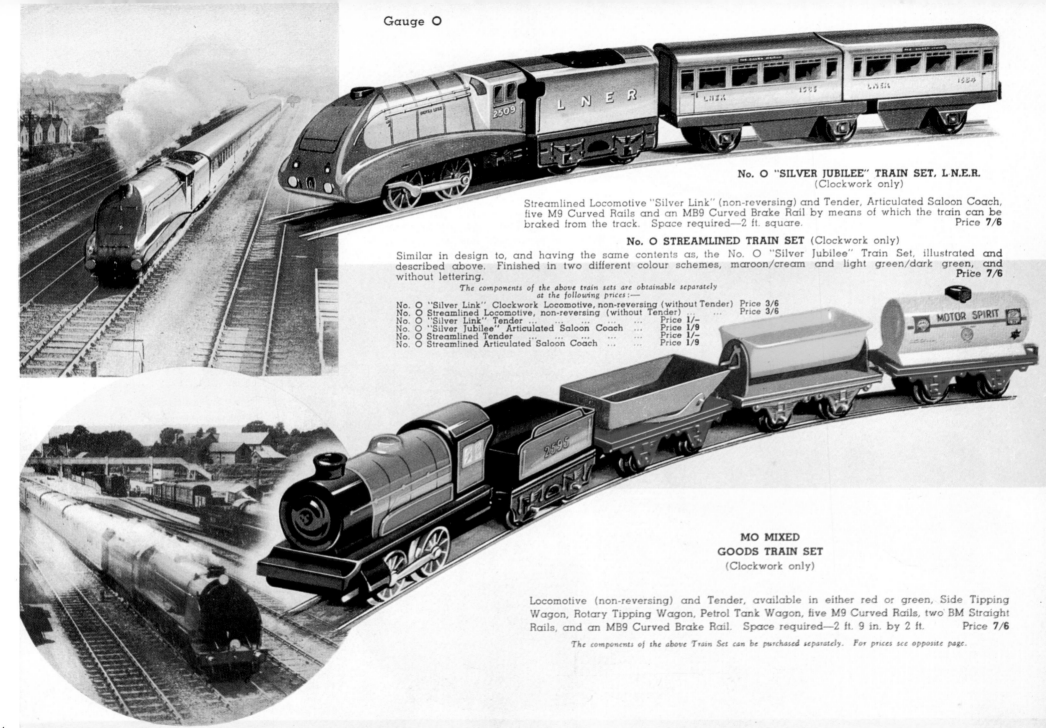

No. O "SILVER JUBILEE" TRAIN SET, L.N.E.R.
(Clockwork only)

Streamlined Locomotive "Silver Link" (non-reversing) and Tender, Articulated Saloon Coach, five M9 Curved Rails and an MB9 Curved Brake Rail by means of which the train can be braked from the track. Space required—2 ft. square.   Price **7/6**

No. O STREAMLINED TRAIN SET (Clockwork only)

Similar in design to, and having the same contents as, the No. O "Silver Jubilee" Train Set, illustrated and described above. Finished in two different colour schemes, maroon/cream and light green/dark green, and without lettering.   Price **7/6**

The components of the above train sets are obtainable separately at the following prices:—

No. O "Silver Link" Clockwork Locomotive, non-reversing (without Tender) Price **3/6**
No. O Streamlined Locomotive, non-reversing (without Tender) ... ... Price **3/6**
No. O "Silver Link" Tender ... ... Price **1/—**
No. O "Silver Jubilee" Articulated Saloon Coach ... ... Price **1/9**
No. O Streamlined Tender ... ... Price **1/—**
No. O Streamlined Articulated Saloon Coach ... ... Price **1/9**

MO MIXED
GOODS TRAIN SET
(Clockwork only)

Locomotive (non-reversing) and Tender, available in either red or green, Side Tipping Wagon, Rotary Tipping Wagon, Petrol Tank Wagon, five M9 Curved Rails, two BM Straight Rails, and an MB9 Curved Brake Rail. Space required—2 ft. 9 in. by 2 ft.   Price **7/6**

The components of the above Train Set can be purchased separately. For prices see opposite page.

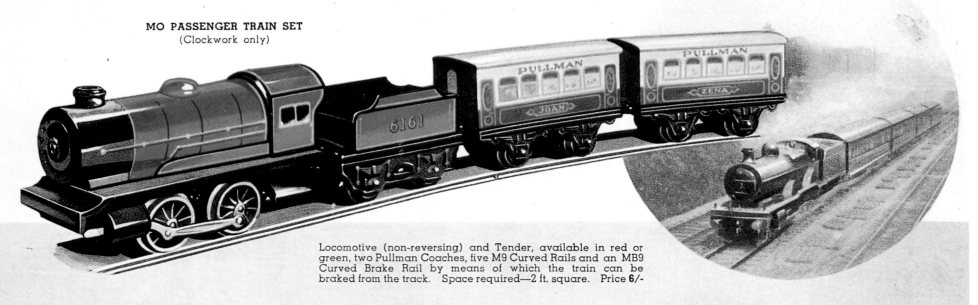

MO PASSENGER TRAIN SET
(Clockwork only)

Locomotive (non-reversing) and Tender, available in red or green, two Pullman Coaches, five M9 Curved Rails and an MB9 Curved Brake Rail by means of which the train can be braked from the track.   Space required—2 ft. square.   Price **6/-**

MO GOODS TRAIN SET
(Clockwork only)

Locomotive (non-reversing) and Tender, available in red or green, two wagons, five M9 Curved Rails and an MB9 Curved Brake Rail by means of which the train can be braked from the track.   Space required—2 ft. square.   Price **5/6**

The components of the MO Passenger and Goods Train Sets can be purchased separately at the following prices:—

MO Locomotive, non-reversing (without Tender) Price **3/-**	MO Tender ... ... Price **6d.**	MO Petrol Tank Wagon ... ... Price **1/-**
MO Pullman Coach ... ... Price **9d.**	MO Wagon ... ... Price **6d.**	MO Rotary Tipping Wagon ... ... Price **1/-**
MO Side Tipping Wagon... ... ... Price **1/-**		

For prices of MO Rails and Points (9 in. radius) see page 51

DINKY TOYS—OVER 300 VARIETIES

STATION STAFF

Dinky Toys No. 1. Price of complete set 1/6
No. 1a Station Master   each **3d.**   No. 1d Driver   ...   each **3d.**
No. 1b Guard   ...   ...   ,, **3d.**   No. 1e Porter with Bags   ,, **3d.**
No. 1c Ticket Collector   ,, **3d.**   No. 1f Porter   ...   ...   ,, **3d.**

ENGINEERING STAFF

Dinky Toys No. 4. Price of complete set 1/6
No. 4a Electrician   ...   each **3d.**   No. 4d Greaser   ...   each **3d.**
No. 4b Fitters (2)   ...   ,, **3d.**   No. 4e Engine Room
No. 4c Storekeeper   ...   ,, **3d.**   Attendant   ...   ,, **3d.**

Many items from the range of over 300 Dinky Toys are ideal for giving the finishing touch to your model railway. A few of them are illustrated here. You must have railway men to deal with your trains, and passengers to travel in them; car attendants to look after the passengers, and engineers for the maintenance of the railway and its equipment. Then there are miniature Train Sets, Tramcar, Motor Bus and various other types of motor vehicle that can be used very effectively in your layout. These toys may all be purchased from your Meccano dealer. Ask him for the latest Dinky Toys Price List.

SHEPHERD SET

Dinky Toys No. 6. Price of complete set 1/-
No. 6a Shepherd   ...   .   each **3d.**
No. 6b Dog   ...   .   ,, **2d.**
No. 2d Sheep (4)   ...   .   ,, **2d.**

PASSENGERS

Dinky Toys No. 3. Price of complete set 1/6
No. 3a Woman & Child   each **3d.**   No. 3d Female Hiker   ...   each **3d.**
No. 3b Business Man   ,, **3d.**   No. 3e Newsboy   ...   ,, **3d.**
No. 3c Male Hiker   ...   ,, **3d.**   No. 3f Woman   ...   ,, **3d.**

TRAIN AND HOTEL STAFF

Dinky Toys No. 5. Price of complete set 1/3
No. 5a Pullman Car Conductor   ...   each **3d.**
No. 5b Pullman Car Waiters (2)   ...   ,, **3d.**
No. 5c Hotel Porters (2)   ...

HORNBY ELECTRIC LOCOMOTIVES

Hornby 20-volt Electric Locomotives are designed to run from the mains supply (Alternating Current) through a 20-volt Transformer capable of supplying 1 amp. at 20 volts. The 6-volt Electric Locomotives may be operated either from a 6-volt accumulator, or (excepting the EPM16 Special Tank) through a Transformer capable of supplying 2.5 amps. at 9-volts direct from the mains supply (Alternating Current).

HORNBY CLOCKWORK LOCOMOTIVES

Hornby Clockwork Locomotives are the longest-running spring-driven locomotives of their respective types in the world. The motors fitted are perfect mechanisms with accurately-cut gears that ensure smooth and steady running.

(1) MO CLOCKWORK LOCOMOTIVE, WITH TENDER
Non-reversing. Available in either red or green.
Locomotive ... Price 3/- Tender ... Price 6d.

(2) M1/2 CLOCKWORK LOCOMOTIVE, WITH TENDER
Reversing. Available in either red or green.
Locomotive ... Price 5/- M1/2 Tender ... Price 9d.

(3) No. O "SILVER LINK" CLOCKWORK LOCOMOTIVE, WITH TENDER
Non-reversing. Streamlined model, finished in silver and grey.
Locomotive, Price 3/6 No. O "Silver Link" Tender, Price 1/-

No. O STREAMLINED CLOCKWORK LOCOMOTIVE, WITH TENDER
Non-reversing. Finished in maroon/cream, or light green/dark green.
Locomotive, Price 3/6 No. O Streamlined Tender, Price 1/-

(4) EM320 (20-VOLT) OR EM36 (6-VOLT) ELECTRIC TANK LOCOMOTIVE
Reversing. L.M.S., L.N.E.R., G.W.R. or S.R.
Price (20-volt or 6-volt) 17/-

M3 CLOCKWORK TANK LOCOMOTIVE
Reversing. L.M.S., L.N.E.R., G.W.R. or S.R. Price 9/-

(5) EO20 (20-VOLT) ELECTRIC LOCOMOTIVE, WITH TENDER
Reversing. L.M.S., L.N.E.R., G.W.R. or S.R.
Locomotive ... Price 19/- No. O/1 Tender ... Price 2/-

No. O CLOCKWORK LOCOMOTIVE, WITH TENDER
Reversing. L.M.S., L.N.E.R., G.W.R. or S.R.
Locomotive . Price 10/- No. O/1 Tender Price 2/-

(6) E120 (20-VOLT) ELECTRIC TANK LOCOMOTIVE
Reversing. L.M.S., L.N.E.R., G.W.R. or S.R. Price 20/-

No. 1 CLOCKWORK TANK LOCOMOTIVE
Reversing. L.M.S., L.N.E.R., G.W.R. or S.R. Price 13/-

(7) E120 (20-VOLT) ELECTRIC LOCOMOTIVE, WITH TENDER
Reversing. L.M.S., L.N.E.R., G.W.R. or S.R.
Locomotive Price 20/- No. O/1 Tender . Price 2/-

No. 1 CLOCKWORK LOCOMOTIVE, WITH TENDER
Reversing. L.M.S., L.N.E.R., G.W.R. or S.R.
Locomotive ... Price 13/- No. O/1 Tender, Price 2/-

E120 (20-VOLT) SPECIAL ELECTRIC LOCOMOTIVE, WITH TENDER

(8) Automatic reversing.   L.M.S., L.N.E.R., G.W.R. or S.R.
Locomotive, Price **30/-**   No. 1 Special Tender, Price **3/6**

No. 1 SPECIAL CLOCKWORK LOCOMOTIVE, WITH TENDER
Reversing.   L.M.S., L.N.E.R., G.W.R. or S.R.
Locomotive, Price **17/6**   No 1 Special Tender, Price **3/6**

E120 (20-VOLT) SPECIAL ELECTRIC TANK LOCOMOTIVE
Automatic reversing. L.M.S., L.N.E.R., G.W.R. or S.R., Price **30/-**

EPM16 (6-VOLT) SPECIAL ELECTRIC TANK LOCOMOTIVE
(9) 6-volt Permanent Magnet type.   Reversing.   Can be run
from a 6-volt accumulator, or from A.C. Mains through the
Hornby Transformer-Rectifier listed on page 34.
L.M.S., L.N.E.R., G.W.R. or S.R.   Price **37/6**

No. 1 SPECIAL CLOCKWORK TANK LOCOMOTIVE
Reversing.   L.M.S., L.N.E.R., G.W.R. or S.R.   Price **17/6**

E220 (20-VOLT) SPECIAL ELECTRIC LOCOMOTIVE, WITH TENDER. Automatic reversing

(10) L.M.S. No. 1185 ("Standard Compound" class).
G.W.R. "County of Bedford" ("County" class).
L.N.E.R. "The Bramham Moor" ("Hunt" class).
S.R. No. 1759 ("L1" class).
Locomotive, Price **38/6**   No. 2 Special Tender, Price **6/6**

No. 2 SPECIAL CLOCKWORK LOCOMOTIVE, WITH TENDER
Reversing
L.M.S. No. 1185 ("Standard Compound" class).
G.W.R. "County of Bedford" ("County" class), (Illustrated).
L.N.E.R. "The Bramham Moor" ("Hunt" class).
S.R. No. 1759 ("L1" class).
Locomotive, Price **28/6**   No. 2 Special Tender, Price **6/6**

E220 (20-VOLT) SPECIAL ELECTRIC TANK LOCOMOTIVE
(11) Automatic reversing. L.M.S., L.N.E.R., G.W.R. or S.R., Price **32/6**

E26 (6-VOLT) SPECIAL ELECTRIC TANK LOCOMOTIVE
Reversing.   L.M.S., L.N.E.R., G.W.R. or S.R.   Price **30/-**

No. 2 SPECIAL CLOCKWORK TANK LOCOMOTIVE
Reversing.   L.M.S., L.N.E.R., G.W.R. or S.R.   Price **21/-**

E320 (20-VOLT) METROPOLITAN ELECTRIC LOCOMOTIVE
Automatic reversing   ...   Price **32/6**

(12) **E36 (6-VOLT) METROPOLITAN ELECTRIC LOCOMOTIVE**
Reversing   ...   ...   Price **30/-**

No. 3C METROPOLITAN CLOCKWORK LOCOMOTIVE
Reversing   ...   ...   Price **21/-**

E320 (20-VOLT) ELECTRIC LOCOMOTIVE, WITH TENDER
Automatic reversing
L.N.E.R. "Flying Scotsman"   G.W.R. "Caerphilly Castle"
L.M.S. "Royal Scot"   S.R. "Lord Nelson"
Locomotive, Price **32/6**   No. 2 Special Tender, Price **6/6**

(13) **No. 3C CLOCKWORK LOCOMOTIVE, WITH TENDER**
Reversing
L.N.E.R. "Flying Scotsman"   G.W.R. "Caerphilly Castle"
L.M.S. "Royal Scot" (Illustrated) S.R. "Lord Nelson"
Locomotive, Price **22/6**   No. 2 Special Tender, Price **6/6**

E320 (20-VOLT) RIVIERA "BLUE" ELECTRIC LOCOMOTIVE WITH TENDER. Automatic reversing
(14) Locomotive, Price **32/6**   No. 3 Riviera "Blue" Tender, Price **5/6**

No. 3C RIVIERA "BLUE" CLOCKWORK LOCOMOTIVE, WITH TENDER. Reversing
Locomotive, Price **22/6**.   No. 3 Riviera "Blue" Tender, Price **5/6**

Full details of the new Hornby Scale Model Locomotives
"Princess Elizabeth" and "Eton" are on pages 15 and 16.

HORNBY COMPLETE MODEL RAILWAYS

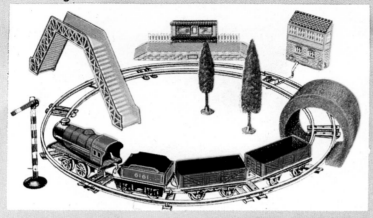

This illustration shows a suitable arrangement of the M8 Complete Model Railway.

These fine Model Railway Sets provide the simplest way of beginning the fascinating Hornby Railway hobby. Unpack the box, lay out the rails and accessories as shown in the illustration provided, put the locomotive and coaches or wagons on the track, and begin to run your own railway! It's the greatest fun in the world!

M8
COMPLETE MODEL RAILWAY
(Clockwork only)

Consists of a fine non-reversing Locomotive that can be braked from the track, Tender, two Goods Wagons and Set of Rails, Wayside Station, Footbridge, a Signal and Signal Cabin, two Trees with Stands, and Tunnel. Packed in a strong carton as illustrated.

Price **9/11**

HOW TO GET MORE FUN

While each of the Hornby M8, M9, M10 and M11 Train Sets is a complete model railway in itself, greater fun can be obtained by the addition of extra rails and other items from the Hornby range. Full details of the complete range of Hornby Trains, Rolling Stock, Accessories and Rails are given in this catalogue.

M9 Complete Model Railway

M8 Complete Model Railway

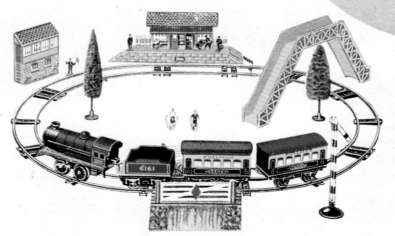

M9
COMPLETE MODEL RAILWAY
(Clockwork only)

This Set includes a non-reversing Locomotive that can be braked from the track, Tender, two Passenger Coaches and Set of Rails; Station, Footbridge, Signal and Signal Cabin, Level Crossing, Guard, Porter, two Trees with Stands and two Hikers. Packed in a strong carton as illustrated.

Price **12/6**

This illustration shows a suitable arrangement of the M9 Complete Model Railway.

M10 Complete Model Railway

M10
COMPLETE MODEL RAILWAY
(CLOCKWORK ONLY)

A larger Set containing a non-reversing Locomotive that can be braked from the track, Tender, two Pullman Coaches and Set of Rails; Footbridge, two Stations, Signal Cabin and two Signals, two Telegraph Poles, Loading Gauge, Tunnel, Cutting, Level Crossing, three Trees with Stands, two Porters, two Hikers, Horse and Cow. The Set is packed in an attractive special cabinet as illustrated.   Price **19/9**

The illustration above shows a suitable arrangement of the M10 Complete Model Railway.

M11
COMPLETE MODEL RAILWAY
(CLOCKWORK ONLY)

This is the largest and best of the Complete Model Railway Sets. It includes a powerful reversing Tank Locomotive that can be braked from the track, Fibre Wagon, Timber Wagon, Open Wagon and Set of Rails and Points, Tunnel, Station, Signal and Signal Cabin, Level Crossing, Footbridge, two Trees with Stands, Guard, one Cow and one Horse. The Set is packed in a strong special cabinet as illustrated. Price **27/6**

The illustration below shows a suitable arrangement of the M11 Complete Model Railway.

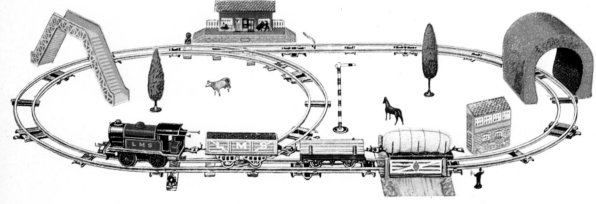

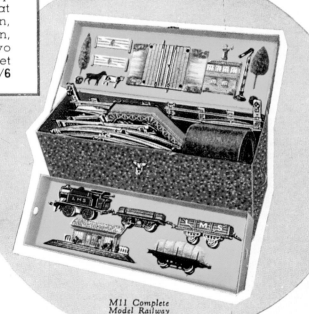

M11 Complete Model Railway

THE HORNBY ELECTRIC RAILWAY SYSTEM

Hornby Electric Trains are of two types—Mains Operated and Accumulator Operated. Mains operation is possible with all the Hornby Electric Train Sets and the chief features of these trains are set out in brief below. Full details in regard to the operation of miniature electric railways are contained in the booklet **"How to Choose and Use a Hornby Electric Railway"**, which may be obtained from any Meccano dealer, price 3d., or from Meccano Ltd., Binns Road, Liverpool 13, for 4d. post free.

MAINS-OPERATED TRAINS

Where the house lighting supply is Alternating Current, power can be obtained through a Meccano Transformer, which reduces the high voltage of the mains to a low voltage that is safe and economical. There is no direct connection between the mains supply and the railway system and therefore no risk of shock. All the Meccano Transformers are scientifically designed and perfectly constructed, and they comply fully with the requirements of the British Standards Institution. To ensure absolute safety the insulation of every Meccano Transformer is tested at a pressure of 2,000 volts.

Direct Current mains supplies must NOT be used to run a model electric locomotive. Any attempt to do so by direct connection is DANGEROUS owing to the risk of shock to which the operator is exposed. Therefore, where the supply is Direct Current, or there is no supply at all, the railway must be accumulator operated.

MECCANO TRANSFORMERS

In order to operate a Hornby Electric Railway, the Transformer is simply plugged into a house lighting socket and the transformed current is led to the railway.

There are two systems in use for Hornby Electric Railways, 20-volt and 6-volt.

The 20-volt system is for transformer operation from Alternating Current mains supplies, and it has the great advantage that the more important Hornby 20-volt Locomotives are fitted with automatic reversing mechanism. With these Locomotives lineside control of every movement is perfect and complete. Therefore, if mains Alternating Current is available, the 20-volt system should be selected.

Four different Transformers are available for use with Hornby 20-volt Locomotives, and these are known respectively as the T20A, T20, T20M and T22M. The T20A and T20 types are each fitted with a five-stud speed regulator, by means of which a train can be started or stopped, and controlled for speed. The T22M and the T20M Transformers have no speed regulator, and a Resistance Controller must be used with them in order to control the speed of the train. The T22M Transformer has an output sufficient to run two trains at once, either on the same track or on two separate tracks. In the latter case two Resistance Controllers are

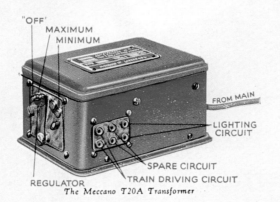

"OFF"
MAXIMUM
MINIMUM
FROM MAIN
LIGHTING CIRCUIT
SPARE CIRCUIT
TRAIN DRIVING CIRCUIT
REGULATOR

The Meccano T20A Transformer

Prices of
TRANSFORMERS, RESISTANCE CONTROLLER AND CIRCUIT BREAKER

All Meccano Transformers, and the Hornby Transformer-Rectifier, are available for the following Alternating Current supplies:—100/110 volts, 50 cycles; 200/225 volts, 50 cycles; 225/250 volts, 50 cycles. They can be specially wound for other supplies. **In ordering a Transformer or a Transformer-Rectifier the voltage and frequency of the supply must be stated.** These particulars are given on the supply meter.

T20A TRANSFORMER
(Output 35 VA at 20/3½ volts) for 20-volt trains. Fitted with speed regulator and output sockets for lighting fourteen 3½-volt lamps.   Price 22/6

T20 TRANSFORMER
(Output 20 VA at 20 volts) for 20-volt Trains. Fitted with speed regulator.   Price **17/6**

T20M TRANSFORMER
(Output 20 VA at 20 volts) for 20-volt Trains. This is similar to No. T20, but is not fitted with speed regulator. Price **12/6**

T22M TRANSFORMER
(Output 50 VA at 20 volts) for running two 20-volt Trains. Not fitted with speed regulator.   Price **13/6**

T6A TRANSFORMER
(Output 40 VA at 9/3½ volts) for 6-volt Trains. Fitted with speed regulator and separate circuit for supplying current for eighteen 3½-volt lamps.   Price **22/6**

T6 TRANSFORMER
(Output 25 VA at 9 volts) for 6-volt Trains. Fitted with speed regulator.   Price **17/6**

T6M TRANSFORMER
(Output 25 VA at 9 volts) for 6-volt Trains. This is similar to No. T6 but is not fitted with a speed regulator. **Price 12/6**

T26M TRANSFORMER
(Output 50 VA at 9 volts) for running two 6-volt Trains. Not fitted with speed regulator.   Price **13/6**

TR6 TRANSFORMER-RECTIFIER
(Output 6 volts at 1½ Amps.) for use with Hornby EPM16 Special Tank Locomotive (6-volt Permanent Magnet)   Price **29/6**

RESISTANCE CONTROLLER
20-volt or 6-volt.   Price 3/9

CIRCUIT BREAKER
20-volt or 6-volt.   Price 3/6

Note—The T22M and T26M Transformers are not available wound for frequencies below 40.

necessary, one connected to each track. The T20A Transformer, in addition to the driving of the train, makes possible the illumination of Hornby Accessories fitted for electric lighting.

ACCUMULATOR-OPERATED TRAINS

Where the mains supply is Direct Current, or there is no supply at all, the 6-volt system must be adopted, and an accumulator then forms the source of power. All Hornby 6-volt Locomotives can be run from a 6-volt accumulator, a Resistance Controller being used to control the speed.

Four Meccano 6-volt Transformers are available, T6A, T6, T6M and T26M, corresponding to the 20-volt types.

One Hornby Electric Locomotive, the EPM16 Special Tank, cannot be run from a transformer, as it requires low voltage Direct Current; but it can be operated from Alternating Current mains supply by means of the Hornby Transformer-Rectifier. This apparatus converts the high voltage Alternating Current to low voltage Direct Current. It is connected to the mains in a similar manner to a Transformer, with the Reverse and Resistance Control Switch made specially for this Locomotive connected between the Transformer-Rectifier and the track.

The source of power for a Hornby Electric Railway, whether Transformer, Transformer-Rectifier or accumulator, is connected to the rails by either Terminal fittings for the Steel Rails or a Terminal Connecting Plate or Combined Switch Rail for Tinplate Rails.

The Terminals for Steel Rails and the Terminal Connecting Plates are separate fittings, and can be attached to the track at any point on the layout as convenient. There are two types of Terminal Connecting Plates, the TCP20, specially intended for use with T20A and T20 Transformers; and the TCP6, for use with T6A and T6 Transformers.

The Combined Switch Rails EMC20 and EMC6, for 20-volt and 6-volt layouts respectively, are self-contained units consisting of a straight length of Hornby electric track fitted with a plate having terminals and a fuse, in addition to an "on-off" switch for starting and stopping a train. These fittings are specially intended for use with the Meccano T20M and T6M Transformers.

Where the Hornby Transformer-Rectifier is used in conjunction with a Reverse and Resistance Control Switch for running the EPM16 Special Tank Locomotive, connection to the track should be made by a TCP6 Terminal Connecting Plate. This fitting should be used also where an accumulator is employed in conjunction with a Resistance Controller.

CIRCUIT BREAKER

The Hornby Circuit Breaker is a useful accessory for either 20-volt or 6-volt systems. It prevents damage to the Transformer or accumulator in the event of a short circuit, and avoids the necessity for the renewal of fuse wire.

No. 2 CORRIDOR COACH L.M.S. (First-Third)

A perfect model of a modern side corridor coach with end doors. Not suitable for 1 ft. radius rails.

Price **7/6**

The Hornby Railway System includes a complete range of Rolling Stock, Accessories, and Rails, Points and Crossings, with which the most elaborate model railway can be constructed. Every component in the Hornby Series is well designed and carefully modelled on its prototype.

Hornby Rolling Stock includes almost every type in use on the big railways. Special attention is directed to the fine Corridor Coaches shown on this page. These splendid models include in their design all the features characteristic of the latest main line stock of the four groups.

The Accessories are now better than ever before, while the Rails, Points and Crossings allow an endless variety of layouts to be constructed.

No. 2 CORRIDOR COACH L.M.S. (Brake Composite)

A realistic vehicle reproducing the latest standard steel-panelled stock. Not suitable for 1 ft. radius rails.

Price **7/6**

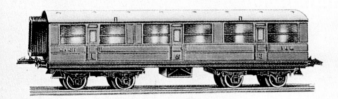

No. 2 CORRIDOR COACH L.N.E.R. (First-Third)

A handsome coach finished to represent the varnished teak stock of the L.N.E.R. Not suitable for 1 ft. radius rails.

Price **7/6**

No. 2 CORRIDOR COACH G.W.R. (First-Third)

The design of this coach is based on the latest corridor stock built for general main line service on the G.W.R. Not suitable for 1 ft. radius rails.

Price **7/6**

No. 2 CORRIDOR COACH S.R. (Third Class)

A model of the latest type "open third" centre-corridor coaches recently introduced on the S.R. Not suitable for 1 ft. radius rails.

Price **7/6**

No. 2 CORRIDOR COACH L.N.E.R. (Brake Composite)

This coach has guard's and luggage compartments at one end and it is a necessary vehicle to complete any miniature L.N.E.R. express train. Not suitable for 1 ft. radius rails. Price **7/6**

No. 2 CORRIDOR COACH G.W.R. (Brake Composite)

This follows the typical G.W.R. arrangement of brake composite coaches, with the guard's compartment between the passenger and the luggage portions. Not suitable for 1 ft. radius rails.

Price **7/6**

No. 2 CORRIDOR COACH S.R. (Brake Composite)

A well-proportioned vehicle modelled on the standard side corridor coaches built for S.R. steam-worked main line services. Not suitable for 1 ft. radius rails. Price **7/6**

191

No. 2 PASSENGER COACH (First/Third)
Available in correct colours of L.M.S., L.N.E., G.W. or Southern Railway Companies' rolling stock. Not suitable for 1 ft. radius rails. Price **7/-**

No. 2 PASSENGER COACH (Brake/Composite)
Available in correct colours of L.M.S., L.N.E., G.W. or Southern Railway Companies' rolling stock. Not suitable for 1 ft. radius rails. Price **7/-**

No. 2 SALOON COACH
Finished in the colours of the L.N.E. (as illustrated) or L.M.S. Railway Companies. Not suitable for 1 ft. radius rails. Price **10/6**

RIVIERA "BLUE" TRAIN COACH
"Dining Car" or "Sleeping Car". Not suitable for 1 ft. radius rails. Price **11/-**

CONTINENTAL "MITROPA" COACH No. 3
Similar in design to the Riviera "Blue" Train Coach. Finished in red, with white roof, and lettered "Mitropa" in gold. Price **11/-**

No. 2 SPECIAL PULLMAN COACH
This coach is perfect in detail and finish. Lettered "Loraine", "Zenobia" and "Grosvenor". Not suitable for 1 ft. radius rails. Price **13/6**

No. 2 SPECIAL PULLMAN COMPOSITE COACH
One part is designed for passenger accommodation and the other for luggage. Lettered "Verona", "Alberta" or "Montana" Not suitable for 1 ft. radius rails. Price **13/6**

No. 2 PULLMAN COACH
Not suitable for 1 ft. radius rails. Price **10/6**

METROPOLITAN COACH C
First class or brake-third. Not suitable for 1 ft. radius rails. Price **7/6**

METROPOLITAN COACH E
First class or brake-third. Fitted for electric lighting. Not suitable for 1 ft. radius rails. Price **11/6**

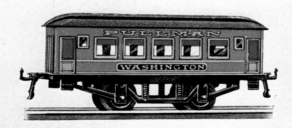

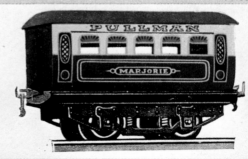

No. O "SILVER JUBILEE" ARTICULATED SALOON COACH
This is an interesting model of the type of coach used with the "Silver Jubilee" train. Finished in silver and grey. Price **1/9**

No. O STREAMLINED ARTICULATED SALOON COACH
Finished in maroon/cream or light green/dark green. Price **1/9**

PULLMAN CAR
American Type (as illustrated). Yellow or green with orange or red roof. Lettered "Washington" or "Madison" Price **1/9**

Continental Type. "Mitropa" No. O. Red with white roof. Lettered "Mitropa". Price **1/9**

MI/2 PULLMAN COACH
Named "Marjorie", "Aurelia" or "Viking". Price **1/-**

No. O PULLMAN COACH
Similar to M1 Pullman Coach, illustrated above, but fitted with automatic couplings. Price **1/3**

HORNBY ROLLING STOCK

Gauge O

FITTED WITH AUTOMATIC COUPLINGS

No. 1 PASSENGER COACH

Available in correct colours of L.M.S., L.N.E.R.,
G.W.R. or S.R.   Price **2/6**

GUARD'S VAN

Available in correct colours of L.M.S., L.N.E.R.,
G.W.R. or S.R.   Price **2/6**

MO PULLMAN COACH

As supplied with MO Passenger Set. Available
named "Joan" or "Zena" (MO coupling).
          Price **9d.**

No. 1 PULLMAN COACH

Distinctive in design and beautifully finished.
Named "Cynthia", "Corsair" or "Niobe".
          Price **2/6**

No. 1 PULLMAN COMPOSITE COACH

One part of this coach is designed for passenger
accommodation and the other for conveyance of
luggage. Named "Ansonia" or "Aurora". Price **2/6**

CABOOSE (American Type)

This is a realistic model of the type of brake
van used on the American railroads.
          Price **2/3**

No. 1 CATTLE TRUCK

Fitted with sliding doors. Available lettered
L.M.S., N.E., G.W. or S.R.   Price **2/3**

No. 2 CATTLE TRUCK

Bogie model fitted with double doors. Not
suitable for 1 ft. radius rails. Available lettered
L.M.S., N.E., G.W. or S.R.   Price **4/6**

BOX CAR (American Type)

A realistic model of the type of vehicle used in
America for the conveyance of luggage and
perishables.   Price **2/6**

HORNBY ROLLING STOCK
FITTED WITH AUTOMATIC COUPLINGS

BRAKE VAN

Fitted with opening doors. Available with S.R. or N.E. lettering. Price **2/9**

BRAKE VAN

Fitted with opening doors. Available with L.M.S. or G.W. lettering. Price **2/9**

GUNPOWDER VAN

Fitted with sliding doors. L.M.S., N.E. and S.R. models in red with gold lettering. G.W.R. model in grey with gold lettering. Price **2/3**

No. O FISH VAN

Available lettered L.M.S., N.E. or G.W. each with correct details. Price **1/6**

No. 1 BANANA VAN "FYFFES"

Sliding doors. Price **2/3**

No. O BANANA VAN

Lettered L.M.S. only. Price **1/6**

No. 1 REFRIGERATOR VAN

Fitted with sliding doors. Available lettered L.M.S., N.E., G.W. or S.R. Price **2/3**

No. O REFRIGERATOR VAN

Available lettered L.M.S., N.E., G.W., or S.R. each with correct details. Price **1/6**

No. 1 MILK TRAFFIC VAN

Fitted with sliding doors and complete with four milk cans. Price **2/3**

Separate Milk Cans. Price, each, **1d.**

No. O MILK TRAFFIC VAN

Lettered G.W. only. Price **1/6**

No. O MEAT VAN

Available lettered L.M.S., N.E. or G.W. each with correct details. Price **1/6**

CADBURY'S CHOCOLATE VAN

Fitted with sliding doors. Price **2/3**

CARR'S BISCUIT VAN

Fitted with sliding doors. Price **2/3**

CRAWFORD'S BISCUIT VAN

Fitted with sliding doors. Price **2/3**

JACOB'S BISCUIT VAN

Fitted with sliding doors. Price **2/3**

FITTED WITH AUTOMATIC COUPLINGS

No. 1 LUGGAGE VAN

Fitted with sliding doors. Available lettered L.M.S., N.E., G.W. or S.R.   Price **2/3**

No. 2 LUGGAGE VAN

Mounted on bogies and fitted with opening double doors. Not suitable for 1 ft. radius rails. Available lettered L.M.S., N.E., G.W. or S.R.   Price **4/6**

BREAKDOWN VAN AND CRANE

Fitted with sliding doors. The crane, which swivels about a pivot, is provided with a handle for hoisting loads. Not suitable for 1 ft. radius rails. Available lettered L.M.S., N.E., G.W. or S.R.   Price **5/11**

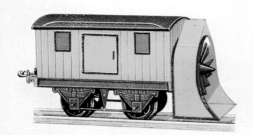

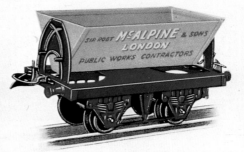

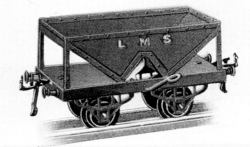

SNOW PLOUGH

Runs on specially designed heavy wheels. The plough is driven from the front axle. Available lettered L.M.S., N.E., G.W. or S.R.   Price **3/11**

MO SIDE TIPPING WAGON

This model will tip to either side of the track. (MO coupling). Price **1/-**

No. 1 SIDE TIPPING WAGON

Lettered Sir Robert McAlpine and Sons, London. Will tip to either side of the track.   Price **2/-**

HOPPER WAGON

This wagon is unloaded by operating the handle shown. Available lettered L.M.S., N.E., G.W. or S.R.   Price **3/-**

SAUSAGE VAN, "PALETHORPES"

Fitted with sliding doors.   Price **2/3**

CEMENT WAGON, "PORTLAND CEMENT"

The door at the top opens.   Price **1/11**

MO ROTARY TIPPING WAGON

Container revolves and tips. (MO coupling).   Price **1/-**

No. O ROTARY TIPPING WAGON (illustrated)

Container revolves and tips.   Price **1/6**

No. 1 ROTARY TIPPING WAGON "TRINIDAD LAKE ASPHALT"

The container revolves on its base and tips.   Price **2/-**

Gauge O

No. O WAGON
Available lettered L.M.S., N.E., G.W. or S.R.
Price **1/3**

No. 1 WAGON
Available lettered L.M.S., N.E., G.W. or S.R.
Price **1/6**

OPEN WAGON B
Similar to No. 1 Wagon but fitted with centre tarpaulin-supporting rail. Available lettered L.M.S., N.E., G.W. or S.R. Price **2/-**

COAL WAGON
This is similar to Hornby No. 1 Wagon, but is lettered Hornby Railway Company (not Meccano) and is fitted with an embossed representation of coal. Price **2/3**

MO WAGON
As supplied with MO Goods Train Set. Finished in red. (MO Coupling.) Price **6d.**

M1 WAGON
As supplied with M1 Goods Train Set. Available lettered L.M.S., N.E., G.W. or S.R. Price **10d.**

TARPAULIN SHEETS
Lettered L.M.S., G.W., N.E., or S.R. For fitting to Hornby Wagons. Price **2d.**

No. 2 HIGH CAPACITY WAGON (L.N.E.R.)
This is a new model of the type of wagon used by the L.N.E. Railway Co. for conveying bricks. Not suitable for 1 ft. radius rails. Price **4/-**

No. 2 HIGH CAPACITY WAGON (L.M.S.)
This is a new model of the type of wagon used by the L.M.S. Railway Co. for conveying coal. Not suitable for 1 ft. radius rails. Price **4/-**

No. 2 HIGH CAPACITY WAGON (G.W.R.)
This is a new model of the type of wagon used by the G.W. Railway Co. for conveying coal. Not suitable for 1 ft. radius rails Price **4/-**

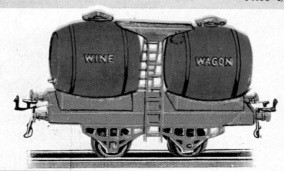

WINE WAGON
This interesting model represents a type of wine wagon used in France. Price **4/6**

COVERED WAGON (French Type)
This attractive looking model is fitted with a special frame and is supplied complete with sheet. French type, lettered NORD. Price **2/6**

WAGON (French Type)
Lettered NORD only. Modelled on a type of goods wagon used in France. Price **3/6**

HORNBY ROLLING STOCK

FITTED WITH AUTOMATIC COUPLINGS

MILK TANK WAGON

"Nestlés"

Price 4/6

PETROL TANK WAGON No. 1

"Esso"

Price 1/11

OIL TANK WAGON

"Royal Daylight"

Price 1/11

PETROL TANK WAGON No. 1

"Power Ethyl"

Price 1/11

COAL FOR HORNBY WAGONS

Imitation coal for loading into Hornby Wagons. It is packed in a box the lid of which fits inside the L.M.S. and G.W.R. No. 2 High Capacity Wagons to provide a base for the load. Price, per box, **6d.**

BRICKS FOR No. 2 HIGH CAPACITY WAGON

A realistic load for Hornby Wagons. They are packed in a box, the lid of which fits inside the No. 2 High Capacity L.N.E.R. Brick Wagon to form a base for the load. Price, per box, **10d.**

PETROL TANK WAGON No. 1

"Redline-Glico"

Price 1/11

OIL TANK WAGON

"Castrol"

Price 1/11

OIL TANK WAGON

"Mobiloil"

Price 1/11

BITUMEN TANK WAGON

"Colas"

Price **4/-**

MO PETROL TANK WAGON

"Shell-Mex B.P."

(MO Coupling).   Price 1/-

TANK CAR (American Type)

Modelled on a type of oil tank wagon used in America. Price 1/11

GAS CYLINDER WAGON

Price 1/8

BARREL WAGON

Price 2/6

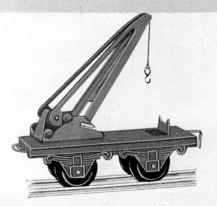

MO CRANE TRUCK

The crane revolves on its base, (MO coupling).   Price **1/-**

No. 1 TIMBER WAGON

Complete with load of timber as shown above.   Price **1/3**

No. 1 LUMBER WAGON

Fitted with bolsters and stanchions.   Price **1/3**

No. 1 CRANE TRUCK

The crane swivels about a pivot and is operated by a crank handle.   Price **2/9**

No. 2 TIMBER WAGON

Highly finished, complete with load of timber as shown above.   Not suitable for 1 ft. radius rails.   Price **2/6**

FIBRE WAGON

This is an interesting model of a type of wagon used in France and other Continental countries.   Price **1/3**

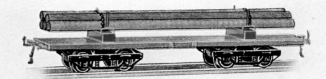

No. 2 LUMBER WAGON

Fitted with bolsters and stanchions for log transport. Not suitable for 1 ft. radius rails.   Price **2/11**

FLAT TRUCK (Complete with Cable Drum)
Available lettered L.M.S., N.E., G.W. or S.R.
          Price **1/9**

FLAT TRUCK (Without Cable Drum)
          Price **1/6**

CABLE DRUM
Liverpool Cables Ltd.   Price **3d.**

TROLLEY WAGON (Complete with two Cable Drums)
Fitted with bolsters and stanchions. Not suitable for 1 ft. radius rails.   Price **4/6**

TROLLEY WAGON (Without Cable Drums).   Price **4/-**

CABLE DRUM
Liverpool Cables Ltd.   Price **3d.**

FLAT TRUCK (Complete with Container)
Available lettered L.M.S., N.E., G.W. or S.R.
          Price **2/-**

FLAT TRUCK (Without Container).   Price **1/6**

CONTAINERS
L.M.S. (Furniture). L.N.E.R. (Goods). G.W.R. (Insulated). S.R. (Ventilated).   Price **6d.** each

HORNBY RAILWAY ACCESSORIES

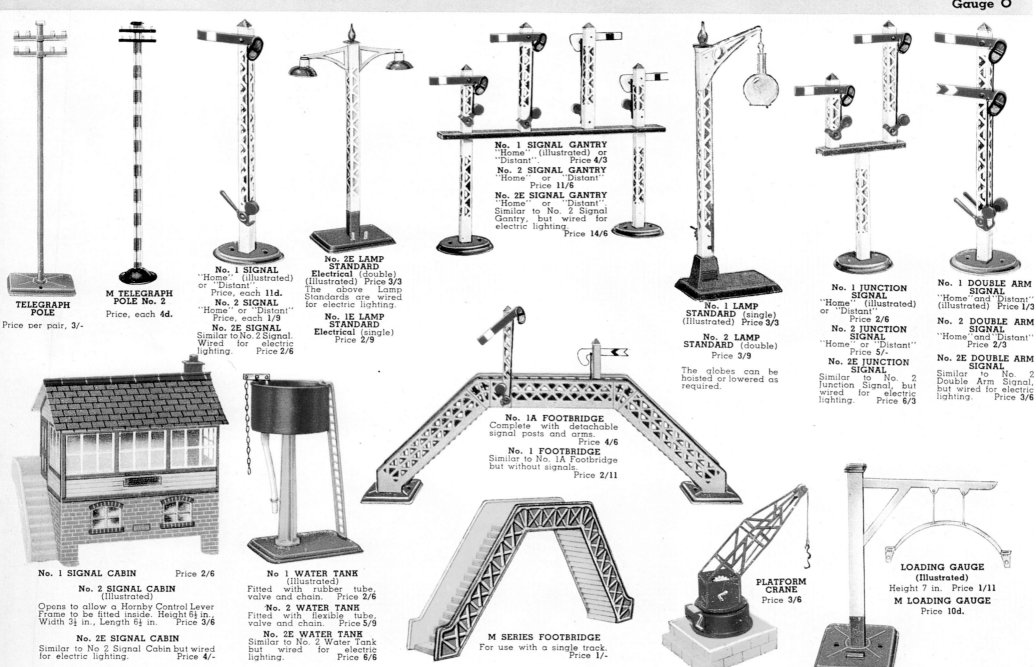

TELEGRAPH POLE

Price per pair, 3/-

M TELEGRAPH POLE No. 2

Price, each 4d.

No. 1 SIGNAL "Home" (illustrated) or "Distant". Price, each 11d.

No. 2 SIGNAL "Home" or "Distant". Price, each 1/9

No. 2E SIGNAL Similar to No. 2 Signal. Wired for electric lighting. Price 2/6

No. 2E LAMP STANDARD Electrical (double) (Illustrated) Price 3/3 The above Lamp Standards are wired for electric lighting.

No. 1E LAMP STANDARD Electrical (single) Price 2/9

No. 1 SIGNAL GANTRY "Home" (illustrated) or "Distant". Price 4/3

No. 2 SIGNAL GANTRY "Home" or "Distant" Price 11/6

No. 2E SIGNAL GANTRY "Home" or "Distant". Similar to No. 2 Signal Gantry, but wired for electric lighting. Price 14/6

No. 1 LAMP STANDARD (single) (Illustrated) Price 3/3

No. 2 LAMP STANDARD (double) Price 3/9

The globes can be hoisted or lowered as required.

No. 1 JUNCTION SIGNAL "Home" (illustrated) or "Distant" Price 2/6

No. 2 JUNCTION SIGNAL "Home" or "Distant" Price 5/-

No. 2E JUNCTION SIGNAL Similar to No. 2 Junction Signal, but wired for electric lighting. Price 6/3

No. 1 DOUBLE ARM SIGNAL "Home" and "Distant" (illustrated) Price 1/3

No. 2 DOUBLE ARM SIGNAL "Home" and "Distant" Price 2/3

No. 2E DOUBLE ARM SIGNAL Similar to No. 2 Double Arm Signal, but wired for electric lighting. Price 3/6

No. 1 SIGNAL CABIN Price 2/6

No. 2 SIGNAL CABIN (Illustrated) Opens to allow a Hornby Control Lever Frame to be fitted inside. Height 6¼ in., Width 3½ in., Length 6½ in. Price 3/6

No. 2E SIGNAL CABIN Similar to No 2 Signal Cabin but wired for electric lighting. Price 4/-

No 1 WATER TANK (Illustrated) Fitted with rubber tube, valve and chain. Price 2/6

No. 2 WATER TANK Fitted with flexible tube, valve and chain. Price 5/9

No. 2E WATER TANK Similar to No. 2 Water Tank but wired for electric lighting. Price 6/6

No. 1A FOOTBRIDGE Complete with detachable signal posts and arms. Price 4/6

No. 1 FOOTBRIDGE Similar to No. 1A Footbridge but without signals. Price 2/11

M SERIES FOOTBRIDGE For use with a single track. Price 1/-

PLATFORM CRANE Price 3/6

LOADING GAUGE (Illustrated) Height 7 in. Price 1/11

M LOADING GAUGE Price 10d.

M LEVEL CROSSING
Suitable for single track only.   Price 1/3
No. 1 LEVEL CROSSING
As illustrated. Suitable for single track only.   Price 2/11
No. E1 LEVEL CROSSING (Electrical)
Similar to No. 1 Level Crossing but fitted with electrical track.   Price 3/9
No. E1E LEVEL CROSSING
Similar to No. E1 Level Crossing but wired for electric lighting.   Price 4/11

No. 3 STATION
This Station is of up-to-date design and realistic appearance. Length 16½ in., width 6 in., height 6 in.   Price 5/9

No. 2 RAILWAY ACCESSORIES
Milk Cans and Truck: Price 1/3

No. 2 LEVEL CROSSING
As illustrated. Fitted with two gauge O tracks.   Price 5/3
No. E2 LEVEL CROSSING (Electrical)
Similar to No. 2 Level Crossing but fitted with two electrical tracks.   Price 7/3
No. E2E LEVEL CROSSING
Similar to No. E2 Level Crossing but fitted for electric lighting.   Price 8/9

No 4 RAILWAY ACCESSORIES
This is a composite set consisting of all the pieces contained in Nos. 1, 2 and 3 Railway Accessories.   Price 3/9

No. 3 RAILWAY ACCESSORIES
Platform Machines, Fire-hose Box, etc.   Price 1/6

No. 1 RAILWAY ACCESSORIES
Miniature Luggage and Truck.   Price 1/-

No. 1 BUFFER STOPS
Spring type.   Price 1/-
No 1E BUFFER STOPS
As No. 1 but suitably wired for electric lighting. Price 1/3

VIADUCT. Price **6/9**   **VIADUCT** (electrical), Price **7/6**
VIADUCT. Centre Section only   Price **4/6**
VIADUCT (electrical), Centre Section only   Price **5/-**

No. 2 BUFFER STOPS
As illustrated. Hydraulic type.   Price 4/11

No. 2A BUFFER STOPS
This new Buffer Stop is of simple but attractive design. It is of the hydraulic type with working heads. Price 2/9
No. 3A BUFFER STOPS
Similar in design to No. 2A Buffer Stops, but fitted for use with Hornby Solid Steel Track.   Price 3/6
LIGHTING ACCESSORY FOR BUFFER STOPS Nos. 2A and 3A
This is a realistic lamp provided with a bracket for affixing to Nos. 2A and 3A Buffer Stops. Price **6d.** (bulb and flex extra).

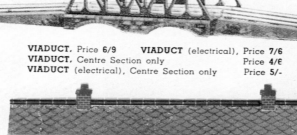

No. 4 STATION
Built up in three detachable sections with accessible Booking Hall and Ticket Office Barrier. Named "Margate", "Wembley", "Ripon" or "Reading"   Length 2 ft. 9 in., breadth 6 in., height 7 in.   Price 10/6

No. 4E STATION
This Station is fitted for electric lighting, otherwise it is the same as No 4 Station.   Price 11/9

HORNBY RAILWAY ACCESSORIES

PLATELAYER'S HUT

This is an extremely attractive accessory, beautifully designed and finished.

Price **1/2**

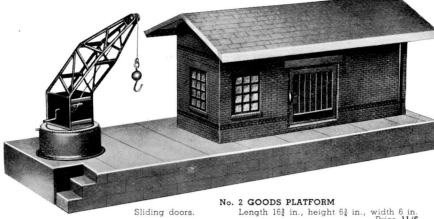

No. 2 GOODS PLATFORM

Sliding doors. Length 16¾ in., height 6¾ in., width 6 in.

Price **11/6**

No. 2E GOODS PLATFORM

No. 2E Goods Platform is wired for electric lighting; otherwise it is the same as No. 2 Goods Platform, illustrated above.

Price **12/6**

Gauge O

No. 1 TURNTABLE (Illustrated above)
Diameter 8½ in.   ...   ...   Price **1/11**

No. 2 TURNTABLE
Diameter 13½ in.   ...   ...   Price **4/-**

No. E2 TURNTABLE (Electrical)
Similar to No. 2 Turntable but fitted with electric rails.   ...   ...   Price **6/-**

No. 1 GOODS PLATFORM

Length 13 in., height 6¾ in., width 6 in.

Price **6/11**

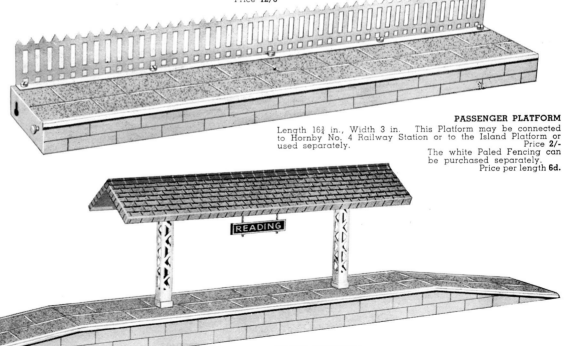

PASSENGER PLATFORM

Length 16¾ in., Width 3 in.   This Platform may be connected to Hornby No. 4 Railway Station or to the Island Platform or used separately.

Price **2/-**

The white Paled Fencing can be purchased separately.

Price per length **6d.**

READING

ISLAND PLATFORM

Length 32¼ in., height 6¾ in., width 3 in.
The Ramps can be purchased separately.

Price **6/3**
Price per pair **1/9**

ISLAND PLATFORM E

This platform is suitably wired for electric lighting. Otherwise it is the same as the Island Platform illustrated above.

Price **7/3**

PERFECT DESIGN AND WORKMANSHIP

Only the very best materials are good enough for the manufacture of Hornby Trains, Rolling Stock and Accessories. The highest quality steel, brass and tinplate are used throughout.

Every Hornby model is the result of prolonged experimental work, and each component is as perfect and efficient as modern methods can make it.

Remember that the simplest Hornby Train Set can be developed into a complete miniature railway by making small additions to it from time to time.

HORNBY RAILWAY ACCESSORIES

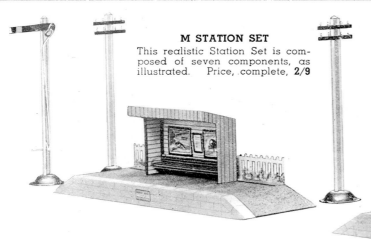

M STATION SET

This realistic Station Set is composed of seven components, as illustrated. Price, complete, **2/9**

The components can be purchased separately at the following prices:—

M Wayside Station Price **8d.** each   M Station ... ... Price **1/-** each
M Signal Box ... ,, **4d.** ,,   M Telegraph Pole No. 1 ,, **3d.**
M Signal ... ... ,, **3d.** ,,

SHUNTER'S POLE ... Price **2d.**

No. 1 ENGINE SHED

This Shed will accommodate any Locomotive and Tender with an overall length not exceeding 8¾ in. It has double doors at each end. Price **15/6**

No. E1E ENGINE SHED

Similar to No. 1 Engine Shed but wired for electric lighting. Provided with electrical track. Price **17/-**

No. 1A ENGINE SHED

This Shed is of the same dimensions as the No. 1 Shed described above but is of more simple design and has doors at one end only. Price **11/3**

POSTER BOARDS

To carry Hornby Miniature Posters. Provided with lugs for attachment to Paled Fencing, etc. Packet of 6 (3 large, 3 small) Price **4d.**

No. 1 Engine Shed

> The more Rolling Stock and Accessories you have the better the fun!

STATION OR FIELD HOARDING

This is a realistic accessory, suitable for placing on the Station platform or in the fields adjacent to the track. Price **3d.**

No. 7 RAILWAY ACCESSORIES

Watchman's Hut, Brazier, Shovel and Poker. Price **10d.**

> Read the 'Meccano Magazine', Price **6d.** from your dealer

No. 2 Engine Shed

No. 2 ENGINE SHED

This Shed will accommodate any Locomotive and Tender with an overall length not exceeding 17½ in. It has double doors at each end. Price **22/-**

No. E2E ENGINE SHED

Similar to No. 2 Engine Shed but wired for electric lighting. Provided with electrical track. Price **24/-**

No. 2A ENGINE SHED

This Shed is of the same dimensions as the No. 2 Shed described above but is of more simple design. Price **18/6**

POSTERS IN MINIATURE

These Posters are reproductions of familiar national advertisements. They are intended to be pasted on the Station Hoarding, or the Poster Boards (described on left of this page), and are beautifully printed in full colours.
No. 1 Series (packet of 51) ... ... Price **6d.**
No. 2 Series (packet of 51) ... ... Price **6d.**

HORNBY RAILWAY ACCESSORIES

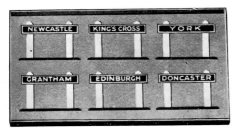

No. 9 RAILWAY ACCESSORIES
Station Name Boards ... ... Price **2/-**

No. 1 OIL CAN
This strongly made Miniature Oil Can functions perfectly.
Price **6d.**

MECCANO LUBRICATING OIL

This is the best oil obtainable for Hornby Rolling Stock, Meccano Models, Clockwork and Electric Motors, and other similar mechanisms.
Price, per bottle, **6d.**

GRAPHITE GREASE

An ideal lubricant for the springs of Hornby Locomotives and Hornby Speed Boats, Meccano and Aero Clockwork Motors, Meccano Motor Cars, and for filling axle-boxes of Hornby Rolling Stock. Price, per tube, **6d.**

POPLAR TREES,
with STANDS
Price, per doz., **2/-**

OAK TREES,
with STANDS
Price, per doz., **2/-**

TREES with STANDS (Assorted)
Price, per dozen, **2/-**

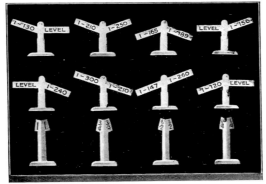

No. 5 RAILWAY ACCESSORIES
Gradient Posts and Mile Posts ... Price **2/-**

ACCESSORIES FITTED FOR ELECTRIC LIGHTING

The Hornby Accessories fitted for Electric Lighting make possible a new development in realism. By means of them, Stations, Engine Sheds, Signal Cabins and Goods Platforms can be lighted up and goods yards and sidings illuminated by Lamp Standards. The various Signals can be made to show their red and green or yellow and green lights, and red lamps fitted to Buffer Stops and Level Crossing Gates will show their warning as in actual practice. No Hornby railway is complete without some of these Accessories.

The following is a complete list of the Hornby Accessories that are available fitted for Electric Lighting. They are specially designed for lighting from the 3½-volt circuit of a Meccano T20A or T6A Transformer, and with each of these Transformers are packed for the purpose a pair of Plugs, a Bonding Clip and a coil of Wire, together with full instructions. For use with clockwork railways the Accessories can be lighted from an accumulator, or if necessary from dry batteries. Each Accessory is accompanied by a Bonding Clip and a leaflet giving full instructions for use. Lamp bulbs are not provided with the Accessories.

	Price		Price
No. E1E Engine Shed ...	17/-	No. 2E Junction Signal ...	6/3
No. E2E Engine Shed ...	24/-	No. 2E Signal Gantry ...	14/6
No. 4E Station ...	11/9	No. E1E Level Crossing...	4/11
Island Platform E ...	7/3	No. E2E Level Crossing...	8/9
No. 2E Goods Platform ...	12/6	No. 1E Buffer Stops ...	1/3
No. 2E Signal Cabin ...	4/-	No. 1E Lamp Standard ...	2/9
No. 2E Signal ...	2/6	No. 2E Lamp Standard ...	3/3
No. 2E Double Arm Signal	3/6		

The following items used in connection with the Hornby system of Accessories lighting are available:—
Plugs for sockets of Transformers T20A and T6A ... Price per pair **6d.**
Bonding Clips ... Price, each, **3d.** Connecting Wire, Price per coil **4d.**
The prices of Meccano Lamp Bulbs are as follows:—Nos. 184a (2.5-volt), each 5½d., 184b (3.5-volt), each 6½d.; 184c (6-volt), each 7½d.; 184d (10-volt), each 8½d., and 184e (20-volt), each **10d.**

HEDGING
Length 10¼ in. Price, per length, **3d.**

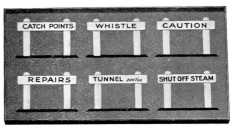

No. 8 RAILWAY ACCESSORIES
Notice Boards ... ... Price **2/-**

No. 2 OIL CAN ("K" Type)
Polished Copper
This miniature Oil Can operates perfectly. The oil is ejected drop by drop by depressing the valve. Price **3/6**

MANSELL WHEELS

These wheels are die-cast and are correctly designed. They may be fitted to Hornby Vans, Coaches, etc.
Price, per pair, **3d.**

DIE-CAST SPOKED WHEELS

These wheels are specially suitable for fitting to Hornby Wagons, Tenders, etc. Price, per pair, **3d.**

FENCING, WITH FOUR TREES
Length 16¾ in. Price, per pair, **2/6**

Two No. 1 and one No. 2 Cuttings are illustrated above

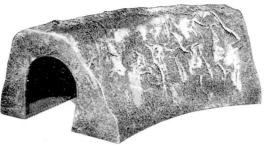

No. O TUNNEL (Straight)
Base measurements—Length 6 in.,
Width 6 in. Price **1/3**

No. 1 TUNNEL (Straight)
As illustrated. Base measurements—
Length 7¾ in., Width 6¼ in. Price **1/6**

No. 2 TUNNEL (Straight)
Base measurements—Length 15¾ in.,
Width 9½ in. Price **2/11**

No. 1 CUTTING (End Section)
Base measurements: Length 7¾ in., Width 6 in. Price per pair **3/-**

No. 2 CUTTING (Centre Section, Straight)
The addition of these centre sections allows a Hornby Railway Cutting to be extended to any length. They are intended to be used in conjunction with the End Sections (Cutting No. 1). Base measurements: Length 10¼ in., Width 6 in. Price **2/-**

No. 3 CUTTING (Centre Section, Curved)
This is used for curved track in the same manner as the straight Centre Section, described above, is used for straight track. It is suitable for 1 ft. and 2 ft. radius rails and also for the Solid Steel track. Price **2/-**

TUNNEL ENDS
Tunnels of varying lengths can be made with cardboard or other material, and then completed with the Tunnel Ends. Price per pair **1/6**

No. 3 TUNNEL (Curved)
Base measurements—Length 13 in., Width 9½ in. For 1 ft. or 2 ft. radius track. Price **3/6**

No. O CUTTING
The base measurement of this Double Cutting is 8⅛ in. square. Price **1/9**

It is important to note that the whole range of Hornby Rolling Stock and all Hornby Accessories can be used in conjunction with both clockwork and electric railways.

Remember that the simplest Hornby Train Set can be developed into a complete miniature railway by making small additions to it from time to time.

No. 4 TUNNEL (Curved)
Base measurements—Length 20 in., Width 9½ in. For 2 ft. radius track only. Price **3/9**

TRAIN NAME BOARDS

These Boards are specially intended for No. 2 Special Pullman Coaches, and No. 2 Corridor Coaches which are fitted with brackets to hold them. The Boards add greatly to the realistic appearance of the coaches. The following are available:—

No. 1 The Flying Scotsman.
No. 2 The Scarborough Flyer.
No. 3 The Royal Scot.
No. 4 The Merseyside Express —London (Euston) and Liverpool (Lime Street).
No. 5 The Golden Arrow.
No. 6 The Bournemouth Belle.
No. 7 Cornish Riviera Limited.
No. 8 Torbay Express.

No. 9 The Yorkshireman — London (St. Pancras) and Bradford (Exchange).
No. 10 King's Cross, Edinburgh and Aberdeen.
No. 11 London (Euston) and Liverpool (Lime Street).
No. 12 The Mancunian — London (Euston) and Manchester (London Road).

No. 13 Queen of Scots.
No. 14 Waterloo, Salisbury and Exeter.
No. 15 The Yorkshire Pullman.
No. 16 The Bristolian.
No. 17 Cheltenham Spa Express.
No. 18 London, Folkestone Dover, Deal.
No. 19 Ocean Liner Express.

Price per packet of four of a kind, **4d.**

The Train Name Boards can be fitted to No. 2 Pullman and Saloon Coaches and Metropolitan Coaches, if desired, by means of No. 2 Roof Clips. Price **1/-** per packet of 12.

SUNDRIES

LAMPS FOR LOCOMOTIVES, Head or Tail ... ... each **1d.**

KEYS FOR HORNBY LOCOMOTIVES

"A" MO, No. O "Silver Link", and No. O Streamlined Locomotives ... each **2d.**
"L" M1, M3 Tank No. O and No. 1 Locomotives ... ... „ **1½d.**
"H" No. 1 Special Locomotives ... ... „ **6d.**
"J" No. 2 Special, No. 3C, No. 4C and Metropolitan Locomotives ... „ **5d.**

COMBINED RAIL GAUGE, SCREWDRIVER AND SPANNER FOR LOCOMOTIVES Price **2d.**

FUSE WIRE, PLUGS AND SOCKETS

Fuse Wire, 41 Gauge, Tinned Copper. For 6-volt circuits ... ... per card **2d.**
„ 32 „ Lead. For 20-volt circuits ... ... „ **3d.**
„ 24 „ Lead. For lighting circuit of Meccano T20A or T6A Transformers ... ... „ **3d.**
The Hornby Circuit Breaker avoids the necessity for replacing Fuse Wire. Price **3/6**
Plugs ... ... each **3d.** Sockets ... . each **3d.**

HORNBY RAILS, POINTS AND CROSSINGS

Gauge O, 1¼ in.   **HORNBY SOLID STEEL TRACK**   3 ft. Radius

ELECTRIC ONLY

Although our standard tinplate rails are the acknowledged best of their class, we have felt that in order to do justice to the speed and hauling power of our locomotives, especially "PRINCESS ELIZABETH" and E420 "ETON", a drawn steel rail was essential. We set out to produce the perfect miniature railway track, and we have achieved our aim in the Hornby Solid Steel Track. The rails and points of this system are of the very highest quality, yet are sold at reasonable prices. We are confident that they will give satisfaction to Hornby Train users and to all model railway enthusiasts. The track is joined up by fishplates which are supplied with each rail.

STRAIGHT RAILS

ELECTRIC

EB3	Straight Rails. (Length 23 in.)	...	each 2/8
EB3½	Straight Half Rails	...	„ 1/7
EB3¼	Straight Quarter Rails	...	„ 1/-
TSR	Electrical Terminal for Solid Section Rail	...	per pair 4d.

CURVED RAILS

ELECTRIC

EA3	Curved Rails	...	each 2/8
EA3½	Curved Half Rails	...	„ 1/7

QUALITY FEATURES
OF HORNBY ELECTRIC SOLID STEEL TRACK
(All-level system)

1. RAILS. Solid drawn steel section, zinc coated to prevent rust and to ensure good electrical contact. The overall diameter of a circle made up of 10 Curved rails is 77 in.

2. SLEEPERS. Pressed steel, of similar design to the steel sleepers used on actual railways. Each sleeper is pierced so that the track can be screwed down to a wood base.

3. POINTS. On solid base, providing the greatest rigidity. Lever movement simple and positive. Right-hand and Left-hand points available.

ELECTRIC POINTS
(Hand Operated)

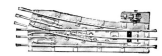

EPR3	Right-hand Points	...	each 8/3
EPL3	Left-hand Points	...	„ 8/3

ADAPTING PIECES

Many owners of Hornby Railways with tinplate rails will want to add solid steel track to their layouts. To enable them to do this special adapting pieces are available.

AP   Adapting Pieces ... Price, per box of six, 1/-

FISHPLATES

FP   For joining up track ... Price, doz. 6d.

HORNBY SOLID STEEL TRACK FORMATIONS

A splendid variety of interesting layouts can be built up with Hornby Solid Steel Track. Simple single-line layouts or intricate double-track systems can be assembled equally easily, as can be seen from the four diagrams below. On double-track systems the curves of both inner and outer tracks are of the same radius, the necessary adjustments between the lengths of the inner and outer straight tracks being made by means of half and quarter-length rails.

The Points are of particularly interesting design. Sidings and loop lines are easily arranged with them, and two Right-hand or two Left-hand Points can be used together to form right-hand or left-hand crossover points connecting adjacent tracks. Tracks so connected are the same distance apart as the standard Gauge O Hornby Tinplate Double Track and double-track accessories, such as the Engine Sheds and the No. E2E Level Crossing.

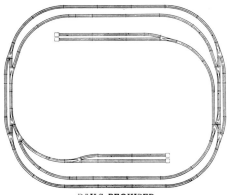

RAILS REQUIRED
19 EA3   22 EB3   8 EPL3
6 EA3½   8 EB3½   4 EPR3
  10 EB3¼
4 No. 3A Buffer Stops

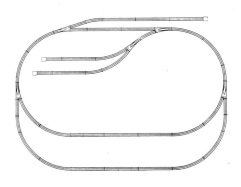

RAILS REQUIRED
14 EA3   13 EB3   2 EPR3
5 EA3½   5 EB3½   3 EPL3
3 No. 3A Buffer Stops

RAILS REQUIRED
14 EA3   1 EPL3
2 EB3½   1 EPR3

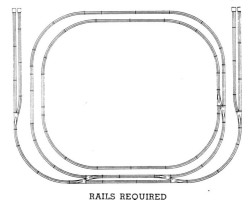

RAILS REQUIRED
20 EA3   22 EB3   5 EPL3
12 EA3½   7 EB3½   3 EPR3
  4 EB3¼
4 No. 3A Buffer Stops

Personal Notes on the Series

Personal Notes on the Series